FOR TIME AND FOREVER

HENRY M. MORRIS

Master
Books

First printing: November 2004

Copyright © 2004 by Henry M. Morris. All rights reserved. No part of this book may be used or reproduced in any manner whatsoever without written permission of the publisher, except in the case of brief quotations in articles and reviews. For information write: Master Books, Inc., P.O. Box 726, Green Forest, AR 72638.

ISBN: 0-89051-427-5
Library of Congress Number: 2004113802

All Scripture is from the King James Version of the Bible

Printed in the United States of America

Please visit our website for other great titles:
www.masterbooks.net

For information regarding author interviews,
please contact the publicity department at (870) 438-5288.

ACKNOWLEDGMENTS

I wish especially to thank Pastor Tom Chesko for writing a foreword to this little book. Mr. Chesko is pastor of the Faith Community Bible Church here in El Cajon, California, where Dr. John Morris, ICR president, is an elder, and where I have spoken occasionally. It is a fine Christ-centered church, founded several years ago by Pastor Chesko, and he is a diligent student and teacher of the Word, so I am grateful to have him review this rather unusual study of mine and then to write the foreword for it.

My two sons, Dr. John and Dr. Henry III, have also reviewed the manuscript, and I appreciate their suggestions. The copy preparation was done by my daughter, Mary Ruth Smith.

Various parts of the book are based on articles of mine published over the past few years in ICR's monthly free periodical *Acts and Facts*, modified and integrated into what I hope is a comprehensive and helpful survey of God's wonderful plan for His creation for time and eternity.

Contents

FOREWORD

In *For Time and Forever*, Dr. Henry M. Morris presents a sound refutation of one "notable myth" that he has labored for over 60 years to expose — *the myth of evolution*. With a good dose of "wit and humor," Dr. Morris addresses the many unresolved problems inherent with biological and cosmic evolution, and advances the case for biblical creationism with clarity.

However, this book is more than an exposé of bad science and the real truth about origins. It explores numerous biblical themes: *the Dominion Mandate revealed in Genesis, the person and work of Christ, heaven and hell, creation evangelism, why bad things happen, and the consummation of God's divine plan.* Concerning the latter, Dr. Morris speculates on the possibility that the Dominion Mandate, which presently involves man's stewardship over the earth, may be extended to cover the whole universe in the ages to come. Though he cannot speak with certainty as to all that this may involve, he prompts his Christian readers to consider what exciting and rewarding opportunities to serve God await them in eternity.

In the meantime, Dr. Morris exhorts the same to exercise their spiritual gifts, talents, intellect, etc., in every vocation to advance the knowledge of God as Creator, Savior, sustainer, and Lord over all. In his judgment, there is no time to waste, little time for trivial pursuits — we must "redeem the time" (Eph. 5:16). Thank you, Dr. Morris, for the example you have been to me in this regard, and for all that you have done to "edify the saints" and "refute those that contradict." I hope that *For Time and Forever* gets a wide reading, to the end that God might be glorified.

Thomas Chesko, Pastor
Faith Community Bible Church

INTRODUCTION

Do you know that God has a wonderful plan for your life?" This question has been a popular way of approaching someone about the way of salvation, often used especially by Christian college students hoping to lead a fellow student to Christ.

And it is a good question. God does have a will and a plan for each individual in his or her life here on earth, and it does require first of all that that person accept the Lord Jesus Christ by faith as personal Savior. Furthermore, God does have an individualized plan for that life, just as He did for the apostle Paul, who testified that, even though he had been bitterly anti-Christian in his early career, nevertheless, God had "*separated me from my mother's womb, and called me by his grace*" (Gal. 1:15).

But God is not interested merely in saving individual souls. That is just part of His wonderful plan for the wonderful planet He has created as the home of all those individual souls. The earth, with its beautiful plains and woodlands, rivers and seas, birds and cattle, and all its myriad complex and marvelous systems for maintaining life and beauty, is itself a very vital part of God's plan in creation.

He also has created a host of angels as His servants, and they may have *their* homes amidst the stars of heaven (angels are often even called stars in the Bible). But only men and women here on earth have been created in the very image of God, and then given the amazing ability to reproduce themselves in their exalted status as human beings in God's image. Obviously, men and women, with the angels serving them as well as God, must have a vital part in God's wonderful plan for the earth. God has even entrusted them with stewardship over the earth and its animal inhabitants, authorizing them to exercise dominion over all of it. This privilege has been called the "Dominion Mandate" and obviously entails great responsibility.

This dominion apparently applies only to the earth, not to the heavens. But what about them, with their apparently endless extent and infinite complexity of stars and other bodies scattered everywhere in space? The visible stars do have a certain limited ministry to the earth's human masters (note Gen. 1:14–16), but what about all the galaxies of stars that cannot even be seen on earth, except through the giant telescopes invented in recent generations?

God must somehow have a wonderful plan — not only for each individual life, but also for the earth and for the whole universe. Although the entrance of sin into His creation has postponed its implementation (first by rebellion of a contingent of the angels led by Satan, then by the first man and woman created), that plan cannot be defeated. The earth one day will be purged of all the effects and evidences of sin, and then made new again by a mighty renewal project. That new earth will then last forever.

The purging of sin, both from individual lives and from the earth itself, would require an amazing intervention by God. That intervention required God himself to become a man and then to pay the awful penalty required for man's redemption. That, of course, is the old, old gospel story so familiar now and so precious to all those who have been redeemed and saved thereby.

Through believing the gospel, men and women can be saved, and eventually the earth itself will be delivered from its *"bondage of corruption into the glorious liberty of the children of God"* (Rom. 8:21).

But what about the mighty cosmos far beyond the earth? Does God have a wonderful plan for that also? One would almost have to think so, because God created it, and He always has a purpose in whatever He does. But the Bible says little about any such plan. There may be a few intriguing hints here and there, but in general we must be content with God's statement through Moses in Deuteronomy 29:29: *"The secret things belong unto the Lord our God: but those things which are revealed belong unto us and to our children for ever, that we may do all the words of this law."*

But one fascinating speculation can at least be mentioned. We who have been redeemed will be in the new Jerusalem (or at least that will be our home base), but it hardly seems that we shall do nothing except enjoy living in our *"mansion"* through all the ages to come. *"His servants shall serve him"* the Scripture says (Rev. 22:3), and we shall have transformed bodies *"fashioned like unto his glorious body"* (Phil. 3:21) in which to carry out that service.

I like to think (although I cannot prove it, and certainly am not dogmatic about it) that in that future age the Dominion Mandate may be extended to cover the entire universe, and we who have been created (and re-created — Col. 3:10) in God's own image may be assigned *that* domain to explore and develop for the glory of God. If that is our assignment for eternity, we can never lack for exciting service to render our Master and Lord, for we shall have endless time to explore and develop the systems of endless space.

Whether that speculation is valid or not, the Scriptures do assure us that *"in the ages to come he might shew the exceeding riches of his grace in his kindness toward us through Christ Jesus"* (Eph. 2:7).

CHAPTER I

A PERSONAL TESTIMONY

(AFTER 60 YEARS)

I have been promoting scientific biblical creationism for at least 60 years, but it was not always so. I was more or less satisfied with theistic evolution for the first 25 years, but that all changed when I started teaching at Rice Institute (now Rice University) back during World War II.

As a young Christian, I felt the need to begin an intense study of both Scripture and evolutionism in order to acquire a clear conviction about origins. During my previous college days, at the same institution, indoctrination in evolution had been the norm, but attending a strong Baptist church after graduation, plus joining the Gideon ministry, had convinced me of the divine authority of the Bible, so this conflict had to be resolved.

And it *was* resolved, decidedly. The Bible was true, and evolution false! This had become to me not simply a matter of faith, as many would maintain, but of true science and history. The evidences for biblical inerrancy were seen to be vast and sound, whereas evolutionism was unscientific and based essentially on the presupposition of total naturalism.

That conviction changed my life, and indeed has become stronger and stronger ever since.

THE TWO MANDATES OF GOD TO MAN

I had majored in civil engineering at Rice and then had worked for three years with the International Boundary and Water Commission as a junior engineer. Then Rice officials unexpectedly called me back to teach the Navy students that had been sent there to study engineering. Trying to witness about Christ and salvation to these scientifically minded students had, in fact, provided the stimulus to begin that study of science and Christianity in the first place.

My choice of engineering as a major had not been for spiritual reasons, but for economic reasons. I don't think I had even prayed about it — as I've tried to do for every important decision since. But apparently God was leading anyway!

I soon reached the strong conviction that civil engineering had been an ideal background for studying evolution and the Bible, and for doing useful service for the Lord in general. The practitioners of so-called "pure science" (physics, biology, etc.) seek to understand how nature works and to organize it in terms of natural "laws" and "processes." But "applied scientists" (engineers, medical doctors, etc.) then use the results obtained from pure science to produce structures, products, systems, etc., which benefit mankind. Pure science often involved theorizing, and even metaphysical speculation. To the engineer, however, the science has to *work*. His designs must be tested. One cannot just theorize about the size of a beam or the stresses on an engine.

Both the pure and applied sciences are basic in carrying out God's very first command to the human beings He had created. That command, found in Genesis 1:26–28, but also expanded, expounded and amplified in later Scriptures, has come to be known as God's "Dominion Mandate." In it, God has made mankind the steward of God's physical and animal creations, giving men and women *"dominion"* over all the earth.

In exercising this dominion, the earth and its processes must first be understood; this is the domain of so-called pure science. But then applying this knowledge in useful systems is the domain of applied science, and this is at least as vital in *"subduing"* the earth and *"having dominion"* over it as simply knowing about it. In fact, engineers have long argued that they are the most critical practitioners of the mandate, because they first have to know the sciences and then know how to apply them in order to attain the stipulated *"dominion."*

In civil engineering, for example, the typical curriculum will include one or more courses in physics, chemistry, biology, geology, hydrology, and astronomy, not to mention much mathematics, as well as courses in engineering design. Although such a thought never entered my mind at the time, I eventually came to understand that the practice and teaching of engineering actually comprised one very significant component of God's Dominion Mandate. But in fact, all honorable human vocations have a role in carrying out that primeval command.[1] Furthermore, the mandate has never been withdrawn, so we have to assume God is still expecting men and women to carry it out.

One's spiritual relationship to God is not a factor. When God told Adam and Eve (and their descendants) to have dominion, He gave no limiting specifications as to who would participate in this responsibility. Thus, all people — regardless of whether they are Jews or Gentiles, Christian or non-Christian — are still responsible to obey and fulfill it, to the extent their occupations permit. In fact, their faithfulness in implementing the Dominion Mandate is very likely one of the criteria by which the nations themselves will be judged by the Lord. A recent book of mine[2] has explored this and other criteria used by God in setting the boundaries and durations of the nations of past and present. This present study will also deal at some length with this subject, especially in chapter II.

Christians often fail to realize their own ongoing responsibility in this connection. Engineers and geologists, doctors and lawyers, teachers and technicians, businessmen and housewives, all are responsible to function under the Dominion Mandate in whatever ways are appropriate for their vocation. Christians especially should not forget to serve as faithfully in their secular jobs as they would if they were pastors or missionaries. The Scriptures often stress this obligation: "*Whatsoever ye do, do it heartily, as to the Lord, and not unto men*" (Col. 3:23). "*Whatsoever thy hand findeth to do, do it with thy might*" (Eccles. 9:10).

Then there is also Christ's so-called Great Commission — the command to believers to "*preach the gospel to every creature*" (Mark 16:15). We could (and should, in fact) actually view the Great Commission as a second great worldwide mandate, this one to be carried out specifically by Christians rather than by mankind in general. Call it the "Missionary

---

1 *The Biblical Basis for Modern Science* (Green Forest, AR: Master Books: 2nd ed., 2002), 474 pages.

2 *God and the Nations* (Green Forest, AR: Master Books: 2002), 176 pages.

Mandate" or some such name, and regard it as supplementary, though vitally important, to the Dominion Mandate.

Christian believers, obviously, are responsible for both. In fact, Christ should be Lord of all creation as well as of His individual followers. He not only created the entire world, but even now is *"upholding all things by the word of his power"* (Heb. 1:3). The entire creation is currently under God's curse because of sin and therefore in bondage to Satan as *"the god of this world"* (2 Cor. 4:4). God has promised, however, that *"the* [creation] *itself also shall be delivered from the bondage of corruption into the glorious liberty of the children of God"* (Rom. 8:21).

The redemption price is the shed blood of the Son of Man. As the one perfect Lamb of God, He *"taketh away the sin of the world"* (John 1:29), and in the renewed earth which God will create after this one fades away, *"there shall be no more curse"* (Rev. 22:3).

In that future world, the Missionary Mandate will no longer be necessary, because all its inhabitants will be happily serving the Lord, and *"there shall in no wise enter into it any thing that defileth"* (Rev. 21:27).

But in all probability, the Dominion Mandate will not only still be in effect, but may well be extended to apply to the whole universe, not merely this earth. God surely had a purpose in creating the myriads and myriads of stars and other marvelous things scattered throughout the infinite reaches of space. Our physical bodies will have been changed to be *"fashioned like unto his glorious body"* (Phil. 3:21), and we, as *"his servants shall serve him"* (Rev. 22:3) in an infinite variety of meaningful job assignments, based in some yet-to-be clarified criteria on our faithfulness in serving Him here in this life.

He has told us, intriguingly, that *"eye hath not seen, nor ear heard, neither have entered into the heart of man, the things which God hath prepared for them that love him"* (1 Cor. 2:9). We may be able, however, to sense some of these, *"by his Spirit"* (1 Cor. 2:10), and I, at least, like to think about having an eternity of time to explore and develop and enjoy the endless marvels of His infinite creation.

Even in this life and this world, we who are Christians have the wonderful challenge of *"bringing into captivity every thought* [and, by extension, every product of those thoughts] *to the obedience of Christ"* (2 Cor. 10:5), which in effect would involve merging both the Dominion Mandate and the Missionary Mandate into one great Kingdom mandate.

We should not only seek to win scientists and musicians and businessmen to Christ, but also to lead the very disciplines of science and music and business to obey and honor Christ. Have Christians not been praying through the centuries: *"Thy kingdom come. Thy will be done in earth, as it is in heaven"* (Matt. 6:10)?

These great themes may exceed our imaginations in this world, but we have much yet to do even here in carrying out the two mandates. Right *now*, we human beings all have been commanded to *"have dominion"* over all the earth and *"over every living thing that moveth upon the earth"* (Gen. 1:26, 28). Beyond that, we Christians have been commanded to witness for Christ as Creator, Redeemer, and coming King *"unto the uttermost part of the earth"* (Acts 1:8). There is much yet to do, right now!

A Christian Educator's Dream

With all due apologies to Dr. Martin Luther King Jr., as a Christian educator I also have long had a dream — a dream of a great Christian creationist university and educational center, with teaching and research programs in all important disciplines at all levels of higher education. Every course and project in that dream university would be developed on strict creationist presuppositions, as well as absolute biblical inerrancy and authority. Evolutionism and secular humanism would be treated adequately, of course, but thereby shown to be false and harmful in every field. It would be great if all universities were like that, but that would be practically impossible even to dream about. But there should be at least one; even in a secularistic world like ours, shouldn't there be?

I have been dreaming such a dream for perhaps 40 years, as a direct result of serving 28 years on the faculties of five great non-Christian, non-creationist universities and trying to maintain a genuine Christian testimony on those campuses while trying also to teach engineering in a God-honoring context to thousands of students from many backgrounds. With all the merits of our systems of higher education, developed over many centuries and countries, it is sad that nowhere in Christendom is there such a fully Christian university or educational center. No wonder our whole world seems to be heading toward chaos, with all students everywhere (except for those in a few small religious institutions here and there) being indoctrinated in evolutionary humanism.

Such an educational center could contribute mightily to the accomplishment of both mandates — the Dominion Mandate and the Missionary Mandate. As to the structure of such a complex, I believe God has given us the basics in the earliest chapters of His Word.

In the Old Testament Scriptures, the emphasis is largely (though not entirely) on God's chosen nation of Israel. In the New Testament, especially after the four gospel narratives, it is largely on the Church.

However, before either one of these even existed, there were some 2,000 years of human history (Adam to Abraham), where mankind was supposed to be functioning under the Dominion Mandate (as outlined in Genesis 1 and 2, supplemented and extended in Genesis 9). Adam and his descendants were supposed to govern and utilize all of God's creation as His stewards, developing it for man's good and to the glory of God.

Such a ministry certainly would have had to build on what we now would call scientific research and development, then extending into construction, transportation, agriculture, communication, and a host of other occupations. Later, with the entrance of the discordance of sin into God's harmonious creation, the disciplines associated with human government would also have to be included — indeed, *all* honorable vocations are now implied in the Dominion Mandate.

And certainly education would be a primary aspect! Its teachers themselves would necessarily accomplish much of the original research, as well as the full-time scientists, but then also it would be essential that all developments for fulfilling the mandate in one generation be transmitted by teachers to the next. Whether any formal schools were ever actually set up in the primeval world has not been recorded, but in principle they *should* have been, for the mandate to be carried out.

This great mandate has never been withdrawn, and is thus still in effect, whether men realize it or not. With the coming of Israel and especially the Church, it has been supplemented by the Missionary Mandate (the so-called Great Commission, Matt. 28:18–20), which in a sense could even include the Dominion Mandate as part of the *"all things"* Jesus has commanded us to teach. The Missionary Mandate applies only to Christians, of course, whereas the Dominion Mandate is still in effect for all men. But *both* mandates do apply to us believing Christians — *especially* to us, in fact.

To me, it is a great tragedy that Christians for the most part, while rightly concerned with their Great Commission (witness the proliferation of seminaries and Bible colleges, as well as denominations and missionary organizations) have allowed all the other components of God's marvelous creation to become almost wholly dominated by secularism and evolutionism. Even the relatively few Christian liberal arts colleges have often yielded to compromise here. What could ever be done to change all this? What *should* be done?

The Structure of a Creationist University System

We do have an effective model to go by, in structure, though not in curricular content. In a sense, human societies have been (no doubt unintentionally, but nevertheless actually) partially implementing the Dominion Mandate as they developed their own educational systems. A great modern university will have "colleges" in all the major disciplines, with undergraduate, graduate, and research programs in all their respective subdivisions. Today these are being augmented to some degree by extension centers and on-line studies. For example, the University of Minnesota, where I taught for 5 years, has colleges of medicine, engineering, agriculture, business, and just about everything useful in our nation's economy. So does Virginia Tech, where I was an engineering department head for 13 years. The university systems of California, New York, Texas, and other large states are even more variegated and far spreading. But they are all dominated and controlled by a philosophy of evolutionary humanism, and this, of course, trickles down into all the elementary and high schools, spills over into the handful of religious schools, and even comes to dominate the political system and the whole culture.

But the structural model is good and has been effective in the development of all the leading nations of the world and their economies. How wonderful it would be if at least one such university system would build all these same programs on the true biblical Christian/creationist world view! Such a university would include these other divisions also — publishing, seminars, radio, television, museums, etc. All great secular universities incorporate these as adjuncts to their ministry as centers of education. Such a biblical, creationist, Christ-centered, educational center should also have all these, with all developed in the context of implementing God's primeval Dominion Mandate, as extended also by His Missionary Mandate.

Can anything be done now? Not very likely, in view of the dominating interests of modern Christians in evangelism and the personal needs of individual believers, not to mention denominational interests, turf wars, and the like. Many years ago, while I was still at Virginia Tech, I talked with administrators at several leading Christian colleges about the possibility of their developing their school into a creationist university, but all felt it was an impossible dream. Later, I helped in the founding of Christian Heritage College and then the ICR Science Graduate School in hopes that they eventually could grow into such a university system. But that's another story, and it all may well be nothing but an idealistic dream.

And yet, as the old chorus goes: *"God specializes in things thought impossible."* In recent years, a number of Christian liberal arts colleges have become solidly committed to true biblical creationism and biblical inerrant authority. In addition to Christian Heritage and the ICR Graduate School, one thinks of Bob Jones, Liberty, Cedarville, Master's, Bryan, Clearwater, Pensacola, Tennessee Temple, Grace, and perhaps others.

If even these could somehow form a cooperating, unselfish coalition of some kind, and then if each could specialize and grow in a few other areas — one in engineering, say, another in earth science, another in business, and so on — it all could amount to at least the foundation of a nationwide truly biblical university system.

Furthermore, a number of other significant creationist ministries have come into existence in recent decades — the Creation Research Society, numerous other creation organizations (some local, some national), the Transnational Association of Christian Colleges and Schools (TRACS, a fully recognized accrediting association), vast numbers of creationist books and videos, and all sorts of things that could help.

The situation is, indeed, much different and much better in many ways than it was 40 years ago when I first began to dream this way.

What about the cost? That's a problem, all right. Practically all existing universities are supported largely by the government — through taxation, research grants, fellowship grants, etc. This is true even of most private universities, though the latter also are often able to generate large endowments through wills and special gifts.

Christian colleges usually do not have access to government money, and most would not accept it if they did, because most modern governments are also committed to evolutionary humanism, and strings are commonly tied to any government largess.

Nevertheless, the wealth of the whole wide world is really in the hands of God. It is more a matter of how He leads those who have tentative earthly jurisdiction over those resources. And this may depend on the prayers and encouragement of those believers who become convinced of the primary (and eternal) importance of the Dominion Mandate in the purposes of God for His creation.

The Bible teaches that, in the new earth which God will create after the last judgment, *"His servants shall serve him"* (Rev. 22:3). This service will not be in evangelism, because everyone who is there is already saved. It just may be, as noted above, that the Dominion Mandate will then apply to the whole universe, and we shall spend eternity studying, developing, and teaching about all God's creation.

Well, I said this was a dream. But it has been a pleasant dream and a challenging and motivating dream.

First, however, we need to understand more fully God's interactions with this present world — both its nations and their inhabitants. Of special concern in this book will be their response to the Creator, and what He will do about it.

CHAPTER II

GOD AND THE NATIONS

The education of the rising generation should certainly play a key role in fulfilling God's Dominion Mandate. The present schools and colleges of the world, however, are obviously far from what God must have intended them to be. Even in Christendom, the schools not only are mostly controlled by the governments in their respective nations but also are largely dominated by an underlying philosophy of humanism and practical atheism. God cannot be pleased.

CRITERIA FOR TIMES AND BOUNDARIES

Whether or not they recognize it officially in a pledge of allegiance or some other way, the fact is, however, that *all* nations with their schools *are* "under God." They were formed by God in the first place, are being evaluated by Him, and eventually have been or will be judged by Him.

A key text on this subject is found in Paul's reminder to the Athenian evolutionists. "[God] *hath made of one blood all nations of men for to dwell on all the face of the earth, and hath determined the times before appointed, and the bounds of their habitation*" (Acts 17:26). Somehow, God has led each nation into the territory it was intended to occupy. After all, *"The earth is the Lord's,"* and He can divide it according to His own will (Ps. 24:1). Furthermore, the duration of that occupation has been controlled by Him, using criteria revealed in His word.

Thus, God has a deep interest in each nation as such (including its schools), as well as in the individual citizens of that nation. In fact, one can discern at least five criteria by which He evaluates the nations and determines their appointed times.

THE RIGHTEOUSNESS CRITERION

One obvious measure God uses is His standards of righteousness. For example, although God told Abraham that his nation would receive the land of the Canaanites, they would have to wait a long time, *"for the iniquity of the Amorites is not yet full"* (Gen. 15:16). Similarly, when God was ready to terminate the period of time allowed Sodom and Gomorrah *"because their sin is very grievous,"* He agreed to spare them if there could be found even ten righteous people there (Gen. 18:20, 32).

There are other biblical references to this effect. *"Righteousness exalteth a nation: but sin is a reproach to any people"* (Prov. 14:34). If anyone wonders how a nation could know what God's standards of righteousness were before the law was written by Moses, an answer is given by Paul: *"For when the Gentiles, which have not the law, do by nature the things contained in the law, these, having not the law, are a law unto themselves: Which shew the work of the law written in their hearts . . ."* (Rom. 2:14–15). God has encoded the fundamentals of His standards of righteousness in each person's conscience.

SEEKING GOD

A second criterion was noted by Paul, who attached it to his testimony about the times and territories appointed to the nations by God. The purpose of this allocation was that *"they should seek the Lord . . . though he be not far from every one of us"* (Acts 17:27). God had promised that *"those that seek me early shall find me"* (Prov. 8:17). *"For the eyes of the Lord run to and fro throughout the whole earth, to shew himself strong in the behalf of them whose heart is perfect toward him"* (2 Chron. 16:9).

Furthermore, God has provided such an abundance of evidence in the creation itself that those who see these wonderful phenomena and still refuse to seriously seek God are *"without excuse"* (Rom. 1:20). Most definitely, *"He left not himself without witness"* (Acts 14:17).

But the sad fact is that all those ancient nations, *"when they knew God . . . did not like to retain God in their knowledge . . ."* (Rom. 1:21–28). By the time of Paul, that Apostle said that, at least as far as the nations themselves were concerned, *"there is none that seeketh after God"* (Rom.

3:11). They did have various "gods" to worship, but all had rejected the true God. *"For all the gods of the nations are idols: but the Lord made the heavens"* (Ps. 96:5).

THE BLESSING OF ISRAEL

A third criterion which God uses to evaluate the nations is their treatment of His chosen nation, Israel. When He called Abraham to found His elect nation, He said: *"I will make of thee a great nation. . . . And I will bless them that bless thee, and curse him that curseth thee"* (Gen. 12:2–3).

God had promised to send a Savior into the world so *"that the world through him might be saved"* (John 3:17). That Savior would have to be God himself, but incarnate as a man, so a nation had to be prepared into which He could be born and carry out His mission of world redemption. Although the nation Israel has often failed miserably, there has always been a remnant true to God and His revealed word. Despite severe divine judgments, Israel has survived and God has promised it will continue forever.

God has occasionally even allowed ungodly and wicked nations (such as Babylonia and Assyria) to chastise Israel, but then terminated those same nations for their wickedness and their treatment of Israel.

RESPONSE TO THE GOSPEL

In this present age, God has raised up another chosen and *"holy nation, a peculiar people . . . now the people of God"* (1 Pet. 2:9–10). This nation has no king but Christ, who has redeemed them with the blood of His cross, so they have become citizens of His heavenly kingdom, serving on the earth as *"ambassadors for Christ,"* seeking to persuade others to *"be . . . reconciled to God"* (2 Cor. 5:20). The response to this wonderful gospel of salvation, as they seek to *"teach all nations"* its saving message (Matt. 28:19), is yet another criterion by which God is evaluating the nations of the present world.

When the Lord sent out His first disciples on a preliminary evangelistic mission — a sort of training mission, as it were — He said: *"And whosoever shall not receive you, nor hear your words, when ye depart out of that house or city, shake off the dust of your feet. . . . It shall be more tolerable for the land of Sodom and Gomorrha in the day of judgment, than for that city"* (Matt. 10:14–15). This very action was taken by Paul and Barnabas when their gospel preaching was rejected (Acts 13:51). Any nation that persecutes either Israel or the Church will eventually regret it.

The Dominion Mandate

A fifth criterion is derived from God's very first command to Adam and Eve and therefore to the nations they would generate. *"Be fruitful, and multiply, and replenish the earth, and subdue it and have dominion over . . . the earth"* (Gen. 1:28). This mandate implies a large population and every honorable occupation — science, commerce, education, etc. This "Dominion Mandate" amounts, in effect, to a magnificent divinely commissioned stewardship for man over God's great creation — to understand its processes and develop its resources to the glory of God and the good of men.

Although man has failed miserably since sin entered the world and the other criteria had to be established, this first command has never been withdrawn, so it is still in effect for all the nations, Jew and Gentile alike, and Christian believers and unbelievers alike.

The mandate was renewed and expanded after the great judgment of the Flood. So far as the record goes, there were no nations as such until the dispersion at Babel, with its supernatural imposition of different languages for different families. There were apparently 70 original nations after Babel, but these have now proliferated into about 200 organized nations and perhaps as many as 7,000 languages and ethnic groups.

Many nations have perished throughout the ages, and new nations have arisen. God has been evaluating and judging them throughout the centuries and millennia, presumably on the basis of the five criteria we have discerned in Scripture (there may be others also that we don't yet see). God is not capricious, and we can be sure that He has good reasons for His *"appointed times and boundaries"* for each nation of past or present.

The Future Nations

We read also in the Bible about a future judgment of whatever nations still exist when Christ returns. *"Before him shall be gathered all nations: and he shall separate them one from another"* (Matt. 25:32). One group *"shall go away into everlasting punishment: but the righteous into life eternal"* (Matt. 25:46). Since the Greek word for nations is, depending on context, also used for both *"Gentile"* and *"heathen"* (the same is true for the Old Testament Hebrew), this judgment apparently applies to individual Gentiles, but seems also to apply to Gentile nations as such.

There will be distinct nations in both the future millennium and the ultimate new earth as well, according to a literal interpretation of the passages dealing with them (see Rev. 20:3, 8; 21:24, 26; 22:2).

Which nations will these be? Certainly not those ancient nations that are already gone and largely forgotten (Sumeria, Phoenicia, Scythia, etc.) Presumably, some of the present nations will make it, but most of them don't seem to rate too highly in terms of the criteria discussed herein. Some have contributed very significantly to the accomplishment of the Dominion Mandate, but few have been friends of Israel, for example. Some nations have responded heartily to the preaching of Christian missionaries (e.g., South Korea), but many Moslem nations have vigorously opposed all who would proclaim the gospel.

What about our own nation? We have been the best friends of Israel and have also contributed more than most other nations to the Dominion Mandate. Our nation was founded in large measure to serve the Lord, and has sent out the largest number of missionaries in modern times. In the past, at least, our moral standards were relatively high.

However, there is no doubt that our positions relative to all five of the criteria have badly declined in recent decades. There is hope that the "good old USA" will be a viable nation in the ages to come, but there is a great need for true biblical revival in *this* age!

THE NATIONS OF TODAY

Despite all the lethal turmoil in the nations of the world today, God is now visiting *"the Gentiles, to take out of them a people for his name"* (Acts 15:14), thereby creating a new nation, the Church, composed of people from every human nation on earth who have trusted Christ for salvation and been *"born again."* That "nation" does not have a capital or a king here on earth.

"For our conversation is in heaven" (Phil. 3:20). The word translated *"conversation"* actually means *"citizenship."* That is, while we may be citizens of the United States or some other nation here in this world, we are also citizens of the heavenly kingdom, which is none other than *"the everlasting kingdom of our Lord and Saviour Jesus Christ"* (2 Pet. 1:11). This kingdom is actually called *"an holy nation"* (1 Pet. 2:9), and we are, in effect, *"ambassadors for Christ"* here on earth (2 Cor. 5:20).

That does not imply, however, that the established early nations are no longer of interest to God as nations. Remember that God *"hath determined the times before appointed, and the bounds of their habitation"* in every case for the individual nations, having made *"all nations of men for to dwell on all the face of the earth"* (Acts 17:26).

Many nations of the past no longer exist, having failed in their God-given opportunities and passed their appointed times. But there are now perhaps 200 viable nations functioning today. These are all still under active observation by God in terms of their faithfulness in seeking Him and in accomplishing His primeval Dominion Mandate.

The Ongoing Dominion Mandate

God's primeval Dominion Mandate (Gen. 1:26–28) has never been withdrawn, and thus is still in effect. It was given originally to Adam and Eve, then confirmed and expanded to Noah (Gen. 9:6–7) after the great Flood. It is, therefore, appropriate to raise the question as to how well the Dominion Mandate is being implemented by the present nations. A basic component in the mandate (Gen. 2:24) was the establishment of monogamous life-long marriage as the basis for producing the population needed to accomplish the other components of the mandate.

It is obvious that the nations have failed miserably in this aspect. The nominally Christian nations of the West have given priority to monogamy in their legal codes, but divorce and "serial" polygamy have become very common, and now even homosexual "marriage" and cohabitation without marriage. The many Moslem nations of the world flagrantly disobey this mandate, as do the others. The Koran allows each man to have four wives, as well as easy divorce.

As far as *"subduing the earth"* is concerned, a number of nations have made contributions in terms of science, technology, commerce, education, and cultural products, although the most important such contributions have come from Europe and America. In spite of all this advance in science and technology, however, mankind is still a long way from subduing the earth. We have not been able to control the weather or make the great deserts fertile and habitable or develop cures for numerous deadly diseases (cancer, Alzheimer's, MS, ALS, etc.).

Long ago, God described the patriarch Job as *"none like him in the earth, a perfect and an upright man, one that feareth God, and escheweth evil"* (Job 1:8). Yet when God finally spoke to Job in Job 38:1–41, He answered none of Job's questions concerning the reason for his suffering. Instead, He gave out a remarkable monologue about His own great creation and its providential maintenance. The monologue took the form of some 70 or more rhetorical questions having to do with that creation and Job's lack of understanding thereof. These were the very phenomena which Adam and his descendants should have been seeking to understand in order truly to subdue the earth and develop it to the glory of God and the benefit of His creation.

If God needed to rebuke Job — not for his wickedness, but for his lack of concern for God's Dominion Mandate — then what must He say about us?

Even those marvels we have been able to comprehend in science have been encrusted with science falsely so-called — that is, evolutionism. And even man's great contributions in the fine arts have been polluted with utter banality and even blasphemy in so much of what now passes for art. The sophisticated realms of economics and business are intermingled with much greed, deception, and even criminality. And true education for transmitting truth has been so undermined that the real truth as found in Christ and His creation has been submerged in humanistic philosophy.

It would seem, despite our so-called high civilization, we are still far from fulfilling God's Dominion Mandate.

In reference to the command to nations to *"seek the Lord,"* as stipulated in Acts 17:27, there has been at least limited obedience on the part of some nations — but it is doubtful whether today any nation as a whole could be described as truly seeking God as revealed in the Bible and in the Lord Jesus Christ.

Human Governments

Another component of the Dominion Mandate was given to Noah and his sons following the great Flood.

That component was the authorization of human government. The command was very simple, yet exceedingly broad in its implications. *"Whoso sheddeth man's blood, by man shall his blood be shed"* (Gen. 9:6). The crime of murder was no longer to be merely the trigger of a series of family "payback" revenge killings, leading to general continuing violence. Instead, God established the principle of human government to exercise authority over the process. This authority would inevitably imply the need to also exercise some kind of control over those human activities which might otherwise lead to murder — such things as robbery, assault, slander, rape, etc. Laws would have to be set up governing many types of human behavior, with appropriate punishment for disobedience.

Over the centuries many different forms of government have developed in the different nations of the world, ranging from pure democracies to total dictatorships. There have been absolute monarchies, limited monarchies, oligarchies, feudal systems, fascist and communist states, religious theocracies, and others. Americans generally believe that the governmental system developed by our founding fathers (Washington, Madison, Jefferson, et al.) is the best of all, although this opinion is not necessarily shared by the rest of the world. Nevertheless, many nations have tried to emulate it, at least in part. Furthermore, both our Constitution and our legal regulations have been largely founded on the English "common law," which in turn was developed mainly as an application of biblical principles centered around the Ten Commandments.

It is significant, however, that the Bible does not specify which form of government should be employed, but only that the nations are responsible to govern themselves, with everything developed around capital punishment as the ultimate enforcement weapon.

Whatever form the government may take, it is important to remember that *"there is no power but of God: the powers that be are ordained of God."* Consequently, God's will is that *"every soul be subject unto the higher powers"* (Rom. 13:1). This is true regardless of whether that "power" is kind or cruel, ungodly or righteous.

Even though we Christians are actually citizens of heaven, we are also commanded to be good citizens of our own nation here on earth. *"Put them in mind to be subject to principalities and powers,"* advised Paul to Pastor Titus concerning his flock, *"to obey magistrates, to be ready to every good work"* (Titus 3:1). And Peter said: *"Submit yourselves to every ordinance of man for the Lord's sake: whether it be to the king, as supreme; Or unto governors, as unto them that are sent by him for the punishment of evildoers, and for the praise of them that do well"* (1 Pet. 2:13–14). The Lord Jesus himself said: *"Render therefore unto Caesar the things which are Caesar's; and unto God the things that are God's"* (Matt. 22:21).

Of course, there is a limit. We are to render to God the service He commands, even if Caesar forbids it. *"We ought to obey God rather than men"* (Acts 5:29), was Peter's response to the decree of the council for the disciples to stop preaching about Christ.

In any case, God is clearly still much aware and concerned about the governments of nations, even though they are neither His chosen nation Israel nor His church. These governments are actually, whether they realize it or care, involved in one key phase of the Dominion Mandate. For the most part, they have fulfilled this role acceptably, at least in preventing the anarchy that prevailed before the Flood, when there were no governments.

However, one concern is that more and more nations have rejected capital punishment, no matter how heinous the murder or other crime. Since this was the very basis for God authorizing human government in the first place, this may turn out to be still another measure of how nations have failed to carry out God's Dominion Mandate, and therefore may soon find their appointed time ending.

There is coming a time, however, when the Lord Jesus Christ returns, that He will establish a better government throughout the earth.

DOES THE MANDATE APPLY TO OUTER SPACE?

As noted above, we need to be aware that God's primeval Dominion Mandate is still in effect for all nations. As a reminder, that mandate — originally given to Adam and Eve — is as follows:

> *And God blessed them, and God said unto them, Be fruitful, and multiply, and replenish the earth, and subdue it: and have dominion over the fish of the sea, and over the fowl of the air, and over every living thing that moveth upon the earth* (Gen. 1:28).

Such dominion and subjugation of the earth would necessarily entail developing a large population, and then much serious research into the systems and processes of the earth and its inhabitants, as well as the control and dissemination of this research to other men and women who can develop and apply it, all carried out as a divine stewardship under God. This project would eventually involve men and women serving in many different occupations — in fact, every honorable human occupation can well be included in this mandate.

Sometimes the word translated "earth" (Hebrew, *erets*) is used to refer particularly just to the ground. This is *not* the connotation here, however. God specifically said that man's dominion was to be *"over the fish of the sea, and over the fowl of the air, and over every living thing that moveth upon the earth."* Thus, the oceans and atmosphere, as well as the continents, are included.

WHAT ABOUT OUTER SPACE?

The outer heavens, on the other hand, were *not* mentioned in the mandate and so were *not* placed under man's dominion. This fact is made clear in later passages of Scripture. For example:

> *The heaven, even the heavens, are the LORD's: but the earth hath he given to the children of men* (Ps. 115:16).

In light of such a definitive prescription by God, should men talk about conquering outer space, as some have done? Consider also, the key sermon by Paul when he preached to the philosophers in Athens.

> *God that made the world and all things therein, seeing that he is Lord of heaven and earth . . . hath made of one blood all nations of men for to dwell on all the face of the earth, and hath determined the times before appointed, and the bounds of their habitation* (Acts 17:24–26).

This inspired assertion by Paul the apostle tells us that God has made all nations of men *"to dwell on all the face of the earth"* — not on Mars or Venus or some distant star, and apparently not even on an orbiting satellite such as Earth's Moon. None of these have the necessities for human life, such as air and water. Planet Earth, alone among all the known planets and satellites in the solar system (or anywhere else), is equipped to sustain man. *"The earth hath he given to the children of men* [literally, 'children of Adam']."

Note also the reference to *"the bounds of their habitation"* in Acts 17:26. God has apparently assigned specific boundaries, both geographically and chronologically, to each nation. All of these, of course, are on *"the face of the earth,"* never anywhere else.

Then, why do many men — especially scientists and politicians — want to spend untold billions of dollars on outer space? As one scientist acknowledged: "Astronomy and cosmology are of little earthly use."[1]

The answer, at least for most cosmologists and theoretical astronomers, is that they hope by such costly research to explain the universe without God and find evidence of life and evolution out there.

One eminent astronomer comments as follows: "It is therefore scientifically plausible to consider a universe with no need for an external

---

1 Horace F. Judson, "Century of the Sciences," *Science 84* (November 1984), p. 42.

creator in the traditional sense."[2] This notion is based on the popular current astronomical idea that some sort of "quantum fluctuation" in the primeval "nothing" produced a particle universe which then proceeded to evolve through inflation and the big bang into our present cosmos. Alan Guth, the inventor of the inflation hypothesis, says that "in the inflationary theory the universe evolves from essentially nothing at all, which is why I frequently refer to it as the ultimate free lunch."[3]

Such far-out ideas are not, of course, based on observation and are also beset by many theoretical difficulties. Nevertheless, they are believed by most cosmologists (at least if the published scientific journal articles and books in the field are any criterion). Even those cosmologists who reject the big bang and have various other cosmogonies to promote are also mostly writing within an atheistic perspective. There are, of course, a few who believe that the big bang confirms the account of creation in Genesis 1:1, but astronomer Paul Davies notes that: ". . . some still regard the big bang as 'the creation.' . . . However, this sort of armchair theology is wide of the mark. The popular idea of a God who sets the universe going like a clockwork toy and then sits back to watch was ditched by the Church in the last century."[4] There is little doubt that the vast majority of astronomers and cosmologists view the cosmos from an atheistic perspective.

The evolutionary world view could be buttressed, of course, if evidence of the development of life in other worlds than Earth alone could ever be found. This is what enables the politicians and cosmologists to obtain continual government funding for their hyper-expensive space projects. An important meeting was held for this very purpose several years ago. "But last week researchers from a host of disciplines gathered in Washington to build a case for protecting and expanding work on the origins of the universe, planetary systems, and life itself. Their goal is to convince the Clinton administration that further cuts to NASA's science budget will endanger efforts to understand how life emerged."[5]

One commentator has noted that: "Given a choice, many people would not spend a dime to explore the universe beyond Earth. They think

2 Paul Davies, "What Hath COBE Wrought?" *Sky and Telescope* (January 1993), p. 4.

3 Alan Guth, "Cooking Up a Cosmos," *Astronomy* (vol. 25, September 1997), p. 54.

4 Paul Davies, op. cit., p. 47.

5 Andrew Lawler, "Building a Bridge between the Big Bang and Theology," *Science* (vol. 274, November 8, 1996), p. 912.

social problems rate funding priority and therefore consider it wasteful to throw billions of tax dollars to achieve who-knows-what in return. . . . It's a 'given' that humans so yearn to discover life elsewhere; this underlying desire can be exploited to 'green light' almost any mission."[6]

Not even the waste of billions of dollars — not to mention sacrificing the lives of many dedicated and brilliant men and women — must be allowed to hinder space research, they say, "So continued planetary funding requires public relations — and glamour."[7]

There have been many valuable "spin-offs" from our space research, especially in the technological tools that have been developed to implement it. Furthermore, astronomy has for centuries had many practical earthly uses (in navigation, surveying, chronology, etc.). Modern research has led to tremendous advances in communications, weather forecasting, etc. These aspects surely are warranted in the Dominion Mandate. Also, many highly motivated men and women — not only engineers and scientists, but even many astronauts themselves — have contributed significantly to the program as sincere Christians, seeking to follow God's will in their lives.

Those aspects of the space program that have contributed specifically to our divinely ordained mandate of dominion over the earth are fully warranted, as far as the mandate itself is concerned. The risk to human life may be questioned, especially in view of the fact that unmanned space shuttles and other vehicles can be programmed to do almost everything that manned vehicles can do.

But space programs whose purpose is mainly to satisfy curiosity about cosmic or organic evolution do *not* seem (to me, at least) to be a part of the Dominion Mandate. It is *"the earth"* that has been *"given to the children of men"*!

However, I am admittedly as curious as anyone about the structure and purpose of all the trillions of stars, planets, and satellites that are out there. But the Bible says that, in the ages to come, we who have truly trusted the Word of God and have believed on the Lord Jesus Christ for forgiveness and salvation have eternity ahead of us to learn about God's creation. We cannot know much about all this right now, but at least we know there will be endless time ahead in which to learn and enjoy everything about God's limitless creation. Maybe the present

---

6 Bob Berman, "Strange Universe," *Astronomy* (vol. 28, August 2000), p. 100.
7 Ibid.

Dominion Mandate will be expanded to become a cosmic mandate. We shall see!

THE CRITICAL ROLE OF EDUCATION

Of all the components of human obedience to the Dominion Mandate, the ministry of teaching is the one of greatest interest to me personally. This would naturally follow from the fact that most of my life has been spent in the field of education — first (1942–70) in teaching engineering, then in teaching creationism and biblical evidences (1970–80), and more recently (1980–present) in graduate science education, especially in its administration and promotion.

Throughout all those years, I have been simultaneously involved in teaching God's Word, both in terms of straightforward Bible exposition and also in terms of defending our Christian faith scientifically. Both engineering teaching and Bible teaching have involved writing many books, many of which have even been used as textbooks by other teachers. All of this clearly involves the teaching implications of the Missionary Mandate as well as the Dominion Mandate, so I rather naturally have become an enthusiastic advocate of true education.

I now believe, as noted earlier, that true education — education as originally implied in the Dominion Mandate and also in the teaching component of the Great Commission — incorporates the premise of biblical inerrant authority and strict creationism in every subject being taught. This does not mean turning every physics course or music class into a Bible study, but rather maintaining this premise always in mind as we teach. On such occasions as a particular Bible passage is actually relevant to the subject matter, or when the question of origins is obviously involved in the exposition of a subject, then that material should be incorporated in a matter-of-fact way. Otherwise the physics class or whatever it is should proceed naturally as in a secular school, but always with the underlying awareness that God is the Creator and His Word is ultimate truth in all things.

The Great Commission, as it is known, is broader than many Christians realize. First of all, it involves Christians being sent into all the world. *"As my Father hath sent me,"* said Jesus to the disciples, *"even so send I you"* (John 20:21). Then, just before His return to heaven, He told them what they would do as they went. *"Ye shall be witnesses unto me . . . unto the uttermost part of the earth."* But how could they (or we) possibly do such a thing? *"Ye shall receive power, after that the Holy Ghost is come upon you"* (Acts 1:8), was His statement.

And what does it mean to be "witnesses"? The actual Greek word also means "martyrs," so this Commission could well involve real sacrifice in many cases. But *what* would be the content of their witness? On another occasion, He had already told them that *"repentance and remission of sins should be preached in his name among all nations"* (Luke 24:47). A more succinct, and yet more comprehensive statement of His Great Commission had been given on still another occasion, when He said, *"Go ye into all the world, and preach the gospel to every creature"* (Mark 16:15).

Yes, but just what is this *"gospel"* that we are to preach? The message clearly must include repentance and remission of sins, of course, but that is only a part. What is it that must be repented of, for example, and on what basis are sins to be forgiven? And then what?

The gospel we are to preach is, of course, the "good news" about Christ. That, in fact, is precisely the meaning of the Greek word itself. It is not "good advice" or "good philosophy." It is the wonderfully glad tidings in the record concerning Jesus Christ — specifically who He is, what He has done, and what He will do in the ages to come.

Its central focus is on the substitutionary death of Christ for our sins, His physical burial, and bodily resurrection (see 1 Corinthians 15:1–4). But it also includes His creation of all things in the beginning (Rev. 14:6–7 calls *that* the *"everlasting gospel"*). Furthermore, it includes the promised *"hope which is laid up for you in heaven, whereof ye heard before in the word of the truth of the gospel"* (Col. 1:5), as well as everything that God in Christ has said or done in anticipation of His promised heavenly kingdom.

The most extensive definition of that Commission was given when Jesus met with His first 11 disciples on a mountain in Galilee, and said:

> *All power is given unto me in heaven and in earth. Go ye therefore, and teach all nations, baptizing them in the name of the Father, and of the Son, and of the Holy Ghost: Teaching them to observe all things whatsoever I have commanded you: and, lo, I am with you alway, even unto the end of the world. Amen* (Matt. 28:18–20).

Twice in this Missionary Mandate, we note that He stressed the ministry of teaching. The scope of the commandment is indeed extensive; *all* nations are to be taught, and the teaching is to incorporate *everything* that Jesus taught.

And even that is not all. There was another great commission given to men and women back at the very beginning of time as we have seen, and it is still in effect. *"Have dominion over…every living thing that moveth upon the earth"* (Gen. 1:28), God had told our first parents. This primeval Dominion Mandate necessarily implies comprehensive scientific research into the nature of the earth and all its living creatures — plant life, animal life, human life. Then, for us to *"subdue"* the earth (Gen. 1:28) must involve the development of all kinds of technology and commerce and — especially — *education!* What is learned and implemented in one generation would be useless if not transmitted to the next generation. That requires the vital ministry of teaching!

When Christ told the disciples to *"teach all nations,"* the actual language He used was "make disciples in all nations." A disciple is not just a listener (like a student whose mind is closed or filled with trivia), but one who is a real learner and user of the information provided by his teacher. The word "disciple" is obviously related to "discipline." True education requires both a disciplined teacher and a disciplined learner. It is appropriate also that the various individual areas of study (science, math, language, etc.) are themselves known as "disciplines."

What is our Teaching to Include?

The *"all things"* we are to *"teach"* must clearly include *everything* that Christ comprehended in both His Dominion Mandate and His Missionary Mandate. Remember that our Lord created them all and has paid the price for their full redemption. He has promised that *"the* [creation] *itself shall be delivered from the bondage of corruption into the glorious liberty of the children of God"* (Rom. 8:21). This responsibility is further implied in Christ's command to *"preach the gospel,"* for, as noted above, the gospel itself also embraces all that Christ is, and does, and says, from creation to consummation. It is infinitely more comprehensive than just the atoning death and bodily resurrection of the Savior, as essential as these are. Belief in this central core of the gospel, along with personal faith in Christ and His Word, is vitally important and is sufficient for one's personal salvation — if truly understood and sincerely believed. But this "simple gospel" is definitely not all that is involved in the Great Commission, nor in the Dominion Mandate, which the Commission incorporates and extends.

The gospel of Christ which we have been commanded to preach, the person and work of Christ of whom we are to be witnesses, and the all-comprehensive teaching implied in the Great Commission and the Dominion Mandate involve nothing less than the wonderful plan of God for His entire creation in the eternal ages to come.

No individual Christian can preach or teach all these things. These orders must involve the entire company of His disciples, each using his or her own individual abilities and opportunities to help in the implementation of God's great plan, and doing it faithfully, as unto the Lord. To help us in doing our part, the Holy Spirit, indwelling each true disciple, has given special "gifts" to each person.

Some of these "gifts of the Spirit" are listed in Romans 12:6–8, some in 1 Corinthians 12:28, and some in Ephesians 4:11. All three listings are different, and each is obviously incomplete. Thus, it is reasonable to conclude that there may be other gifts not covered in any of these three sample lists, that would be given as people and needs vary over the years. *"There are diversities of gifts, but the same Spirit"* (1 Cor. 12:4).

It is significant that the only gifts mentioned in all three of the biblical lists are those of prophecy and teaching. However, the apostle Paul said that the prophetic gift (that is, of conveying new, inspired revelation from God to those early believers) would soon vanish away, presumably when the New Testament Scriptures had been completed (see 1 Cor. 13:8; also note John's warning at the end of his Book of Revelation not to add anything more — Rev. 22:18). That tells us that the gift of teaching has the distinction of being the one *permanent* gift of the Spirit stressed in all three of the Bible's listings, and therefore needed permanently in the accomplishment of the Great Commission.

Furthermore, there is surely more than one type of teaching gift. Teaching the Bible is different from teaching music, for example. Also, teaching middle-school children is very different from teaching graduate students in science or teaching pastoral students in a seminary. But all teaching, too, requires good preparation, sincere interest in students as well as subject matter, and — for Christian teachers in particular — doing it as unto the Lord, *"Whatsoever ye do, do it heartily, as to the Lord, and not unto men"* (Col. 3:23).

The Lord does not call everyone to be a teacher. In fact, He warns those who are *not* truly called to a teaching ministry against trying to be one. *"My brethren, be not many masters* [same Greek word as 'teachers'], *knowing that we shall receive the greater condemnation"* (James 3:1). Recognizing the basic importance of training the younger generation, Satan has managed to deceive many pseudo-disciples into becoming *false* teachers, thereby incurring severe judgment on themselves. *"There* [shall be] *false teachers also among you . . . who privily shall bring in damnable heresies, even denying the Lord that bought them and bring upon themselves swift destruction"* (2 Pet. 2:1).

We need to realize that the Dominion Mandate still applies to all people, both Christians and non-Christians, whereas the Great Commission is the responsibility of Christians only. The latter, therefore, have a double responsibility in "subduing" the earth. With respect to science, for example, we not only want to win individual scientists to salvation in Christ, but also to bring the sciences themselves under submission to God and His Word. This includes warning students about the deadly fallacies of evolutionary philosophy, and secular humanism in general (whether the teacher is a parent in a home school, a dedicated teacher in a Christian school, or one of the occasional Christian teachers in the modern mission field called public schools). It applies in an extreme sense to college and university teachers, especially to those teaching science at the graduate level as they prepare our future scientific researchers and educators.

Considering the importance Christ placed on teaching in His Great Commission, as well as its pre-eminent position among the gifts of the Holy Spirit (the gift of evangelism is mentioned in only one of the three lists, for example; the gift of teaching is in all three), as well as its essential importance in implementing God's Dominion Mandate, the entire Christian community is surely responsible to provide whatever support is needed to enable these teaching ministries to function effectively.

This discussion of teaching and learning obviously implies the use of teaching tools — especially books. Books, of course, have been produced and in use since men first learned how to write. This goes back to Adam himself! The Bible actually mentions *"the book of the generations of Adam"* (Gen. 5:1), with the implication that Adam wrote down the material in Genesis 2–4.

CHAPTER III

THE NEED TO READ

As important as reading is in the implementation of true education, it is necessary also to remind ourselves to be *"redeeming the time"* (Eph. 5:16; Col. 4:5), and not to waste time reading books that are harmful or useless. Time is our most valuable possession; once lost, it can never be regained, unlike lost money or lost health.

THE IMPORTANCE OF RIGHT READING

Among the very last words written by the great apostle Paul were these: *"The cloak that I left at Troas with Carpus, when thou comest, bring with thee, and the books, but especially the parchments"* (2 Tim. 4:13). When he wrote, Paul was in a cold, damp, dark Roman dungeon, awaiting his imminent execution by Nero and knowing that *"the time of my departure is at hand"* (verse 6).

Yet he still wanted to read! Evidently his arrest by the emperor's officers had been so abrupt there at the home of his friend Carpus that he could not even gather up his winter coat, let alone his personal library. As to what these books were (the parchments were probably the Old Testament Scriptures) we can only speculate, but we do know that Paul was well educated and well read.

Whatever they were, we can be sure they were books that would be helpful in understanding and teaching the Word of God. He had urged his followers always to redeem the time, and he certainly would not have wasted his last days in reading *"profane and vain babblings"* (1 Tim. 6:20), nor *"the wisdom of this world, nor of the princes of this world, that come to nought"* (1 Cor. 2:6).

And he surely would not want books dealing with the "curious arts" of occultism or mysticism — books such as those which his Christian converts at Corinth had once used but, after receiving Christ, had voluntarily decided to destroy — even though they could probably have been sold (at today's prices) for a million dollars (Acts 19:18–20).

Paul's books may well have included books dealing with creation and ancient history (it is fascinating to note that Paul quoted from three early Greek writers who had dealt with this theme, when he debated with the evolutionary philosophers at Athens — Acts 17:23–28). It is also worth noting that Paul quoted from or alluded to references in the Book of Genesis approximately 100 times in his epistles. He was profoundly interested in the primeval origin of the world and of the nations, especially Israel.

In any case, he had previously urged young Timothy (who had *"from a child…known the holy scriptures"*; see 2 Tim. 3:15) to *"give attendance to reading, to exhortation, to doctrine"* (1 Tim. 4:13), and Paul would surely continue to do so himself as long as he lived.

Now, if reading good books was of such vital importance for Paul and the early Christians, it is surely even more important for us today.

Actually, books have *always* been important. The very first man on earth probably wrote the very first book on earth — *"the book of the generations of Adam"* (Gen. 5:1) — in which he recorded the great events that took place at the creation, the Fall, and the Curse. Archaeology has shown that people have been able to read and write throughout all known history. Literally thousands of clay and stone tablets have been unearthed at Ebla, Ur, and other ancient cities, dating back to well before the days of Abraham. Furthermore, these were not just books written by scholars for other scholars. They included grocery lists, property transactions, and all kinds of mundane documents. *Everyone* knew how to read and write, long before Abraham or Moses.

There is good evidence that the Book of Genesis was written by Adam, Noah, and the other ancient patriarchs, then finally compiled and edited by Moses as the first book in the Pentateuch. People have been reading books since the beginning of history.

Interestingly, the first mention of "book" in Scripture had to do with Adam's book, as noted above. The first mention in the New Testament is in Matthew 1:1 — *"The book of the generation of Jesus Christ."*

Thus, the Old Testament deals with the heritage of *"the first man Adam"*; the New Testament with that of *"the second man . . . the Lord from heaven"* (1 Cor. 15:45–47), and both were written in books as the Lord's Word . . . forever *"settled in heaven"* (Ps. 119:89).

The truly indispensable books, of course, are the 66 books of the Bible, from Genesis through Revelation. In fact, this collection is called *THE* Book — the Bible. The word "Bible" comes from the Greek *biblion*, which means "book" and is used some 30 times in the New Testament. The final occurrence of *biblion* seems clearly to refer to the *completed* Bible, warning men not to take any of the words away *"from the things which are written in this book"* (Rev. 22:19). Like Paul, however, we do need to be selective in what we read. Many authors have had great influence for bad (Darwin, Marx, Mao, Kinsey, etc.), and time is too precious to waste on harmful or trivial reading.

We now are living in what many are calling "the information age," though much of the information being disseminated might better be called "disinformation," just as much of what is called "science" is really *"science falsely so called"* (1 Tim. 6:20). Serious reading, whether of the Bible or substantive books of any kind, is being phased out of the lives of many people — even Christians — in this "information age." Movies and live entertainment, television and video, and now the great web, are providing so much mini-information and absorbing so much time that good books and the Good Book itself are being forgotten.

This is not good. Communication via video and the Internet can be greatly used by Christians, as well as others, of course, and ICR itself *has* produced many fine videos and has a significant web page, but the best way to *really* learn is still through direct personal reading and study — especially of the Bible, but also of other good books — books that are sound and substantive, biblically as well as scientifically and historically.

Dr. Gertrude Himmelfarb, one of our finest living historians, recently made the following insightful comment concerning the Bible:

> If we want, for example, a concordance to the Bible, we can find no better medium than the Internet. But if we want to read the Bible, to study it, think about it, reflect upon it, we should have it in our hands, for that is the only way of getting it into our minds and hearts.[1]

1 Gertrude Himmelfarb, "Revolution in the Library," *American Scholar* (Spring 1997).

Dr. Himmelfarb was using the Bible as an example, but, in context, she was stressing the unique importance of reading good books in general. She herself is not writing as a Christian, but merely as a distinguished scholar concerned about the decline of the humanities in modern thought. She is professor emeritus of the Graduate School of the City University of New York.

One of her early books, *Darwin and the Darwinian Revolution* (London: Chatto and Windus, 1959, 422 p.), was a devastating critique of the social impact of Darwinism. Her latest book, *The De-Moralization of Society: From Victorian Virtues to Modern Values* (New York: Alfred A. Knopf, 1995), won the annual Templeton Foundation Prize as the Outstanding Contemporary Book for 1997.

In her article for the *American Scholar* (the journal of the Phi Beta Kappa honorary society), Dr. Himmelfarb was deploring the over-computerization of modern university libraries. While appreciative of computer catalogs and the ability to retrieve information rapidly, as well as other advantages, she was concerned with the fact that "workstations" were replacing carrels and that students and faculty were consulting the Internet more than the books, especially the great books that reach both mind and heart. She concluded her study with these words:

> *These are the books that sustain our mind and inspire our imagination. It is there that we look for truth, for knowledge, for wisdom. And it is these ideals that we hope will survive our latest revolution.*[2]

Professor Himmelfarb was concerned (and rightly so) about the decline of reading the great books of the past (Augustine, Milton, etc.), and we need to encourage Christians as well to *"give attendance to reading"* — both the Bible and substantive Christian books of both past and present. It is especially important to get our young people in the habit of reading good Christian books that are both sound biblically (particularly with reference to creation and history) and also reliable factually.

In the closing words of his gospel, the apostle John made an amazing claim: *"And there are also many other things which Jesus did, the which, if they should be written every one, I suppose that even the world itself could not contain the books that should be written. Amen"* (John 21:25).

---

2 Ibid.

How could this be? Such a statement seems like a gross exaggeration. But there is at least one intriguing possibility.

The footnote on this verse in *The Defender's Study Bible* makes this comment:

> *This apparently hyperbolic statement is actually quite realistic. The four Gospels only record what Jesus began both to do and teach (Acts 1:1). These works and words have been continued throughout the world for 2,000 years by all those in whom Christ dwells by the Holy Spirit. If every such person could write a complete autobiography about all that the indwelling Spirit of God has done in and through him, the number of books would indeed be astronomical. And this will continue throughout eternity.*[3]

In this sense, another seemingly exaggerated observation, way back in the days of King Solomon, might also turn out to be precisely true. *". . . of making many books there is no end"* (Eccles. 12:12). Solomon then complained, however, that *"much study is a weariness of the flesh,"* and this can be true today as well. Serious reading does take time, of course, and may well involve discipline and prioritizing of one's time commitments. Remember that the good can be the enemy of the best.

For whatever my personal testimony may be worth, studying the Bible and good books have been of inestimable blessing to me for almost 65 years. I believe many others could say the same.

Therefore, I would commend it to you as well!

MANY BOOKS

With the worldwide proliferation of television sets and personal computers, along with the proposed global superhighway of information, one wonders if books may soon become as outdated as slide rules.

I hope not, of course, because I have always loved books myself, and they do have a long and vitally useful history. King Solomon could say, a thousand years before Christ, that *"of making many books there is no end"* (Eccles. 12:12).

The Bible, of course, is *the* Book, written by God himself, using the talents and resources of divinely prepared men to convey it down

---

3 Henry M. Morris, *The Defender's Study Bible* (Grand Rapids, MI: World Publishing Inc., 1995), 1620 p.

to man, after it had been *"for ever . . . settled in heaven"* (Ps. 119:89). God is still writing books in heaven (note His *"book of remembrance"* — Malachi 3:16 — and *"the books"* in which are written *"their works,"* books which are to be opened at the judgment — Revelation 20:12). There is also the wonderful *"book of life"* with the names of all who have been redeemed through faith in Jesus Christ as their great Creator, Savior, and coming King. The very last section of the Bible then contains a grave warning against altering even the words of God's Book (Rev. 22:18–19).

The Bible, of course, has been the most *widely* read and most influential book ever written, but many other books have also had great impact on the life of the world — not always for good.

One thinks immediately of the deadly effects of such books as *Mein Kampf* and *Das Kapital*, leading multitudes into misery and death. And what about Darwin's *Origin of Species*, the influence of which has dominated every course in the schools and colleges of the world for over a hundred years now?

So books are important, and people ought to read, but it is important *which* books they read! Every Christian, of course, should seek to be a diligent reader and student of the Bible, as well as sound books defending and expounding its teachings, not wasting his limited and precious time on harmful or trivial reading, but rather *"redeeming the time, because the days are evil"* (Eph. 5:16).

A BOOKWORM AUTHOR

I am open to the charge of bias on this subject, but I know what a blessing the Bible, as well as many other books, have been in my own life. As a child and teenager, I must have spent all my spare time either playing ball (I once had the soon-aborted hope of becoming a professional baseball player, believe it or not!) or reading books. I read all the Oz books, the Tarzan books, the Sherlock Holmes books, and countless other library books — even *Pilgrim's Progress* — as well as the Bible my mother had given me, and which, more than anything else, led me to Christ.

It was more or less natural, then, that I would soon think of becoming a writer. I was editor of my junior high school paper and sports editor of my senior high school paper, so I had hopes of then majoring in journalism in college. Those were the years of the depression, however, and finances would not allow going off to the University of Texas to do this.

Instead, I enrolled at Rice University to study engineering, so I could live at home and go to a (then) tuition-free university.

This was all in the providence of God, although I certainly did not realize it at the time. The Lord has given me, by His grace, a productive career in *both* science (engineering is "applied science") and writing. This combination has turned out to be effective in encouraging people to return to true biblical Christianity at a time when our nation was rapidly drifting away from its theistic foundations into deep paganism and materialism.

When I returned to Rice as a teacher in 1942, I soon felt the need for a small book scientifically and biblically explaining and defending the Christian gospel. I had begun trying to win students to Christ, and this led to the publication of my first Christian book, *That You Might Believe*. That was almost 60 years ago, in 1946, and that book has gone through several revisions and has been used to lead many to salvation. It is still available through Moody Press under the title *Science and the Bible*.

My *first* book, however, was an engineering monograph, *The Rio Grande Water Conservation Investigation*, explaining various hydrological studies which led eventually to the construction of a number of large dams on the Rio Grande and tributaries. I later wrote a number of other engineering books, one of which, *Applied Hydraulics in Engineering* (John Wiley and Sons) was used as a textbook in over 100 universities.

Most of my books, however, have been written in defense and exposition of our Christian faith, especially upholding the truth of literal biblical creationism and opposing all forms of evolutionism. Again in God's providence, the most influential of these, co-authored with Dr. John Whitcomb, was *The Genesis Flood*, published in 1961 by Presbyterian and Reformed. Many subsequent writers, both creationists and evolutionists, have said it was this book that catalyzed the modern revival of creationism, leading to a great proliferation of other creationist books and ministries around the world. Although it was not written as an evangelistic book, the Lord did use this book also to lead many to faith and a changed life through Christ.

I guess that, after this, writing became sort of an "occupational disease" with me, and I seem to have averaged about a book a year since catching it. Many of these books are still in print, and all have been wonderfully used by the Lord in reaching people for Christ and in strengthening the faith and testimony of believers.

Among the more significant of these books have been: *The Genesis Record*, a widely-used commentary on the foundational book of the Bible; *Scientific Creationism*, a text and reference book on creationism; *Many Infallible Proofs*, an equally influential book on the practical evidences of the truth of Christianity; *The Biblical Basis for Modern Science*, the only textbook dealing in depth with each major science in its biblical context; *The Long War Against God*, the most complete and documented exposition of the history and modern influence of evolutionism; *History of Modern Creationism*, the only complete history of the creation movement written from a sympathetic perspective; and *Biblical Creationism*, an exposition of every passage in the Bible dealing with creation or the other events of early earth history.

Most recently published is *The Defender's Study Bible*, with extensive footnotes and appendices especially written with the purpose of defending and expounding literal biblical Christianity. I can speak firsthand about God's blessing on my own books, but whether people read any of my books or not, I strongly encourage them to maintain a lifelong practice of reading sound God-honoring, faith-stimulating Christian literature.

So — use the Internet and other modern technologies judicially, but I trust you will also keep on reading and studying the Bible and good books that support the Bible, whether mine or others. There can really be no substitute for this component in developing and maintaining a consistently sound and fruitful Christian life and witness.

God, in His grace and providential leading, thus allowed me to be involved in both writing (my early interest and desire) and practical science (my training and experience). He has enabled me to combine the two in the much-needed defense and propagation of biblical creationism, supporting the full integrity and authority of the wonderful, written Word of God.

Most importantly, good books on many subjects by many authors must always be vital in carrying out the education component of God's Dominion and Missionary Mandates.

God's Library in Heaven

As one might guess by now, I have always loved libraries. As a child, I spent much time in the Houston Public Library and read many books. As an engineering student (later, also as a teacher), spending my spare time at the Rice University Library was a favorite activity — then even more so in the library at the University of Minnesota where I was both an instructor and a graduate student. Still later, when I was an engineering department head, the Virginia Tech Library provided much of my documentation for the book *The Genesis Flood*. Now we have our own ICR Research Library, and all of the ICR scientists (certainly including myself) are finding it extremely useful.

But I believe that God must also have a library — or at least some system that serves the purpose of a library. There are many, many books there, and the number is constantly increasing. Christ himself is called *"the Word,"* with the specific purposing of *"declaring"* God's nature and purpose to man (John 1:1, 18, 15).

The core of God's library is, of course, the Word as declared in written form by the Living Word to holy men of old through the Holy Spirit. We call this the 66 "books" of the Bible, and God has assured us that *this* part of His library was established before He created the world. *"For ever, O Lord, thy word is settled in heaven"* (Ps. 119:89).

The initial section of this Book ("Bible" means "Book") was probably written by the first man, Adam. At its conclusion, he appended his signature: *"This is the book of the generations of Adam"* (Gen. 5:1). Later, Noah added his record of the antediluvian patriarchs, signing it: *"These are the generations of Noah"* (Gen. 10:1). The post-Flood records were kept by Shem, Terah, Isaac, Jacob, and probably Joseph, each normally terminating his record by the standard closing phrase: *"These are the generations of..."* (Gen. 11:10, 27; 25:19; 37:2; Exod. 1:1). All these record tablets were eventually collected and edited by Moses into the Book of Genesis.[4]

Then, *"at sundry times and in divers manners [God] spake in time past unto the fathers by the prophets"* (Heb. 1:1) until eventually all the books of the Old Testament had been conveyed down from heaven to man (the "original" possibly still being kept in the heavenly ark of the covenant for eternal reference — note Hebrews 9:4; Revelation 11:19).

The books of the New Testament were then *"revealed unto his holy apostles and prophets by the Spirit"* (Eph. 3:5), one by one, until the last book was inscribed by the last living apostle. When John finished writing down the book entitled *"The Revelation of Jesus Christ"* (Rev. 1:1), he signaled that the written word from heaven was now complete on earth,

---

4 See my book, *The Genesis Record* (Grand Rapids, MI: Baker Book House, 1976), p. 22–30 for further discussion.

with a sober warning neither to *"add unto these things,"* nor to *"take away from the words of the book of this prophecy"* (Rev. 22:18–19).

This entire New Testament section of these books of God was introduced as *"the book of the generation of Jesus Christ"* (Matt. 1:1), corresponding fittingly to the *"book of the generations of Adam"* (Gen. 5:1). Thus, in one sense, the entire Bible is composed of two books — one being the history of the first Adam and his physical seed, the second comprising the history of *"the last Adam"* (1 Cor. 15:45) and His spiritual seed. And all of these wonderful books are surely maintained in God's great heavenly library, as well as in countless human libraries on earth.

But then there are other books there, too — possibly a separate book recording the details of the life of each individual who has ever lived. When believers meet Christ at His judgment seat, there will be rewards assigned (or loss of rewards) *"according to that he hath done, whether it be good or bad"* (1 Cor. 3:11–15; 2 Cor. 5:10). *"The fire shall try every man's work* [according to] *what sort it is"* (1 Cor. 3:13). Perhaps the fire will burn up those portions of his "book" that are "bad," leaving only the "good" on his permanent record.

When unbelievers later go before God's great judgment throne, John said: *"I saw the dead, small and great, stand before God; and the books were opened: and another book was opened, which is the book of life: and the dead were judged out of those things which were written in the books, according to their works"* (Rev. 20:12).

These books evidently list all the "works" of each person, but since no one has kept all God's commands, therefore no one will be saved by his works (James 2:10; Rom. 3:10, 20, 23; etc.). So the judge will then turn to His *"book of life,"* in which are inscribed all the names of those redeemed by faith in the shed blood of the Lamb of God, the Lord Jesus Christ (1 Pet. 1:18–21; Rev. 13:8). *"And whosoever was not found written in the book of life was cast into the lake of fire"* (Rev. 20:15).

There is yet another very special book in God's library. *"Then they that feared the Lord spake often one to another: and the Lord hearkened, and heard it, and a book of remembrance was written before him for them that feared the Lord, and that thought upon his name"* (Mal. 3:16).

This little insight into the personal library records of God was given in connection with the band of Israelites who had returned from exile in Babylon. It is reasonable to think, however, that God is keeping the same kind of book for every group of believers who fear the Lord, think often on His name, and speak frequently to one another about Him.

But that is not all. John 21:25 is a very intriguing verse, concluding John's gospel as it does, *"And there are also many other things which Jesus did, the which, if they should be written every one, I suppose that even the world itself could not contain the books that should be written."*

That seems, on the surface, like an exaggeration, but it opens up an intriguing possibility. The very next verses are Acts 1:1–2: *"The former treatise have I made, O Theophilus, of all that Jesus began both to do and teach, Until the day in which he was taken up. . . ."* The implication is that the four gospel records of the life of Christ need to be supplemented with what He did and taught *after* He was taken up.

He would shortly be sending His Holy Spirit to indwell, teach, and guide each of His followers. Thus, He would continue His work through them, and all that *they* accomplished in His name down through the years would, in effect, be a continuation of what *He began*!

Thus, there could well be a special book written for each of His millions of disciples, describing all that their indwelling Lord accomplished through them as they studied and worked and witnessed in His name. Jesus had promised, when the Holy Spirit would come to *"abide with you for ever,"* that *"if a man love me, he will keep my words: and my Father will love him, and we will come unto him, and make our abode with him"* (John 14:16, 23). The Lord Jesus thus is continuing *"to do and teach"* through each of us, and all of these activities and their results could indeed be the subject of literally millions of *"books that should be written"* (John 21:25).

But even that is not all. Jesus Christ was himself the Creator of *"all things . . . that are in heaven, and that are in earth"* (Col. 1:16). Furthermore, He continues even now in His ongoing work of *"upholding all things by the word of his power"* (Heb. 1:3). Therefore, in Him *"are hid all the treasures of wisdom and knowledge"* (Col. 2:3), and He has given us the high privilege of "thinking His thoughts after Him," as many godly scientists through the years have described this calling.

When He first created Adam and Eve, He gave them the responsibility of subduing the earth and exercising dominion over it (Gen. 1:26–28). This necessarily implied research and technology, communications and education — indeed, all honorable occupations. Many books would need to be written describing the processes and systems of earth and all its inhabitants, finally filling many libraries around the world.

In the eternal ages to come, however, when the earth and its heavens have been purged of all corruption and then made new again (2 Pet. 3:10–13), we shall have the honor of serving Him in this *"new heaven and new earth"* (Rev. 21:1). *"And there shall be no more curse...and his servants shall serve him"* (Rev. 22:3).

No doubt there will be many and varied occupations by which we shall serve Him, just as there are in this present world. It seems most likely that we shall no longer be limited to this one planet, for He *"shall change our vile body, that it may be fashioned like unto his glorious body"* (Phil. 3:21). We shall be no longer bound by gravity, but, like Him, have access to His entire magnificent created universe!

The Bible teaches that the universe is as infinitely great as the very thoughts and ways of God (Isa. 55:9), and that it will endure forever (Eccles. 3:14; Ps. 148:1–6; Dan. 12:3; etc.). We can study it and describe it and serve in it eternally without ever exhausting its infinite beauties and mysteries.

And we can probably write books about what *we* learn and do there, as well as reading the books of what our fellow believers are learning and doing there. It may finally be literally true that *"of making many books there is no end"* (Eccles. 12:12).

What a library that will become some day! God's thoughts will, more and more, forever, be becoming our thoughts, though we can never reach the end, for there *is* no end! *"Unto him be glory in the church by Christ Jesus throughout all ages, world without end. Amen"* (Eph. 3:21).

It seems clear that — regardless of television, the Internet and other modern technologies for conveying information — books will always be of primary importance in this component of the Dominion Mandate. So get in the habit of reading — especially the Bible, as well as other good books expounding the Word of God, the world of God, and the works of God.

CHAPTER IV

The Miracle Named Jesus

We need to reemphasize, before delving more deeply into this complex theme involving God's two mandates, along with the issue of origins and judgment to come, just how infinitely important this man Jesus Christ really is. Not only was it He who pronounced the Missionary Mandate, but who also issued the Dominion Mandate back in the beginning.

After all, Jesus Christ is God — the incarnate Word made flesh (John 1:14)! In the mystery of the triune godhead, He is the eternally begotten Son of the Father, the God/Man. *"All things were made by him"* (John 1:3), so He was the One with whom Adam and Eve conversed there in Eden's garden. It was there they first received the Dominion Mandate, when *"God said unto them, Be fruitful, and multiply . . . and have dominion . . . over every living thing that moveth upon the earth"* (Gen. 1:28).

He was our Creator but, when He also was made *"in the likeness of sinful flesh, and for sin, condemned sin in the flesh"* (Rom. 8:3), He became our Redeemer as well when He died for our sins. In that mission, He has become personal Lord and Savior to us who believe, giving *us* (not all, but just us Christians) the Missionary Mandate, the Great Commission, to combine with the Dominion Mandate.

But even that is not all that He is. *"For the Father judgeth no man, but hath committed all judgment unto the Son"* (John 5:22). It is none other than *"the Lord Jesus Christ, who shall judge the quick and the dead at his appearing and his kingdom"* (2 Tim. 4:1).

He is thus the final judge of all, as well as Creator of all, and Redeemer, Savior, and Lord of all who believe on Him. We do well, therefore, to carefully heed His words, for He also said: *"He that rejecteth me, and receiveth not my words, hath one that judgeth him: the word that I have spoken, the same shall judge him in the last day"* (John 12:48).

Now some might say that they are willing to believe the words spoken by the great teacher, Jesus. It is the words of the Old Testament which they can no longer accept — especially those "legendary" accounts back in the early chapters of Genesis.

But any such temporizers should also think about *these* words of Jesus: *"For had ye believed Moses, ye would believe me, for he wrote of me. But if ye believe not his writings, how shall ye believe my words?"* (John 5:46–47).

For example, consider the words of Christ, when He said, *"But from the beginning of the creation God made them male and female. For this cause shall a man leave his father and mother, and cleave to his wife"* (Mark 10:6–7).

In this very brief exposition, Christ was not only confirming the priority of monogamous marriage but also quoting as divinely authoritative two brief excerpts from two chapters in Genesis (Gen. 1:27 and Gen. 2:24). The problem is that modern-day evolutionists make the dogmatic claim that these two chapters contradict each other, and they also claim that "the beginning of the creation" had taken place about 4½ billion years before "God made them male and female." Not only was the Bible scientifically wrong, they claim, but also self-contradictory.

The Lord Jesus Christ obviously would not endorse this skeptical denial of the creation record, and He was there! Are modern skeptical intellectuals willing to call Him ignorant, or careless, or even deceptive? I hope not.

But so many modern intellectuals — not only atheistic unbelievers but even many "liberal" professing Christians — are beginning to think of Jesus as only a gifted human teacher rather than as incarnate Deity, infallible in His teachings. We need to emphasize as strongly as we can that He was the God/man. Whatever He said and did was perfectly right — just by definition.

Not only could He perform miracles, He himself was a living miracle — born supernaturally, lived sinlessly, died volitionally, and raised in perfection eternally. As people read the profoundly simple records of His words and deeds in the New Testament, they naturally think mostly in terms of His humanity. But they need to look much deeper, especially in light of history.

THE LIGHT OF THE WORLD

For example, one of the most amazing statements ever made was the assertion of Jesus Christ in the temple in Jerusalem one early morning long ago, speaking to a group of bigoted religionists who were seeking an excuse to condemn Him. This claim immediately brands Him as either a raving lunatic or a conniving charlatan — or — (could it conceivably be true?) as the very Son of God himself!

THE AMAZING CLAIM

Here is what He said: *"I am the light of the world: he that followeth me shall not walk in darkness, but shall have the light of life"* (John 8:12).

A listener may have thought, *But, Sir, it is the mighty sun that illumines the world, not some wandering preacher from Galilee like yourself. The sun moving high in the sky provides light so that men do not have to walk around in the dark, so how can you claim to be the sun? The sun does, indeed, make life possible, with its radiant energy causing plants to grow and rivers to flow; it can certainly be said to be "the light of life." But how can you, of all creatures, claim to give life?*

"Oh," His followers might reply, "He was just speaking metaphorically. He is the *spiritual* light, giving *spiritual* life, conquering *spiritual* darkness, not really claiming to produce sunlight."

But that's just as bad, isn't it? — this country preacher with no formal education and only a motley group of deluded followers! Yet here He is professing to provide the spiritual, as well as moral and intellectual guidance for the whole wide world, when neither He nor His disciples have ever even traveled beyond the borders of Israel! How could this Jesus, from Nazareth, possibly expect anyone to believe *that?*

THE ASTOUNDING FULFILLMENT

Yet, for the past two thousand years there have indeed been millions of people from all over this whole wide world who have believed just that, and whose lives have been transformed because of it. Further, not only have individual men and women been transformed; so have whole societies and cultures. Great educational institutions have been established in His name, as well as hospitals and charities of all kinds, not to mention multiplied thousands of churches and helpful ministries in great variety. Nations have been established to serve Him; even the worldwide evil of slavery has almost been abolished.

Most of the founding fathers of science were sincere followers of Jesus, as well as the greatest medical researchers of the past. The Lord Jesus Christ, even though despised by so many of His contemporaries that He was judicially executed in a uniquely cruel manner by their leaders, has indeed been the Light of the World ever since, not only spiritually, but also intellectually and morally. Those who choose to follow Him have not walked in darkness but gladly testify that they have found the Light of life, just as He promised.

But that is not all, by any means! By overcoming death and rising from His tomb in a glorified physical body (which many would evaluate as the best-proved fact in history), He proved himself to be (as He also claimed) the omnipotent Son of God, equal with the Heavenly Father — the very Word of God made flesh!

But there is more! As His early disciples soon began to proclaim on His authority, it was also He who had actually created all things. He was not the sun (the physical light of the world), but He is greater than the sun, for He created the sun! *"By him were all things created, that are in heaven . . ."* (Col. 1:16). *"All things were made by him"* (John 1:3). It was obvious that God, in the beginning, created heaven and earth, but He *"created all things by Jesus Christ"* (Eph. 3:9).

Not only was the physical light of the world — the sun — created by Christ, but it is He who has kept it shining ever since. It is the eternal Son of God — *"whose goings forth have been from of old, from everlasting"* (Mic. 5:2), *"Who being the brightness of* [God's] *glory, and the express image of his person"* — who is still *"upholding all things by the word of his power"* (Heb. 1:3). Scientists are still somewhat uncertain as to what keeps the sun shining, though most of them promote the theory of thermonuclear fusion processes in its deep interior. There are unsolved difficulties even with this explanation, however, and no one really *knows.*

We do know, however, since the Bible is God's Word, that Jesus Christ the Creator is also the conserver. He upholds everything by His own power! *"By him all things consist"* (Col. 1:17). Not only our sun, in fact, but all the suns of the cosmos! Indeed, He *is* the light — not only of our little world, but of the entire physical universe! In the promised future new earth, in fact, with its magnificent holy city, we are told that the city will not even need the sun for its light, *"for the glory of God did lighten it, and the Lamb is the light thereof"* (Rev. 21:23).

Note, incidentally, the anticipatory intimation in such verses of the modern scientific concept of the equivalence of mass and energy. *Things are held together by* *power*. And that power is nothing less than the power of Christ himself. In Him, all things *"consist"* (literally, "are sustained" or "held together"). Our gentle, loving Savior is the mighty Creator of all things who is now upholding all things and someday will restore all things to their primeval perfection.

As far as physical life is concerned, He also claimed that those who follow Him not only would no longer *"walk in darkness"* but also would possess *"the light of life."*

Modern physical science (at least classical physics) was centered around the electro-magnetic spectrum, which included all the varieties of force and energy in nature — light, heat, sound, electricity, magnetism, chemical energy, etc. — everything except gravity and nuclear energy. Light, of course, in a sense covers the whole spectrum, from long-wavelength infra-red to short-wave ultra-violet radiation, with the visible light spectrum occupying the key center, as it were.

In a significant sense, light energy is thus the most basic energy of all, and it is not surprising that the first words recorded by the living Word of God were: *"Let there be light"* (Gen. 1:3). There were no "lights" as such at that point, however, until He said: *"Let there be lights"* (Gen. 1:14). Then, instantaneously appeared in the sky the two great lights for the earth and *"the stars also"* (Gen. 1:16) scattered throughout the vast cosmos.

And all of these lights — and the light which they generated and sent forth to be *"for signs, and for seasons, and for days, and years"* (Gen. 1:14) — would also serve life itself through the many marvelous mechanisms it would energize for earth's coming inhabitants (photosynthesis, etc.).

Thus it is that: *"In him* [that is, the Word of God] *was life; and the life was the light of men"* (John 1:4). It then follows also that Christ is *"the true Light, which lighteth every man that cometh into the world"* (John 1:9).

And that is true in both the physical sense and spiritual sense. Physically, *"in him we live, and move, and have our being"* so that He is *"not far from every one of us"* (Acts 17:28, 27). It should be painfully sobering for even those who refuse to believe on Him to realize suddenly (as they must, someday) that their very existence — even the cellular structure of their bodies — depends on His moment-by-moment maintenance. If

He were to withdraw His power for an instant, we would collapse into nothingness.

Spiritually, we are likewise assured that He enlightens *"every man that cometh into the world"* (John 1:9). That is, even those born in some heathen home and those who may spend all their lives without ever hearing of Christ have been given some spiritual light (in nature, in conscience, in history, etc.), so that if they respond positively to the light they have, they will then somehow be given more and more light, eventually enough to be saved. The classic biblical example is the Roman Cornelius, to whom God eventually sent Peter with the full message of salvation through Christ. As Peter said at that time: *"God is no respecter of persons: But in every nation he that feareth him, and worketh righteousness, is accepted with him"* (Acts 10:34–35).

The warning, however, is that those who do not respond to whatever light they have are *"without excuse"* and thus will *"die in* [their] *sins"* (Rom. 1:20, John 8:24), because they do not believe on Christ. And the tragedy is that *"light is come into the world, and men loved darkness rather than light, because their deeds were evil"* (John 3:19). Nevertheless, *"the eyes of the Lord run to and fro throughout the whole earth, to shew himself strong in the behalf of them whose heart is perfect toward him"* (2 Chron. 16:9). After all, God does desire everyone *"to be saved"* (1 Tim. 2:4) and to *"turn them from darkness to light"* (Acts 26:18), but they will not come.

Jesus also said to His disciples: *"Ye are the light of the world"* (Matt. 5:14), obviously here referring just to spiritual light. Thus, since He is no longer here in the flesh, His enlightening ministry is to be mediated through us Christians, passing His torch, as it were, to us. *"As my Father hath sent me, even so send I you"* (John 20:21). This is our Missionary Mandate.

Our mission and challenge, therefore, — as those who know the Lord Jesus as both Creator and Savior — is to *"shine as lights in the world; Holding forth the word of life"* (Phil. 2:15–16). *"For there is none other name under heaven given among men, whereby we must be saved"* (Acts 4:12).

THE BREAD OF LIFE

Another incredible claim of the Lord Jesus Christ is found in John 6:35:

> I am the bread of life: he that cometh to me shall never hunger; and he that believeth on me shall never thirst.

It seems obvious that this assertion, like His other "I am" claims (*the light of the world," "the door," "the true vine,"* etc.), has to be interpreted spiritually.

Or does it? There may be more here also than meets the literal eye, in light of the often ignored truth that Jesus Christ is both our Creator and sustainer. Remember Colossians 1:16–17, which reminds us that *"by [Christ] were all things created . . . And he is before all things, and by him all things consist."*

Bread in one form or another is beyond question the most basic form of food in practically every human society, past or present, so much so that it is often called "the staff of life." Fossilized cakes of bread have even been found in a number of ancient archaeological sites. In the Bible the term "bread" is sometimes used to refer to food in general and is often used symbolically also.

Although the first foods mentioned were the seed-bearing herbs and fruit trees (Gen. 1:29), it is clear that man's basic foodstuff was bread. This becomes clear when God pronounced His great Curse on man and all man's dominion because of sin. *". . . cursed is the ground for thy sake . . . In the sweat of thy face shalt thou eat bread, till thou return unto the ground . . ."* (Gen. 3:17–19).

Bread has been made from many different kinds of grain, with the wheat or barley or other grain first being ground into flour, then mixed with water, then formed into cakes or loaves and baked. Various other ingredients are often added to produce different varieties of bread, but each type of bread so made almost inevitably becomes the most essential foodstuff of that society.

Thus, "making one's living" involves growing the grain and making the bread, either directly or indirectly. But the curse on the ground makes this or any other work difficult, involving hard work in a reluctant environment, but *". . . if any would not work, neither should he eat"* (2 Thess. 3:10).

There was one special time when God's chosen people had to live in a hostile desert environment for 40 years and could neither plant grain nor produce bread. In answer to their prayers, however, God *"satisfied them with the bread of heaven"* (Ps. 105:40).

That was the wonderful manna, which miraculously appeared on the ground each day there in the wilderness. All the work required in this special case was the effort by each person to gather as much as needed for that day (or, on the day before the Sabbath, for two days). The manna bread was actually called *"the corn of heaven,"* and *"angels' food"* (Ps. 78:24–25).

Years later, when God had become man in the person of Christ, the Jews challenged Him to give them a miraculous sign, such as Moses had given them when he called for God to send the manna. But note the astounding response given then by the Lord Jesus:

> *Moses gave you not that bread from heaven . . . For the bread of God is he which cometh down from heaven, and giveth life unto the world* (John 6:32–33).

The Lord thus claimed not only to have *sent* the bread which came from heaven, but to *have been* that bread!

> *I am that bread of life. Your fathers did eat manna in the wilderness, and are dead. This is the bread which cometh down from heaven, that a man may eat thereof and not die. I am the living bread which came down from heaven . . . and the bread that I will give is my flesh, which I will give for the life of the world* (John 6:48–51).

But how can *we* eat such *"living bread"* as this? Not just our daily bread like the wilderness manna, but bread that will impart eternal life? *"It is the Spirit that quickeneth,"* said Jesus, *"the words that I speak unto you, they are spirit, and they are life"* (John 6:63). When we hear — or read — His words, and believe Him by faith, whether or not we fully understand all the depths of spiritual truth they convey, that is enough! *"Verily, verily, I say unto you, he that believeth on me hath everlasting life"* (John 6:47).

When we recall that Jesus not only spoke the words of God, but also that He *is* the Word of God (the Living Word), then we can remember that there is yet another marvelous meaning in the living bread. God told His loved ones back in the awful wilderness: *"man doth not live by bread only, but by every word that proceedeth out of the mouth of the Lord doth man live"* (Deut. 8:3). It was not some magic ingredient in the manna that kept them alive in the desert, but the integrity of God's Word. Jesus even rebuked Satan as He, in His humanity, was being tempted, by simply quoting this Scripture: *"It is written,"* He said, *"That man shall not live by bread alone, but by every word of God"* (Luke 4:4).

Note that it is not just the general theme of the Bible that is vital, but *"every word of God."* It is important that each person appropriate the words of Scriptures into his own life, for they are life-giving food for the soul. As Jeremiah said: *"Thy words were found, and I did eat them; and thy word was unto me the joy and rejoicing of mine heart"* (Jer. 15:16). Or, as Job said: *"I have esteemed the words of his mouth more than my necessary food"* (Job 23:12). And in the longest psalm, there is this testimony: *"How sweet are thy words unto my taste! yea, sweeter than honey to my mouth!"* (Ps. 119:103). The words of God (that is, to say, the words of Scripture) are not only spiritual bread, but also honey and milk and meat (note Heb. 5:12), our *"necessary food,"* just as they were to Job long ago.

Even as Christ is the living bread that gives life to all who partake of that bread by faith, He is also the living Word, of whom it was said that *"In him was life"* (John 1:4). Just so, the written word of God is *"quick* [that is, 'living'], *and powerful"* (Heb. 4:12), and can give life to those who believe. It is only through the Scriptures, in fact, that we learn of Christ and His gift of eternal life.

"Search the scriptures," said Jesus, *"for in them ye think ye have eternal life: and they are they which testify of me"* (John 5:39). The apostle Paul wrote to young pastor Timothy concerning the power of the Scriptures as follows: *". . . thou hast known the holy scriptures, which are able to make thee wise unto salvation through faith which is in Christ Jesus"* (2 Tim. 3:15). The chief responsibility of Christians, therefore, is to be *"Holding forth the word of life"* (Phil. 2:16).

Bread is the staff of life for all people, wicked as well as righteous, but it is especially appropriate to speak of the living bread from heaven as received by those who believe in Christ and His word.

To believers, out of fellowship with God, however, the spiritual bread that God sends can be very bitter. The Bible speaks, for example, of *"the bread of tears"* and *"the bread of sorrows"* (Ps. 80:5; 127:2). This was said to be the spiritual food of those members of His elect nation Israel who were being chastened by God because of disobeying His word (by logical extension, this same principle would apply to disobedient Christians).

The figure of bread can also be used to describe the chosen beliefs and life styles of those who deny or refuse to submit to God. For example: *"Bread of deceit is sweet to a man; but afterwards his mouth shall be filled with gravel"* (Prov. 20:17). Bitter bread indeed!

Another form of sin — that of careless and unfruitful living — is contrasted with the life style of the truly godly woman who *"eateth not the bread of idleness"* (Prov. 31:27). Idle hands are the workshop of the devil, as the old maxim goes, for God intended man to work — even more so after sin came in, *"In the sweat of thy face shalt thou eat bread"* (Gen. 3:19), He has said.

In general, the spiritual food of the ungodly is their commitment to opposing the true bread from heaven. *"For they eat the bread of wickedness"* (Prov. 4:17). The Bible also mentions *"the bread of affliction"* (1 Kings 22:27), *"the bread of adversity"* (Isa. 30:20), and *"the bread of mourners"* (Hos. 9:4). Bread is thus both the widespread physical food of all mankind and also the preferred universal symbol of man's spiritual food, whether wholesome and life-giving or sad and bitter.

OUR DAILY BREAD FROM HEAVEN

For true life, men and women must live on both the written word of God and the Living Word. Likewise, they must have both the physical bread and the Living Bread, the true Bread of Life.

We should also remember that even our physical bread — and all our physical food — has been made and provided by God *"who created all things by Jesus Christ"* (Eph. 3:9). In one sense, the Lord Jesus is even in the very molecular structure of the bread itself, as also in His entire creation, for *"by him all things consist"* (Col. 1:17), and He is now *"upholding all things by the word of his power"* (Heb. 1:3).

No wonder the apostle Paul could tell even the skeptical evolutionary Stoic and Epicurean philosophers in first-century Greece that the God who created the world was *"not far from every one of us: For in him we live, and move, and have our being"* (Acts 17:27–28). How foolish and wicked it is, therefore, to continue living on the stale and bitter bread of worldly deceit and sinfulness when one could be thriving on the Bread of Heaven!

And, therefore, we pray as the Lord taught us, *"Give us this day our daily bread"* (Matt. 6:11) — not only bread earned from the reluctant earth, but also bread from the opened windows of heaven!

But how can we know all this is really true about Jesus and what He does for us and for the world? It is true that He made these remarkable claims, but there have been and still are many other great religions and their founders and leaders. What about all these?

THE TESTIMONY OF THE RESURRECTION

There have indeed been many competing religions to that of Jesus, but the one great difference is that all their founders are dead and buried. But the tomb of Jesus Christ is empty, for He defeated death itself, and rose from the dead, never to die again!

The two greatest miracles in all history have been the creation of the world and the resurrection of its Creator from physical death. Without the first, none of us would even exist, and without the second, we would have no hope of life after death. The wonderful fact is, however, that we do have life and, through personal faith in that Creator and His bodily resurrection, we also have assurance of everlasting life with Him in the ages to come.

Modern scientists, on the other hand — at least the leaders of the scientific establishment — believe in neither creation nor resurrection. Their premise is total naturalism, so they must try to explain all events of past, present, or future in terms of present natural laws and processes. Miracles of any kind must be explained away as unscientific — especially miracles that are worldwide in scope or effect. They say that creation would contradict the most basic law of all science — that is, the law of conservation of mass/energy, or the first law of thermodynamics. The conservation principle says, in effect, that *nothing* can be truly created (though things can be changed in form).

Similarly, the idea that a person could be restored to life after being dead for three days would contradict the second law of thermodynamics, or the law of increasing entropy — that is, the law which describes the tendency of all systems to decrease in organized complexity. Once death overtakes an organism, all its functions cease, and it soon returns to dust — the ultimate disintegration.

Thus, both creation and resurrection are impossible, as far as naturalistic science is concerned. No exception to the two laws of thermodynamics has ever been found. For an exception to either one to occur, an enormous miracle would be required, and these scientists tell us miracles can't happen.

But they are wrong!

Jesus Christ *did* rise from the dead! This event is a fact of history, capable of being investigated by the same criteria that are used to test other alleged historical events. When this is done — and it *has* been done by many fully qualified historians and experts on evidence — Christ's resurrection passes all tests of historicity with flying colors.

The many contacts with His followers after His resurrection (at least ten appearances, under many circumstances, and to many different people), the sure testimony of His empty tomb (along with the utter inability of His enemies to produce His body), and the drastic changes in the disciples (from fearful fugitives to bold proclaimers of

His resurrection) are among the *"many infallible proofs"* (Acts 1:3) that assure us that *"He is risen, as he said"* (Matt. 28:6). It is not too much to say that the bodily resurrection of Jesus Christ, after He died and was buried for three days in a sealed tomb, is the best-proved fact of ancient history.[1]

That being the case, consider the implications. Principally, it proves that Jesus Christ is God. Only God could conquer death, for the law of death was imposed by God in the first place when the first man brought sin into the dominion entrusted to him by His Creator (Rom. 5:12).

It also means that the Lord Jesus Christ was the Creator of heaven and earth. Only the Creator could create new matter, as He did when He multiplied the loaves and fishes, or new energy, as He did when He walked on the water and when He stilled the storm waves with a word. The Bible, of course, clearly confirms the fact that He was Creator. *"All things were made by him,"* and *"the world was made by him"* (John 1:3, 10). *"For by him were all things created, that are in heaven, and that are in earth . . . all things were created by him, and for him"* (Col. 1:16).

This great fact further assures us that whatever He does, he does it right, and whatever He says is true. When He said, for example, referring to Genesis 1:27, that *"from the beginning of the creation God made them male and female"* (Mark 10:6), we know for a certainty that the earth and the universe are *not* millions or billions of years old, regardless of the uniformitarian misuse of astronomic and geologic data by evolutionists. Christ was *there*, for He was the creating Word of God, and He has told us that the human race dates from the *beginning* of the creation, not 15 billion years *after* the beginning. Would He lie, or perhaps deliberately mislead us? Did He think we could not understand or appreciate the evolutionist idea of billions of years of a suffering, groaning creation before He got around to creating men and women for fellowship with himself? The very thought seems — to us, at least — to be absurd and even blasphemous.

Furthermore, whether or not we like the idea of His creating an endless hell for those who reject Him as their Lord and Savior, we must deal with it, for He spoke more often about hell than did anyone else in the Bible (note Matt. 5:30; 25:41; etc.). He also accepted the Bible as inerrant

---

1 Many volumes have been written setting forth these evidences, and the case is compelling. For the writer's own summary of the evidence, see the ICR booklet *The Resurrection of Jesus Christ*. Available from ICR (one copy free on request).

and authoritative (Matt. 5:18; John 10:35). At the very end of His Book, He warned against tampering with its words, saying: *"If any man shall take away from the words of the book of this prophecy, God shall take away his part out of the book of life . . ."* (Rev. 22:19).

There is, of course, one more glorious consequence of the certain fact of His bodily resurrection. He has defeated death, not only for himself but also for all those who have trusted Him for their own forgiveness and salvation. He has promised that *"because I live, ye shall live also"* (John 14:19). *"For as in Adam all die, even so in Christ shall all be made alive"* (1 Cor. 15:22).

Our resurrection, like that of Christ himself, will be a physical resurrection, not just spiritual. When God pronounced the judgment of death on Adam and all his dominion, it was physical death, not spiritual only. That is why the Lord Jesus, in dying for our sins, had to die *physically* — a terrible physical death, not just temporary spiritual separation from God, though that also was part of it.

Similarly, our promised resurrection will be a physical, bodily resurrection, like that of Christ. The resurrected body will *not*, however, include the pains and defects that characterize our present physical bodies. Our bodies will be *glorified* bodies, like that of Christ when He rose from the dead — no longer subject to pain and death but raised to eternal perfection. When John saw Him in his great vision on the Isle of Patmos, Christ said: *"Behold, I am alive for evermore"* (Rev. 1:18).

And we too shall be alive forever! *"It doth not yet appear what we shall be: but we know that, when he shall appear, we shall be like him"* (1 John 3:2). *"In a moment, in the twinkling of an eye . . . the trumpet shall sound . . . and we shall be changed"* (1 Cor. 15:52). The Lord Jesus Christ *"shall change our vile body, that it may be fashioned like unto his glorious body"* (Phil. 3:21).

"For if we believe that Jesus died and rose again, even so them also which sleep in Jesus will God bring with him. . . . For the Lord himself shall descend from heaven . . . and the dead in Christ shall rise first: Then we which are alive and remain shall be caught up together with them in the clouds, to meet the Lord in the air: and so shall we ever be with the Lord" (1 Thess. 4:14–17). The law of entropy in our bodies will be forever repealed, and *"there shall be no more death"* (Rev. 21:4), *". . . neither shall there be any more pain."*

But even that is not all that Christ's resurrection will accomplish. God's curse had applied not only to Adam and his descendants but also to his whole dominion — and *that* shall be made whole again! *"There shall be no more curse"* (Rev. 22:3). *"Because the* [creation] *itself also shall be delivered from the bondage of corruption into the glorious liberty of the children of God"* (Rom. 8:21).

Ever since sin entered the world and God pronounced His great curse *"on the ground"* (Gen. 3:17) — that is, on the basic elements, the dust from which all things had been made — the whole world has been in a state of decay, or increasing entropy, travailing in pain.

"...the earth shall wax old like a garment" (Isa. 51:6). *"Heaven and earth* [are passing] *away"* (Matt. 24:35). *". . . as a vesture shalt thou fold them up, and they shall be changed"* (Heb. 1:12). Finally, *". . . the elements shall melt with fervent heat, the earth also and the works that are therein shall be burned up. . . . all these things shall be dissolved"* (2 Pet. 3:10–11).

But when Christ the Creator became the Savior, He not only died *"for the sins of the whole world"* (1 John 2:2), but also became *"the Saviour of the world* [Greek *kosmos*]*"* (1 John 4:14). *"The world [kosmos] was made by him"* (John 1:10), and He has paid the terrible price to redeem the world from its *"bondage of corruption into the glorious liberty of the children of God."*

Finally, after the last judgment, and after this present earth — defiled as it is with the age-long scars of suffering and death — has been *"burned up,"* then *"we, according to his promise, look for new heavens and a new earth, wherein dwelleth righteousness"* (2 Pet. 3:10, 13).

And there we shall live forever. *"For as the new heavens and the new earth, which I will make, shall remain before me, saith the Lord, so shall your seed and your name remain"* (Isa. 66:22).

The old law of entropy, along with *"the law of sin and death"* (Rom. 8:2) which accompanied it, will be gone once and for all — all because Christ lives!

The supreme importance of the resurrection of Christ becomes especially clear when we compare genuine biblical Christianity with the other great religions of the world — Islam, Buddhism, Hinduism, Confucianism and others — with their own convinced followers. What about these?

Other Religions and Resurrection

A common opinion, even in "Christian" America and Europe, in the secular street-corner philosophy of the world is that all the different world religions are just different ways of reaching God and getting to heaven, if there is such a place or such a goal. The fact is that each religion has its own distinctive belief about God and the future life, as well as heaven and how to get there. But then, how do we know which is true?

The only world religions which include faith in one supreme God who created all things are Christianity, Judaism, and Islam. Several of the eastern religions teach that one's future life will be in the form of another person or perhaps an animal. This is the idea of reincarnation and transmigration of souls — an idea which even seems to appeal to many westerners.

But the only religions which teach an actual bodily resurrection of each individual person are those three which teach one great Creator God and His special creation of all things. Even those three in many cases have capitulated to modern evolutionism so that only the traditional orthodox branches of Christianity, Judaism, and Islam continue to teach special creation. It is significant, therefore, that these three — and only these three — also teach a future special bodily resurrection of all people.

It is true that all other religions (except doctrinaire atheism) do believe in a future life of some kind, and that fact is also very significant. Most people intuitively realize somehow that this life, so often unfair and seemingly meaningless, cannot possibly be all there is.

So we have all the different religions, each with its own version of the future life. As noted, many of the religions of Asia, such as Hinduism, Buddhism, Jainism, and Sikhism, with all their internal cults and external offshoots, believe in transmigration and reincarnation, a process terminating eventually perhaps in nirvana, a state of universal oneness (or perhaps nothingness). Individual resurrection is never considered even a possibility.

The Chinese religion (before communism, that is) has been a sort of synthesis of Confucianism, Buddhism, and Taoism, with many hold-over elements of a still earlier animism. Confucianism is primarily an ethical system, though with occasional overtones of belief in a high God back in the beginning. Buddhism in its original form was also mainly ethical and meditational. Taoism was more mystical. Again, however, in none of these religions has there ever been any notion of resurrection.

The various forms of animism, whether ancient or modern, seem often to include the concept of a high God, but one who is very distant and who is involved in individual lives mainly through a host of lesser "gods," usually understood either as benevolent or demonic spirits. This is all quite similar also to the ancient pantheistic/polytheistic religions of Babylonia, Egypt, Greece, Rome, and others.

But once again there is never in any of these the promise of individual bodily resurrection. There is commonly a belief in some sort of immortality, but never resurrection. When a loved one dies, his or her family and friends have no hope of ever seeing that one again, except possibly as a disembodied spirit somewhere.

Not so in Christianity! As the apostle Paul urged those Christians who had suffered such losses: *"Sorrow not, even as others which have no hope. For if we believe that Jesus died and rose again . . . the dead in Christ shall rise first: Then we . . . shall be caught up together with them . . . to meet the Lord"* (1 Thess. 4:13–17). *"He that believeth in me,"* Jesus said, *"though he were dead, yet shall he live. . . . Because I live, ye shall live also"* (John 11:25; 14:19).

What about the other two monotheistic religions, Islam and Judaism? These do indeed teach resurrection, at least in the orthodox form of these religions.

But they are hardly like the resurrection promised in the Bible to Christians. In the holy city where Christians will dwell, they *"neither marry, nor are given in marriage"* (Luke 20:35) and *"there shall in no wise enter into it any thing that defileth"* (Rev. 21:27). The Muslim "Paradise," on the other hand, will be a very sensual place; the men there will have free access to many "houris" or maidens of paradise, and they can marry as many as they please. They will recline on soft couches near flowing rivers, quaffing cups of wine served by their own personal virgins. There are no equivalent promises to faithful Muslim women, however; in fact, the Koran seems almost to ignore their future life.

As far as Judaism is concerned, there is little in the Old Testament concerning the future life at all. There are, however, a few clear references to a future resurrection. The prophet Daniel, for example, predicts that *"many of them that sleep in the dust of the earth shall awake, some to everlasting life, and some to shame and everlasting contempt"* (Dan. 12:2). Also note the prophet Isaiah's promise to the faithful in Israel: *"Thy dead men shall live, together with my dead body shall they arise. Awake and sing, ye that dwell in dust: for thy dew is as the dew of herbs, and the earth shall cast out the dead"* (Isa. 26:19). There is also the promise of Hosea 13:14: *"I will ransom them from the power of the grave; I will redeem them from death: I will be thy plagues; O grave, I will be thy destruction."* And, of course, there is the wonderful assurance in the very ancient record of Job: *"For I know that my redeemer liveth, and that he shall stand at the latter day upon the earth . . . yet in my flesh shall I see God: Whom I shall see for myself, and mine eyes shall behold, and not another"* (Job 19:25–27). Job was answering his own earlier question: *"If a man die, shall he live again?"* (Job 14:14).

The Old Testament answer clearly is yes — though admittedly such promises are few and far between in that portion of Scripture, and the result was that many Jews at the time of Christ believed it only superficially if at all. They seemed more concerned with the problems of their current situation, especially their subjugation to Rome, from which they were seeking deliverance.

One of the main Jewish parties, in fact, denied any future resurrection altogether and, of course, these Sadducees did all they could to try to stop the preaching of Christ's resurrection. The Sadducees were not atheists, but downplayed any ideas of a future life, the reason being that the Torah had only the vaguest references to it, and they regarded these five books of Moses as the most authoritative of all. The Pharisees, on the other hand, did believe in a future resurrection and eventually became more powerful than the Sadducees.

As far as modern Judaism is concerned, only those known as the ultra-orthodox still believe in the inerrancy of the Old Testament. The general belief of most Jews today — at least those who have not become atheistic — is that all Jews will eventually end up in heaven, perhaps after a short time in what amounts to a purgatory.

It must also be noted that, in recent years, many Jews have become Christians and often have organized themselves into Hebrew Christian churches. Such Christian Jews, of course, have come to believe also in the Christian doctrine of resurrection.

In any case, the one truth especially significant in this very brief study of comparative religion is that the promise of resurrection is found only in those faiths that are monotheistic and also believe in special creation, and only the orthodox forms of those faiths at that. It is clear, too, that this commonality depends largely on the fact that all three of these accept special creation because they all accept the first book of Moses as the divinely inspired record of creation.

It is also obvious that the ideas of creation and resurrection go together. The Creator had an eternal purpose in creating men and women and cannot fail in that purpose. Therefore, He is the only one who can and must overcome death. Death is the wages of sin and must be paid either by those who are guilty (which means all men) or by an innocent human substitute for sinners who is himself sinless and is willing to take their place in death. Only the Creator himself could meet this criterion, and therefore He must become man, die, and then restore himself to life by resurrecting himself from the grave.

The glorious truth is that the bodily resurrection of the Word made flesh, the Lord Jesus Christ, has been shown to be a true fact of history by *"many infallible proofs"* (Acts 1:3), and He is the only man in all history who has thus been victorious over death and the grave.

Mohammed is dead, and so are Buddha and Confucius and all other religious founders and leaders. But Jesus Christ was living and then was dead and now is *"alive for evermore"* (Rev. 1:18). We need never be in doubt as to which religion is *true*. True salvation is provided only through the Lord Jesus Christ, who died for us to pay for our redemption from sin and death, and then rose again from the grave to assure us that the price has been fully settled and paid. Now, all who receive this free gift of salvation by faith can be assured that they also will be raised out of death into a glorious heavenly future which will never end.

The confrontation of the apostle Paul with the Greek philosophers at Athens is especially significant in relation to these questions and issues we have been considering. Athens was the cultural center of the world during those times, and its religious philosophies at that period have influenced the nations ever since.

It is interesting, at least to me, that Paul, in his message to the Epicureans and Stoics (atheistic evolutionists and pantheistic evolutionists, respectively) there at Mars Hill near the Acropolis, dealt with some of the key topics I have tried to discuss in this book in these first four chapters. This message is all found in Acts 17:22–31.

Paul first affirmed the Creator and His creation. *"God that made the world and all things therein. . . ."* Then he mentioned the nations (Greece and all the others) as having their geographical and chronological boundaries determined by God. *"And hath made...all nations of men . . . and hath determined the times before appointed, and the bounds of their habitation,"* one criterion of continuance being *". . . that they should seek the Lord."* He made it clear also that their impersonal pantheistic, polytheistic concept of God was all wrong. *"He be not far from every one of us: For in him we live, and move, and have our being."*

Their attempts to depict their nature-god in terms of various idolatrous personifications was especially *"too superstitious,"* and they *"ought not to think that the Godhead is like unto gold, or silver, or stone, graven by art and man's device."* The notion that all religions were basically legitimate attempts to serve God especially came under God's rebuke, through Paul. These were *"the times of this ignorance,"* said Paul, for God *"now commandeth all men everywhere to repent."* No exception!

They and people in all these nations were each one going to come under the judgment of God. They had rejected the Creator, the *"Lord of heaven and earth,"* the one who alone *"giveth to all life, and breath, and all things,"* in favor of idols and the evolutionary pantheism they personified.

Furthermore, they were all going to be judged one day and, by clear implication, condemned as a result of this inexcusable defection from the true Creator. *"Because [God] hath appointed a day, in the which he will judge the world in righteousness by that man whom he hath ordained."*

That man, the coming Judge, will be plainly identified and clearly recognized right now; there is no need to wait until the appointed day comes. God *"hath given assurance unto all men, in that he hath raised him from the dead."*

Therefore, if any should really want to know which religion is uniquely true and can lead to God, he need only look for the one whose founder died and then rose from the dead. For that man will be Judge of all and thus must first have been Maker of all. That man is Jesus Christ, and none other!

As noted above, Mohammed is dead and buried. So are Buddha and Confucius and all the others. Jesus Christ, our Creator, became man and then died for *"the sins of the whole world,"* rose from the grave and is now *"alive for evermore"* (1 John 2:2; Rev. 1:18). This is the great truth that sets biblical Christianity apart from all so-called "religions."

> *Wherefore he is able also to save them to the uttermost that come unto God by him, seeing he ever liveth to make intercession for them* (Heb. 7:25).

> *Blessed are all they that put their trust in him* (Ps. 2:12).

CHAPTER V

THE GLORIOUS GOSPEL OF THE BLESSED GOD

The bodily resurrection of Christ, along with the promised future resurrection and glorification of all His true followers, constitutes the crowning distinctive of biblical Christianity with respect to all the varied other religions of the world, past or present. We have a *living* Savior, not a revered (but dead) founder.

But Christianity also has a number of other distinctives that set it apart from the rest. Probably the most important is its wonderful gospel. Other religions emphasize a set of rules or rituals or both which their adherents must *do* if they would achieve salvation. They are religions of *works*, in other words. The gospel of Christ, on the other hand, provides salvation as a free gift, not of works. Therefore, Paul calls it *"the glorious gospel of the blessed God"* (1 Tim. 1:11).

The word itself comes from an Anglo-Saxon word meaning "God's story." The Greek word from which it is translated means essentially "good tidings." The gospel of Christ is not "good advice" as to how to obtain salvation, but simply "good news," telling how the Lord Jesus Christ has provided free and full salvation to all believers. It is, indeed, a *glorious* gospel! To those who reject such a glorious gift, however, there is no other way, and they must simply await God's future judgment.

THE FINISHED WORKS OF GOD

God, by definition, can never fail in what He undertakes to accomplish. Most Christians naturally place special emphasis on the death and resurrection of Christ, and the Bible verse that always springs first to my own mind is His great victory cry on the cross: *"It is finished!"* (John 19:30).

Right at the beginning of His ministry, He told His mother: *"...mine hour is not yet come"* (John 2:4). Later He told His brothers, *"My time is not yet full come"* (John 7:8). Whether or not He told them what He had come to do, or when He would do it, the record does not say.

Even before this, however, John the Baptist had introduced Him as *"the Lamb of God, which taketh away the sin of the world"* (John 1:29), and this great purpose had guided His whole ministry. Finally, His hour did come, and He *"became obedient unto death, even the death of the cross"* (Phil. 2:8), bearing *"our sins in his own body on the tree"* (1 Pet. 2:24).

There, during the awful three hours of supernatural darkness, the Father had to forsake Him (Matt. 27:46), because He had *"made him to be sin for us, who knew no sin; that we might be made the righteousness of God in him"* (2 Cor. 5:21). After enduring this unspeakable period of utter separation from God (which is the essence of hell itself), then He could finally shout *"with a loud voice"* (Luke 23:46), the great cry of triumph, *"It is finished!"*

The divine approval and acceptance of His substitutionary offering was signaled once and for all by His bodily resurrection on the third day following His burial.

Now, if Christ's wonderful work of paying for our forgiveness and salvation is finished, what is there left for us to do to implement it for ourselves personally?

There is *nothing* left for us to do! *"The wages of sin is death; but the gift of God is eternal life through Jesus Christ our Lord"* (Rom. 6:23). One does not receive a free gift by working for it, or by doing something more to be sure he gets it.

He can refuse to accept it, of course, if he does not want it. But if he considers the proffered gift to be desirable, and truly wants to have it, he must simply accept it gratefully, thanking the one providing it. *"In* [Christ] *we have redemption through his blood, the forgiveness of sins, according to the riches of his grace"* (Eph. 1:7).

We are saved, of course, entirely by God's grace — plus nothing. We then, however, become *"His workmanship, created in Christ Jesus unto*

good works, which God hath before ordained that we should walk in them"
(Eph. 2:10).

THE WORK OF CREATION

Long before the Lord Jesus undertook and then completed His heaven-sent work of redeeming lost sinners, He had completed another great work — that of creation. The first chapter of God's written record tells us about His sequential creating and making of all things in six days, climaxed by the creation of the first man and woman, all of whose descendants He would later have to redeem if He were truly to accomplish His great purpose in creating them.

> *Thus the heavens and the earth were finished, and all the host of them. And on the seventh day God ended his work which he had made* (Gen. 2:1–2).

Once it was finished, of course, there was no more creating to be done. Just like salvation, with the price fully paid, the creation was complete, with all the work of creating and making fully done. Just as a redeemed sinner can never augment the payment for his redemption, neither can some imaginary creative process called evolution augment the completed creation.

Furthermore, the completed creation was *"very good"* (Gen. 1:31), with nothing bad or unfair or hurtful — certainly no "struggle for existence" or "survival of the fittest," or any lack of anything needed by any of God's created beings or systems. In analogous fashion, our finished salvation is *"so great salvation"* (Heb. 2:3) and *"eternal redemption"* (Heb. 9:12), fully meeting our need for forgiveness and endless life with God.

The creation is not *"very good"* at present, of course, for sin and death have entered the world and, therefore, Christ's work of redemption had to be undertaken. Nevertheless, the creation, like salvation and redemption, is eternal.

Speaking of the stars and all the physical creation, the Bible says that *"He commanded, and they were created. He hath also stablished them for ever and ever"* (Ps. 148:5–6). There will, indeed, be drastic changes in the earth and heaven when sin and all its effects are purged out of it (2 Pet. 3:10), but then once again the creation will be very good, with *"no more death,"* and *"no more curse,"* as nothing can ever again enter it that *"worketh abomination, or maketh a lie"* (Rev. 21:4; 22:3; 21:27).

God is the Creator, not an "un-Creator," and His works of both creation and redemption are eternal. *"Whatsoever God doeth, it shall be for ever: nothing can be put to it, nor any thing taken from it"* (Eccles. 3:14).

It is significant that, as far as creation is concerned, the most universal and certain law of science is the law of conservation of matter and energy. Energy can be changed in form (electrical energy to light energy, for example), and matter can be changed in state (solid to liquid, for example). Matter can even be changed into energy (e.g., nuclear fission) and energy into matter (thermonuclear fusion), but the totality of matter and energy can be neither augmented nor diminished. Energy (including matter) can be neither created nor destroyed.

At the end of the six days of creation, Christ the Creator (John 1:3, 14) *"rested from all his work which God created and made"* (Gen. 2:3), and He is now *"upholding all things by the word of his power"* (Heb. 1:3). His present work is one of conservation, as He is resting from His finished work of creation, as far as the physical world is concerned.

Our salvation is now also eternal, and our life is everlasting because of Christ's finished work on the cross. After He died and rose again, He could say: *"I am he that liveth, and was dead; and, behold I am alive for evermore"* (Rev. 1:18). Therefore, He could also promise concerning those who have accepted His gift of salvation: *"I give unto them eternal life; and they shall never perish. . . . I am the resurrection and the life: he that believeth in me, though he were dead, yet shall he live"* (John 10:28; 11:25).

THE FINISHED WORD OF GOD

There is another very important finished work of God — vitally important, in fact — because it is *this* work that tells us about God's finished works of creation and redemption. I am referring, of course, to His work of revelation and inscripturation of that revelation in the written Word. This has given us all we need to know about His great purpose in creating and saving us for fellowship with himself in the eternal ages to come.

That wonderful Word of God was *"for ever . . . settled in heaven"* (Ps. 119:89) before the world began. Then God *"at sundry times and in divers manners spake in time past unto the fathers by the prophets"* (Heb. 1:1). He revealed some to Moses, some to David, some to Isaiah, and some to all the other human writers of the Old Testament. All these Old Testament Scriptures were *"given by inspiration of God,"* or literally, *"God-breathed"* (2 Tim. 3:16).

Then, when Christ came, He promised His chosen apostles that the Holy Spirit would *"teach you all things, and bring all things to your remembrance, whatsoever I have said unto you"* (John 14:26), so that they could write the New Testament.

Finally, when the last of the apostles, John, completed his final book, Revelation, the inspired record was finished. It was still settled forever in heaven, but now also had been sent to the earth.

This fact was firmly emphasized by Christ himself in the final section of John's prophecy:

> *For I testify unto every man that heareth the words of the prophecy of this book, If any man shall add unto these things, God shall add unto him the plagues that are written in this book; And if any man shall take away from the words of the book of this prophecy, God shall take away his part out of the book of life, and out of the holy city, and from the things which are written in this book* (Rev. 22:18–19).

Thus the book of God is completed, just as the creation of God was finished and the salvation of God was accomplished once and for all when Christ died and rose again.

Therefore, there can be no such thing as origin of new kinds of plants or animals by evolution, no extra-biblical "Scriptures" or "prophecies" that can be added to God's Word, and no works of any kind (other than the "work" of believing on Christ and accepting His gift of eternal life) that can produce or add to our redemption and salvation.

The conclusion, as we contemplate the death and resurrection of Christ is: *"That, according as it is written, he that glorieth, let him glory in the Lord"* (1 Cor. 1:31).

Throughout All Ages

Our glorious gospel of salvation by grace through the finished work of Christ has not only been finished for our time here on the earth, but also for our future life on the new earth. As the prophet Isaiah said long before even the time of Christ's first coming: *"For as the new heavens and the new earth, which I will make, shall remain before me, saith the Lord, so shall your seed and your name remain"* (Isa. 66:22).

Although Isaiah was speaking mainly concerning the redeemed Israelites, the truth certainly applies to all the redeemed children of God in every nation. As Peter said in the New Testament: *"Nevertheless we, according to his promise, look for new heavens and a new earth, wherein dwelleth righteousness"* (2 Pet. 3:13).

There will be no need for any further judgment after that, because nothing "dwells" there except righteousness! When John, translated into the future, saw *"a new heaven and a new earth . . . coming down from God out of heaven"* (Rev. 21:1–2), he noted that *"there shall in no wise enter into it any thing that defileth . . . but they which are written in the Lamb's book of life"* (Rev. 21:27).

That does not mean, however, that eternity will consist only of one unchanging existence forever. The eternal "ages" will actually consist of a "series of ages." Just how these will change from age to age has not been revealed, but it will all be good! God has said that we shall *"ever be with the Lord"* (1 Thess. 4:17), *"That in the ages to come he might shew the exceeding riches of his grace in his kindness toward us through Christ Jesus"* (Eph. 2:7).

When Isaiah said the new earth would *"remain,"* he used the same Hebrew word used by the Psalmist when he wrote that the present earth some day would perish, but that *"thou shalt endure"* (Ps. 102:26). That is, no matter how many future ages there may be, the new earth will endure through all of them, just as God will continue forever. *"Thy years shall have no end"* (Ps. 102:27). Therefore, as Paul said: *"Unto him be glory in the church by Christ Jesus throughout all ages, world without end. Amen"* (Eph. 3:21).

We do not know what we shall be doing in all these ages to come, but we do know we shall not be idle, nor will there be any sickness or pain or natural resistance on the part of the natural creation to hinder us from performing whatever services we may be assigned to render. *"And there shall be no more curse: but the throne of God and of the Lamb shall be in it; and his servants shall serve him"* (Rev. 22:3).

In fact, as suggested earlier, I like to think that the realm of the Dominion Mandate may be expanded from just this earth to the entire universe. With innumerable stars in the cosmos (every one of them known from its light spectrum to be unique and different from all others), not to mention possible unknown multitudes of planets and other bodies in the heavens, there could be endless possibilities for exploration and development throughout the cosmos.

With new bodies like that of the glorified Christ himself (Phil. 3:21), we can travel quickly and safely everywhere in God's created universe. With endless space and endless time, we can never run out of useful, enjoyable things to do in the service of our Lord.

It would be presumptuous to speculate too much about the activities of these future ages. *"For since the beginning of the world men have not heard, nor perceived by the ear, neither hath the eye seen, O God, beside thee, what he hath prepared for him that waiteth for him"* (Isa. 64:4). God undoubtedly has had a glorious purpose in creating such a wonderful cosmos, and these will be the times when His purpose will finally be accomplished. It is enough now just to know that we shall have a part in it.

That is, those of us who have been given salvation through faith in Christ will have a part of it. Most people, as the Lord Jesus sadly told us when He was here on earth (Matt. 7:13–14), will *not* be involved. They have rejected or ignored His loving forgiveness and free gift offer of eternal salvation, and so can only look forward to judgment and condemnation. *"Of how much sorer punishment, suppose ye, shall he be thought worthy, who hath trodden under foot the Son of God, and hath counted the blood of the covenant, wherewith he was sanctified, an unholy thing, and hath done despite unto the Spirit of grace?"* (Heb. 10:29).

In the meantime, we have work to do right here. We don't know yet what will be our service assignments in the ages to come, but we *do* know that we have definite responsibilities in *this* age under both the Dominion Mandate and the Missionary Mandate, and each of us, like the Lord Jesus, need to *"be about my Father's business"* (Luke 2:49). Paul, therefore, would admonish us: *"See then that ye walk circumspectly, not as fools, but as wise, Redeeming the time, because the days are evil"* (Eph. 5:15–16).

One vital aspect of our double mandate is that we are to *"preach the gospel to every creature"* (Mark 16:15), within the scope of our opportunities and abilities, by both direct and indirect means. Too few Christians, however, even those who are genuinely concerned about winning souls for Christ, realize that the gospel includes the whole scope of the work of the Lord Jesus Christ — past, present, and future.

Creation is the foundation of that work, and thus should be an important component of our gospel preaching. In fact, doubts about creation often are the most important barriers in the path of those who need Christ, and these barriers should be removed by those seeking to win them.

Creation Evangelism

Creation evangelism is the ministry of using scientific biblical creationism as a help in winning people to Christ. The biblical record of creation is not only historically and scientifically accurate, but it is also the foundation of all the saving doctrines of the Bible. In recent decades, many have come to accept Christ because (at least partially) of the scientific and biblical evidences for creation.

Note especially that the marvelous truths of the person and work of Jesus Christ are based upon His finished work of creation.

> *For by him were all things created, that are in heaven, and that are in earth. . . . And he is before all things, and by him all things consist. . . . And, having made peace through the blood of his cross, by him to reconcile all things unto himself* (Col. 1:16–20).

This wonderful passage summarizes the past, present, and future work of Christ — creation, conservation, and consummation of all things. And the foundation of His saving and reconciling work is His work of creation.

Similarly, the foundation of the gospel of Christ is also His creation and our worship of Him as Creator. The final (of over 100) biblical use of the word "gospel" is as follows:

> *And I saw another angel fly in the midst of heaven, having the everlasting gospel to preach unto them that dwell on the earth. . . . Saying with a loud voice . . . worship him that made heaven, and earth, and the sea, and the fountains of waters* (Rev. 14:6–7).

This is a key component of the gospel of God's saving grace in Christ, for it was, and will be *"everlasting."* Paul warned against even any angel that would preach some other gospel than he was preaching (Gal. 1:8). In fact, he indicated that Christ's past, present, and future work as discussed above (Col. 1:16–20) is incorporated in the truth and hope of the gospel (Col. 1:5, 23).

The fact that creation is the foundation of true and effective evangelism is also indicated by the apostle John, who affirmed that his wonderful book was *"written, that ye might believe that Jesus is the Christ, the Son of God; and that believing ye might have life through his name"* (John 20:31).

That being John's motive and purpose in writing, it is very significant that he began by stressing the fact of creation by Jesus Christ!

In the beginning was the Word, and the Word was with God, and the Word was God. . . . All things were made by him; and without him was not any thing made that was made. . . . He was in the world, and the world was made by him, and the world knew him not. . . . And the Word was made flesh, and dwelt among us (John 1:1–14).

Thereafter, John's record of Christ's person and work is structured around His seven great "I am" assertions of deity (*"I am the light of the world,"* etc.) and His seven great miracles of creation (creating new eyes for a man born blind, etc.).

There should be no doubt that Jesus is the Creator, the eternal Son of God, and that this very fact made it possible for Him also to become our Redeemer and Savior.

Therefore, creation is absolutely basic in true evangelism, not secondary or even irrelevant, as many seem to think. In fact, belief in creation by the Word of God is the very first item in a saving, justifying, living faith (one should read carefully Hebrews 10:38–11:3 in this connection).

This does not *necessarily* mean that a born-again Christian cannot believe that Christ used evolutionary processes in creating things. But he should be willing to deal honestly with the fact that any such "evolutionary creation" is completely contrary to the Bible. Jesus Christ himself believed in the recent creation of all things (note Mark 10:6, for example). He even inscribed the fact of the literal, six-day creation on a table of stone in the Ten Commandments (Exod. 20:8, 11; 31:18).

Assuming, then, that scientific biblical creationism is a valid component of true evangelism, we can note the example of the early Christians, Paul in particular, as they went out to preach the gospel in obedience to Christ's Great Commission. Paul and his companions normally would go first to the Jewish synagogue in any new city, and there would preach Christ from the Scriptures.

The best example is in Acts 17 when Paul came to Thessalonica, in Greece.

And Paul, as his manner was, went in unto them, and three sabbath days reasoned with them out of the Scriptures, Opening and alleging, that Christ must needs have suffered, and risen again from the dead; and that this Jesus, whom I preach unto you is Christ (Acts 17:2–3).

Note that he did not have to convince the Jews that the Scriptures were inspired and true and authoritative, for they already believed that. Neither did he have to talk about the creation of the world by God, for they already believed that, too.

But he did use what we might call apologetics, or Christian evidences, stressing fulfilled prophecy in Christ, along with His death and resurrection as prophecies that had been wonderfully fulfilled, confirming that He was indeed the promised Messiah.

He next went to Berea, where he did the same, and the Bereans *"received the word with all readiness of mind, and searched the Scriptures daily, whether these things were so"* (Acts 17:11).

Then Paul went to Athens, the great cultural and intellectual center of the world at that time. There he encountered the Epicurean and Stoic *"philosophers"* (Acts 17:18). These men were all evolutionists — the Epicureans, atheists, and the Stoics pantheists. They did not believe the Scriptures, and they certainly did not believe in the special creation of all things by an omnipotent God.

Paul, therefore, began with creation, using as a point of reference their awareness of an *"unknown god"* among their many nature gods and goddesses, whose shrines abounded in Athens. The definitive passage, briefly discussed in the previous chapter, is the following:

> *God that made the world and all things therein, seeing that he is Lord of heaven and earth, dwelleth not in temples made with hands . . . He giveth to all life, and breath, and all things; And hath made of one blood all nations of men for to dwell on all the face of the earth, and hath determined the times before appointed, and the bounds of their habitation; That they should seek the Lord. . . . For in him we live, and move, and have our being* (Acts 17:24–28).

Paul recognized that laying the creation foundation was necessary first of all, but the foundation is never the whole structure. Thus he then went on to preach Christ and the resurrection.

> [God] *hath appointed a day, in the which he will judge the world in righteousness by that man whom he hath ordained; whereof he hath given assurance unto all men, in that he hath raised him from the dead* (Acts 17:31).

There is no need to cite his whole message here. For that matter, the account of Paul's message as given by Luke in Acts 17 no doubt is itself a summary of a more detailed exposition given by Paul, but the essential point is that, when Paul dealt with those who believed the Bible, he began with the Scriptures, but when dealing with pagan unbelievers, he began with the fact of primeval special creation.

Another example is Paul's challenge to the pagan idolaters at Lystra.

> We . . . preach unto you that ye should turn from these vanities unto the living God, which made heaven, and earth, and the sea, and all things that are therein: Who in times past suffered all nations to walk in their own ways. Nevertheless he left not himself without witness, in that he did good, and gave us rain from heaven, and fruitful seasons, filling our hearts with food and gladness (Acts 14:15–17).

That Paul often preached against idol worship (which is tantamount to pantheistic evolution) and, therefore, for creation is indicated also by the charges lodged against him at Ephesus, namely that *"almost throughout all Asia, this Paul hath persuaded and turned away much people, saying that they be no gods, which are made with hands"* (Acts 19:26).

Thus, if we would follow the evangelistic example of the early Christians, we would preach from the Scriptures to those who already believe in the Bible and creation, urging them to accept Christ as revealed therein. To those who do not so believe, however, we need first of all to show them the truth of creation (as opposed to the false nature of all forms of evolutionism), and then proceed to the fact of Christ's substitutionary death and resurrection, as revealed in the inerrant written Word of God.

CHAPTER VI

BE READY TO ANSWER

We do indeed have a glorious gospel to share with people all over the world. The way of eternal salvation, provided by the finished work of the Lord Jesus Christ, through His substitutionary death and triumphant resurrection, is so clear and wonderful that it would seem everyone would rush to receive it.

If anyone should ask: *"What shall we do, that we might work the works of God?"* then Jesus would reply: *"This is the work of God, that ye believe on him whom he hath sent"* (John 6:28, 29). But then, Jesus also said: *". . . if ye believe not that I am he, ye shall die in your sins"* (John 8:24). *"And this is the record, that God hath given to us eternal life, and this life is in his Son. he that hath the Son hath life; and he that hath not the Son of God hath not life"* (1 John 5:11–12).

Yet, despite the simplicity of the saving gospel of Christ, the certainty of its validity, and the wonderful future it promises, most people continue to ignore it or even to blatantly reject it, often persecuting those who teach it. Furthermore, there are many in this category who are capable and sincere and who have, in their own minds at least, what they think are good reasons for rejecting Christ and His Word.

The Christian witness, when encountering such reactions, needs to be able to recognize their objections (especially if they are sincere) and answer them. Because there *are* good answers to all of them! *"Be ready always to give an answer to every man that asketh you a reason of the hope that is in you with meekness and fear"* (1 Pet. 3:15).

Note that this Scripture verse is actually a command. The Lord expects Christian believers, as His chosen and called witnesses, to be *able* to give an answer, and this implies life-long study of both His Word and His world, since there seems no end to the questions people are able to come up with as they seek to justify their rejection of Christ and the Bible.

Our answer, however, must not be given in an attitude of arrogance or belligerence, but *"with meekness and fear."* As Paul has said, *"The servant of the Lord must…be gentle unto all men, apt to teach, patient, In meekness instructing those that oppose themselves; if God peradventure will give them repentance to the acknowledging of the truth"* (2 Tim. 2:24–25).

At the same time, the gospel itself must not be compromised in our witnessing. Men do not really accept Christ if they think they can do so with reservations of their own. That is, if a man says he will become a Christian provided he does not have to quit smoking or to be baptized by immersion or to renounce evolution — or any other condition he might pose — then he is not ready. The Lord may not ask him to do these things, but he cannot make conditions of any kind.

All unsaved people are, spiritually speaking, *"dead in trespasses and sins"* (Eph. 2:1), and dead people cannot impose conditions to the only one who can give them life. They must first be *"born again"* (John 3:7), and then they should, like Paul, say, *"Lord, what wilt thou have me to do?"* (Acts 9:6).

There already are numerous books and tracts available to help Christian witnesses with their answers, so this chapter will deal only with those questions and objections which are being raised especially in this present day and age. First of all, consider the question of creation — especially creation as taught in the Bible.

As noted above, God does not ask a person to renounce evolution before he comes to Christ, but neither can that person make his own belief in evolution a condition before he will come. The fact is, however, that creation by God in Christ is the foundational component of His saving gospel, as just pointed out in the previous chapter.

It is true that some genuine Christians believe that creation could have occurred over long ages or even by the process of evolution, while they also still believe in Christ as Creator and Redeemer. This is inconsistent thinking, of course, for it is certainly not what Christ and the Bible teach, but it is a fairly common opinion anyway. People can manage to be inconsistent about many things, including this.

The real stumbling block is *recent* creation. Evolution and long ages can be interpreted by compromising Christians to be consistent with "creation," but not with "recent creation." Non-Christians in most cases are well aware that the Bible teaches creation in six days, so this is certainly a question that needs to be answered, especially if such inquirers believe that geologists and other scientists have proved the earth to be billions of years old.

Therefore, we need to know whether the long-ages view of creation is a legitimate compromise or whether we need a better answer.

IMPORTANCE OF RECENT CREATION

Those of us who believe not only that the Bible is the inerrant Word of God but also that God intended it to be understood by ordinary people (not just by scholarly specialists in science or theology) have been labeled "young-earth creationists."

We did not choose that name for ourselves, but it is true that, since we believe that God is capable of saying what He means and means what He says, we have to believe that the whole creation is far younger than evolutionists can accept.

It would be much more comfortable for us *not* to believe in a young earth, of course. Not only are the entire scientific and educational establishments committed to "old-earth evolutionism," but so also are the supposedly more intellectual segments of the religious world. The seminaries and colleges of the so-called mainline denominations have almost all capitulated to "theistic evolutionism," and most evangelical colleges and seminaries espouse "old-earth creationism," or what many call "progressive creationism."

So "young-earth creationism" is not a comfortable position to hold, especially for scientists or ambitious students, and it would be tempting either to give it up (as many have, under the persuasive influence of such winsome speakers as Hugh Ross, Robert Gange, and other popular evangelicals) or else just to say it really doesn't matter how or when God created (as do most modern churches and para-church organizations), as long as we believe that He is our Creator.

But it *does* matter. That is why ICR was formed in the first place over 30 years ago. Our very statement of faith specifies this position. Therefore, I want to emphasize once again why it is vitally important to continue to believe, as our Christian forefathers did, that *"in six days, the Lord made heaven and earth, the sea, and all that in them is, and rested the seventh day"* (Exod. 20:11).

IMPLICATIONS OF THE OLD EARTH POSITION

It is obvious that belief in a 4.6 billion-year-old earth and a 15 billion-year-old universe did not come from the Bible, for there is not a hint of evolution or long geological ages anywhere in the Bible. My book *Biblical Creationism*, for example, examines every relevant verse in every book of the Bible, and there is no suggestion anywhere of the geological or astronomical ages that are widely assumed today. The concepts of evolution and an infinitely old cosmos are often found in the ancient pagan religions, but never in the original Judaeo-Christian literature.

Therefore, Christians who want to harmonize the standard geological/astronomical age system with Scripture must use eisegesis, not exegesis, to do so. That is, they have to try to interpret Scripture in such a way as to make it fit modern scientism. We believe, on the other hand, that the only way we can really honor the Bible as God's inspired Word is to assume it as authoritative on all subjects with which it deals. That means we must use the Bible to interpret scientific data, not use naturalistic presuppositions to direct our Bible interpretations.

Those who choose the latter course, however, embark on a very slippery slope that ends in a precipice. For if the long geological ages really took place, that means there were at least a billion years of suffering and death in the animal kingdom before the arrival of men and women in the world. Each geological "age" is identified by the types of dead organisms now preserved as fossils in the rocks of that age, and there are literally billions of such fossils buried in the earth's crust. This fact leads to the following very disturbing chain of conclusions, as follows:

1. God is not really a God of grace and mercy after all, for He seems to have created a world filled with animals suffering and dying for a billion years, and He did so for no apparent reason whatever, assuming that His ultimate goal was to create human beings for fellowship with himself.

2. The Bible is not really an authoritative guide, for if it is wrong in these important matters of science and history, which we supposedly can check for ourselves, using the usual criteria of scientific and historical investigation, then how can we trust it in matters of salvation, heaven, and everlasting life, which we have *no* means of verifying scientifically?

"If I have told you earthly things, and ye believe not," said Jesus, *"how shall ye believe, if I tell you of heavenly things?"* (John 3:12).

3. Death is not really the wages of sin, as the Bible says, for violence, pain, and death reigned in the world long before sin came in. God is directly responsible for this cruel regime, not Adam. Furthermore, when God observed the completed creation of *"every thing that he had made . . . the heavens and the earth . . . and all the host of them,"* He pronounced it all to be *"very good"* (Gen. 1:31; 2:1). This seems to imply that God is sadistic, taking pleasure in observing the suffering and dying of His creatures.

4. The Bible teaches that Jesus Christ was our Creator before He became our Savior (John 1:1–3, 10; Col. 1:16; etc.). But Christ taught that it was *"from the beginning of the creation"* (not billions of years *after* the beginning of the creation) that *"God made them male and female"* (Mark 10:6), quoting from the record of the creation of Adam and Eve (Gen. 1:27). If He had really been there at the beginning, He would have known better. Furthermore, if God had really created a world of nature "red in tooth and claw," leading to "the survival of the fittest," how is it that His Son later taught His followers that *"Whosoever will save his life shall lose it"* (Mark 8:35), and that they should love their enemies and *"do good to them that hate you"* (Matt. 5:44)?

5. Still more significantly, if physical human death was not really an important part of the penalty for sin, then the agonizingly cruel *physical* death of Christ on the cross was not necessary to pay that penalty, and thus would be a gross miscarriage of justice on God's part.

6. This would lead us to conclude further that we have no real Savior. Christ is no longer here on earth, but sin and death are still here, so the promises in the Bible concerning future salvation seem to have been just empty rhetoric. If God's Word was wrong about creation and about the meaning of Christ's death, it becomes obvious that its prophecies and promises concerning the future are of no value either.

7. Finally, there remains no reason to believe in God at all — at least not in the personal, loving, omniscient, omnipotent, holy, righteous God that the Bible makes Him out to be. If *that* kind of God really existed, He would never have created the groaning, suffering, dying world implied by the long ages required for evolution. If suffering and death in the world — especially the suffering and death of Christ — are not the result of God's judgment on sin in the world, then the most reasonable inference is that the God of the Bible does not exist. The slippery slope

of compromise finally ends in the dark chasm of atheism, at least for those who travel to its logical termination.

Where We Must Stand

Therefore, no matter how much more convenient it would be to adopt the old-earth approach or the "doesn't matter" approach, we cannot do it. We might get converts more easily if we could just say it doesn't matter, but this would be dishonest, so we cannot. We don't have to raise the issue ourselves when we seek to win souls, but if the skeptic brings it up, we must be truthful.

The Bible *is* the inerrant, infallible, inspired Word of the living, gracious, omnipotent Creator, and the Lord Jesus Christ *is* our crucified and risen Savior, and all the *real* facts of science and history support these truths.

On the other hand, there is *no* genuine scientific evidence for evolutionism. No true evolution from one kind of organism to a more complex kind has ever been observed in all human history, and there is no *recorded* history beyond the six thousand or so years of biblical history. Any alleged earlier ages have to be postulated on the discredited assumption of uniformitarianism. Even if such imaginary ages ever existed, they left no credible fossil records of real evolutionary transitions among the billions of fossils preserved in the rocks.

What the fossils *do* show is *death* — rapid death and burial, in fact, or else they would not have been preserved at all. And death speaks of sin and judgment, not evolution and long ages. Pain and death are not "good" things, and a loving God would not call them good. They are instead, *"the wages of sin"* (Rom. 6:23). This judgment by our all-holy Creator necessarily fell on Adam and his descendants and also on all the *"dominion"* over which God had placed him in charge.

In the new earth which God in Christ will create after sin is finally purged out of this groaning creation, however, *"there shall be no more death, neither sorrow, nor crying, neither shall there be any more pain"* (Rev. 21:4). Once again, God's creation will all be *"very good"*!

In the meantime, we do well to continue to believe His Word just as it stands. God forbid that we should ever *"love the praise of men more than the praise of God"* (John 12:43).

There are many scientific reasons for believing in recent creation, and some will be discussed later in this book, but the fact is that the Bible teaches it, and Jesus Christ believed it. This is the most important reason of all. Whether it is possible that a real Christian, instructed in God's Word, can or will continue to believe in evolution or progressive creation is not a question I can answer. At least, I know he *should not* do so.

Uniformitarianism and the Laws of Science

Closely associated with evolutionism is the so-called principle of uniformitarianism. This principle rejects the idea of the supernatural, assuming that science requires everything to be explained in terms of naturalism. That is, even creation must be explained in terms of natural processes, operating in the past just as they do in the present.

This assumption obviously requires long ages and some form of evolution even to try to account for the amazingly complex functioning earth and its inhabitants. Creationism, on the other hand, not only assumes miraculous processes at the time of creation but also some form of catastrophic interruption of the world's natural processes at some later time or times in the past to account for the tremendous sedimentary and fossil-bearing formations in the earth's crust. The Bible provides a plausible explanation for this "geologic column" in terms of the global deluge that was sent by God in the days of Noah.

The so-called "natural scientists," who wish to explain the origin and history of everything in terms of purely "natural" processes, must try to explain away both the evidence of supernatural creative processes in the world's origin and the evidence of extra-natural processes at the time of the destruction of the world by the great Flood. Thus, they have developed a scheme of long geological ages, supposedly identified by the fossils preserved in the rocks of each "age," comprising in effect a fossil-documented record of the evolution of life over the ages. The whole system is called evolutionary uniformitarianism (or, perhaps, uniformitarian evolutionism). This has been the best scientific "proof" of evolution, as well as the main vehicle for rejecting the biblical record of earth history and even for rejecting God and the gospel of salvation in Christ.

Christians who believe the biblical record of recent creation and the worldwide Flood have long recognized the key significance of the apostle Peter's commentary on these two defining events in world history:

> *There shall come in the last days scoffers, walking after their own lusts, And saying, Where is the promise of his coming? for since the fathers fell asleep, all things continue as they were from the beginning of the creation. For this they willingly are*

ignorant of, that by the word of God the heavens were of old, and
the earth standing out of the water and in the water: Whereby
the world that then was, being overflowed with water, perished
(2 Pet. 3:3–6).

Peter was writing to all *"them that have obtained like precious faith*
with us through the righteousness of God and our Saviour Jesus Christ"
(2 Pet. 1:1). This declaration surely includes all true Christians and (under divine inspiration) is written in the context of future trends *"in the*
last days" (2 Pet. 3:3).

Consequently, his warnings and exhortations are more relevant to
us today than to anyone before us, for we are closer to the last days (and
quite possibly *in* them) than any one before us. A truly biblical world
view for these days, therefore, must correlate with Peter's divinely inspired prophecy.

Although I was probably not the first to do so, I remember teaching on this passage to a Bible class more than 55 years ago, while on
the faculty of Rice University, and I discussed it in my first book, *That*
You Might Believe, published in 1946. I stressed its significance at the
1953 convention of the American Scientific Affiliation in a paper entitled "Biblical Evidence for Recent Creation and a Worldwide Deluge,"
and this paper was reprinted in the January 1954 issue of *His* (the magazine of the Inter-Varsity Christian Fellowship). It was emphasized also in
the book *The Genesis Flood*, written by Dr. John Whitcomb and myself
and published in 1961 (see especially the conclusion of the book, pages
451–453). In its context (the last chapter written by Peter before his
martyrdom), it is surely a critically important component of God's Word
to professing Christians today.

The reason why it is so relevant today is because of both its prophecy
of the dominant secular uniformitarianism of the last days, which has
just been discussed, and also because of its cogent answer to this philosophy.

"All things continue as they were from the beginning of the creation."
This is as succinct a definition of the dogma of uniformitarianism as
one could find. Not only the basic "laws of nature" but also all natural
processes are assumed to be always essentially equivalent to those operating today — similar rates of erosion and deposition, similar rates of
salt influx to the sea, similar rates of radioactive decay, similar rates of
biological variation, similar rates even of local flooding and volcanism,

etc. No sudden global change in earth processes, and certainly no divine intervention in these processes is allowed. This has been the accepted scientific world view for the past two centuries.

But this assumption is very wrong. There have been two tremendous global divine interventions in the uniform course of natural processes in the past — creation and the Flood! *"By the word of God, the heavens were of old, and the earth. . . . "* The cosmos was created, not by continuing natural processes, but by one supernatural "process" — the spoken Word of God!

Secondly, *"the world that then was, being overflowed with water, perished."* This cataclysmic destruction of the prediluvian cosmos necessarily implies a sudden drastic change in all process rates — the *world itself* perished during the great Flood!

The changed world that later emerged as the waters retreated following the year of the Flood, when the present continents were uplifted, the present ocean basins established, and all the residual catastrophism following the Flood (Ice Age, etc.) settled down, soon became a world where uniform processes would prevail thereafter. God himself promised: *"I will not again curse the ground any more for man's sake . . . neither will I again smite any more every thing living, as I have done. While the earth remaineth, seedtime and harvest, and cold and heat, and summer and winter, and day and night shall not cease"* (Gen. 8:21–22).

That is, as long as the present earth remains (though not forever, for the earth will eventually be purged by fire — 2 Pet. 3:10), there would be no other global cataclysm, and the basic geophysical processes — the rotation of the earth and its orbital revolution and inclination of its axis around the sun — which basically control or influence all other natural processes, would be constant. This naturalistic uniformitarianism would be a valid principle with which to study all natural phenomena since the end of the Flood period.

But not before! The Flood caused such a drastic change in most natural processes — especially those of erosion and deposition, but of most others as well — that scientists cannot *legitimately* extrapolate present processes beyond that period in the past.

This is true *biblical uniformitarianism*. Even then, however, the *basic laws of nature* did not change. These were established at the end of the period of creation, including the Fall and Curse. The two most basic and certain natural laws are those of conservation and decay, the first law of thermodynamics (conservation of mass/energy) and the second law of thermodynamics (increasing entropy or decreasing organizational complexity). All natural processes operate within the constraints imposed by these two universal divinely imposed laws of nature and nature's God.

The first law was established following the completion of God's work of creation, when the Creator (the Lord Jesus Christ) *"rested from all his work which God created and made"* (Gen. 2:3). He is ever since *"upholding all things by the word of his power"* (Heb. 1:3). No matter or energy can be naturally either created or destroyed, because God is *conserving* what He created. (Special local miracles are an exception to this principle, but there must be strong reason and evidence for any such alleged miracle.)

Then the second law was enacted by God following Adam's sin, introducing the great Curse of pain, decay, and death, not only on Adam but also on all his dominion. *"Cursed is the ground for thy sake . . . and unto dust shalt thou return"* (Gen. 3:17–19). Ever since that time, *"the whole creation groaneth and travaileth in pain together until now"* (Rom. 8:22).

Thus, the basic laws of science go back just to the end of the creation/Fall period, while the natural processes operating within the constraints of the two laws have been operating uniformly only since the end of the Flood period. Recognition of this biblical fact means that one cannot estimate the age of the earth with any process based on the premise of uniformitarianism, since that premise is valid at best only back to the end of the Flood period.

This conclusion is of fundamental importance in dealing with the question of origins. Evolutionism depends for its supposed evidence entirely on the assumed billions of years of geologic history. However, all such estimates of age must necessarily be based on the assumption of uniformitarianism as applicable back to the very beginning. This fact applies to age calculations based on any geological, biological, or cosmological process whatever. This constraint must also affect radioactive decay processes, which are those few processes that have been used to support the argument that the earth is billions of years old. The so-called "daughter/parent" isotope ratios in certain minerals found in igneous rocks, therefore, are *not* a legitimate indicator of the age of those rocks or of the mantle from which they may have emerged. They cannot really be the product of the decay of the daughter isotope from the parent at present decay rates, if the biblical record is inerrant, as most Christians believe. Rather, these ratios must be viewed either as created directly during the creation period or by vastly accelerated decay rates during either that period or the Flood period, or perhaps by profound contamination during the Flood.

To say that such a conclusion is "unscientific" is to say much more than one knows and is essentially an admission of intolerant atheism. If God exists, and if the overwhelming evidences that the Bible is God's Word are valid evidences, then God could indeed miraculously have created the whole world in a state of functioning maturity (a better term than "apparent age"), and He could also miraculously increase process rates (including radioactive decay rates) in connection with His global intervention in natural processes at the times of the Curse and/or the Flood. Both these periods were times of special divine activity in respect to the earth and its processes, as clearly revealed in the Bible.

Biblical uniformitarianism is a valid premise back to the end of the Flood period, but secular uniformitarianism back to *the beginning of the creation* is not. If we really want to *know* the time when the world began, we must ask the One who created it, for only He was there. He has provided this information in His inspired Word, the Holy Scriptures, but the tragedy is that the modern world — including, sadly, many leaders in the evangelical world — are afraid to believe what He has said.

WHAT ABOUT THE NON-CHRISTIAN RELIGIONS?

There are many other religions in the world besides that of Christ, of course, and Christians are coming much more frequently in contact with their adherents than they used to. One does not have to go to Asia or Africa to encounter Muslims or Buddhists or Hindus, for example. For a whole generation, large numbers of these people have been coming to America — whether as students or tourists or actual immigrants. We need to witness to them also, of course, as they need the Lord just like Americans do. We cannot ignore the fact that Christ said, *"No man cometh unto the Father, but by me."*

Many Muslims are very devout and sincere believers in Islam, for example, and the same type of commitment is true for many in the other great religions, but the fact remains that they are all unsaved sinners, for there is no *"salvation in any other: for there is none other name under heaven given among men, whereby we must be saved"* than that of the Lord Jesus Christ (Acts 4:12).

That is why American and European Christians have been sending out foreign missionaries for many years, and that is still vitally important.

But many of us who will never go out in this way are now meeting many such people right here in our own lands, and we need to witness to them also.

We cannot consider all these different religions here in this small book, but I do want to discuss the Muslim religion briefly. They are surely coming here in the greatest numbers, and their reasons for rejecting Christ are similar in some respects to the reasons offered by Jews, and even by many among the Hindus and others. Furthermore, because of the similarity of their faith to that of Christians in many ways (they believe in the virgin birth of Christ, for example, and in His second coming, as well as being monotheists), many professing Christians seem ready to believe that Allah is the same God in whom we believe, and that sincere followers of Mohammed can be saved in their own religion. Some even believe that sincere practitioners of *any* religion will be saved. That is wrong, however, and we really do need to try to win them to Christ.

I am writing this section during the month of Ramadan, and I have just finished re-reading the Koran,[1] which good Muslims are also instructed to do at this time. I have been trying to compare its teaching with those of the Bible, and would urge our Muslim friends to do the same. Mohammed himself, writing in the years around A.D. 600, frequently referred to the narratives in the books of Moses, as well as those associated with Jesus in the New Testament. Many of the teachings on practical living are similar in the two books.

One important point of commonality is the clear teaching in the Koran that there is only one omnipotent, omniscient Creator and that He created all things in six days.[2] Some Muslims say these "days" were really long ages, but the Koran itself doesn't say this, often noting that God created instantaneously,[3] just as the Bible teaches (e.g., Ps. 33:6–9). However, there is one very significant difference.

---

1 There are a number of English translations of the Koran. The one I have been using was given to me many years ago by a Muslim friend, so I assume that it is a good translation. The Koran contains 114 "Suras," more or less equivalent to chapters, but each representing a special "revelation" of God to Mohammed. The passages quoted below are typical passages.

2 "We created the heavens and the earth and all that is between them in six days, and no weariness touched us" (Sura 50:38). Allah frequently uses "we" and "us" when speaking of himself, even though he vehemently denies the Trinity, as well as polytheism.

3 "And when he decreeth a thing, he only saith to it, 'Be,' and it is" (Sura 2:111).

Allah displays many characteristics of the God of the Bible; he is called "compassionate," "merciful," "almighty," "the Lord of the world," "wise," "the first and the last," "forgiving," "gracious," and so on. These characteristics certainly apply also to our God of the Bible.

But there are almost no mentions in the Koran of Allah as "Love." The God of the Bible is, above all, a God of love! In fact, *"God is love"* (1 John 4:8), and *"God so loved the world, that he gave his only begotten Son, that whosoever believeth in him should not perish, but have everlasting life"* (John 3:16).

Therein is another key difference, of course. The Koran denies categorically that Jesus was the Son of God.[4] He was said to be merely one in a long line of prophets, Adam being the first, with Mohammed the last and greatest.

However, Mohammed is dead and Jesus is alive! Jesus was crucified and died, all right, but then He defeated death forever; His resurrection to a glorified physical body is, as many volumes on Christian evidences have shown, the best-proved fact of all ancient history.[5]

The Koran denies this fact, but the Koran is wrong, as the evidence of real history proves conclusively. After Christ's resurrection, *"He shewed himself alive . . . by many infallible proofs, being seen of* [His followers] *forty days"* (Acts 1:3). John later saw Him again and heard Him say, *"I am he that liveth, and was dead; and, behold, I am alive for evermore, Amen; and have the keys of hell and of death"* (Rev. 1:18).

The Koran does agree with the Bible on the fact of the virgin birth of Christ and on His future second coming. But when it denies His atoning death[6] for our sins and then further denies His resurrection (which proved beyond doubt that His claims were all true), then it is seeking to destroy the very heart of Christianity. It would thereby also undermine God's plan for forgiving our sins and offering eternal salvation to all who

---

4 "Infidels now are they who say, 'Verily God is the Messiah, Ibn Maryam [son of Mary]!' " (Sura 5:19). "Believe therefore in God and his apostles, and say not, 'Three' [there is a Trinity] — Forbear — it will be better for you. God is only one God! Far be it from his glory that he should have a son!" (Sura 4:169).

5 For a brief summary of proofs of the resurrection, see the ICR booklet *The Resurrection of Christ*, sent free on request through ICR Customer Service or the web at [http://www.icr.org/bible/bible.htm].

6 "And for their saying, 'Verily we have slain the Messiah, Jesus the son of Mary, and Apostle of God.' Yet they slew him not, and they crucified him not, but they had only his likeness. . . . they did not really slay him, but God took him to himself." (Sura 4:157).

would put their trust in Him. Thus, the loving God of the Bible cannot be the same one as the counterfeit god called Allah.

Every person — Muslim, Jew, Catholic, Protestant — is a guilty sinner before our holy Creator God. Even Mohammed was a sinner, needing forgiveness and salvation. Our Lord Jesus was *not* a sinner, however. Being virgin-born, He alone had no innate sin, and His whole life was without any sinful act. Thus, He alone could die as an innocent sacrifice for all other men and women. He allowed himself to be crucified and to die as their substitute. Because He *loved* us! As the great apostle Paul said: *"The life which I now live in the flesh I live by the faith of the Son of God, who loved me, and gave himself for me"* (Gal. 2:20).

Does Mohammed love us? Does Allah love us? Absolutely not! The Koran is replete with threats of eternal burning in hell for all kinds of forbidden human activities. Even faithful Muslims have no assurance of salvation and heaven. Infidels, of course, have no chance at all; they are all consigned directly to hell.

And who are infidels? The Koran says that all Jews, Christians, and, in fact, all non-Muslims are infidels and must either convert to Islam or, if possible, be slain, thereafter proceeding to endless torture in hell. In fact, only those Muslims whose good deeds outweigh their sins (or who die fighting non-Muslims) will get to Paradise with all its sensual rewards.[7]

On the other hand, the *true* God, as revealed in the Bible, is a *loving* God who is *"not willing that any should perish, but that all should come to repentance"* (2 Pet. 3:9). No one deserves to be saved, *"For all have sinned, and come short of the glory of God"* (Rom. 3:23), and God will not force anyone to accept His free gift of salvation through Christ. Nevertheless, *"In this was manifested the love of God toward us, because that God sent his only begotten Son into the world, that we might live through him"* (1 John 4:9).

---

7 "Infidels now are they who say, 'God is the Messiah, Son of Mary.' . . . They surely are infidels who say, 'God is the third of three;' for there is no God but one God" (Sura 5:76–77). "Whoso desireth any other religion than Islam, that religion shall never be accepted from him, and in the next world he shall be among the lost" (Sura 3:79). "When ye encounter the infidels, strike off their heads till ye have made a great slaughter among them, and of the rest make fast the fetters" (Sura 47:4). "And when the trumpet shall be sounded . . . They whose balances shall be heavy, shall be the blest. But they whose balances shall be light, — these are they who shall lose their souls, abiding in hell for ever" (Sura 23:3–5). "And whoso fight for the cause of God . . . he will bring them into the Paradise, of which he hath told them" (Sura 47:5–7).

God loves Muslims, too, even though the Koran (allegedly the inspired words dictated to Mohammed by Allah) does not say that. God has, in love, provided a Savior for all who will accept His free gift of total forgiveness and eternal salvation through faith in the Lord Jesus Christ, and He has told all Christians to go and *"preach the gospel to every creature"* (Mark 16:15), not only here in America, but *"unto the uttermost part of the earth"* (Acts 1:8). This is to be done, not with the sword, but by love and reason. Every person needs to come to his or her own personal decision to accept Christ as Savior, whether they are Americans or Asians, men or women, Muslim or Christian in background, rich or poor, or whatever. And that is the most important decision they can ever make! *"For the wages of sin is death; but the gift of God is eternal life through Jesus Christ our Lord"* (Rom. 6:23). One does not have to have his work weighed in balances to earn a gift. He simply accepts the gift — or turns it down!

We would love to see our many Muslim friends — here in America and everywhere — receive this wonderful gift. I personally have enjoyed knowing many Muslims in the engineering schools where we worked and studied together, and have great appreciation for their abilities and contributions to the world. These friends of former days included Iranians, Iraqis, Egyptians, Afghans, Pakistanis, Arabs, and others.

My family and I were even making arrangements back in the late 1940s to move to Afghanistan to help that nation by teaching in a proposed engineering college there. That door closed, but in the process I tried to study as much as I could about Afghanistan and the Muslim people and their religion in general.

Muslim people have indeed been well taught to fear the God of creation, and that is good, for He is all powerful and most holy. But He is also, in the person of His only begotten Son (not begotten by natural generation through Mary, of course, but by eternal and continual heavenly generation), the God of salvation, for He is a loving and caring God. Therefore, He became a man, the eternal Word made flesh (John 1:1–3, 14) in order to pay the infinite price to redeem lost men from sin and death and hell.

We would dearly love to see our Muslim friends — especially the seven million American Muslims who have chosen to live here in the United States as a great country of freedom — now to exercise that freedom (which they could never have done openly in their own native lands) to accept the eternal freedom found only in our Lord Jesus. We would say the same about those who believe in Buddhism or Hinduism or any other religion. They all need salvation in Christ.

Why?

One of the most common objections to belief in Christ is the fact that so many bad things can happen to apparently innocent people. Christians themselves often are called on to suffer for no obvious reason, so why accept Christ?

"Why — why did this happen to me?" How often this unanswerable question bursts from the lips of a grief-stricken parent, or an innocent accident victim, or most anyone hurting in some way for some unknown reason. In fact, such problems and unexplainable sufferings are often used as an excuse for rejecting God altogether. *"How could a loving God permit bad things to happen to good people?"* That was actually the sort of reason given by Charles Darwin himself for turning away from Christianity and the God of the Bible early in his adult life. No doubt every reader of these lines (including their author) has had difficult experiences for which he or she could find no obvious answer to the *"Why?"* question.

Even the Lord Jesus Christ, perfectly sinless throughout His life, yet suffering and dying a terrible death on the cross, cried out: *"My God, my God, why hast thou forsaken me?"* (Matt. 27:46). We now understand that Christ was dying for our sins, but why does God so often leave our own questions unanswered?

As a matter of fact, one of the longest books of the Bible, and probably its oldest, devotes all of its 42 chapters to this very question. The patriarch Job was said by God himself to be *"perfect and upright, and one that feared God, and eschewed evil"* (Job 1:1, 8; 2:3). Yet he suffered more than just about anyone who ever lived, and could not understand why, in spite of repeatedly calling on God for an answer.

It is true, of course, that all people — good and bad alike — live in a wonderful world that has come under God's curse because of human sin. Every person experiences much that is good in God's creation, but also much that is not good. *"He maketh his sun to rise on the evil and on the good, and sendeth rain on the just and on the unjust"* (Matt. 5:45). Yet, in Job's case (and often in ours as well), his sufferings were more than could be explained by the ordinary vicissitudes of life. In one day, all his great wealth and possessions and even his ten grown sons and daughters were taken from him in violent catastrophes. On another day soon afterward, his health was also taken away, and he was stricken with a painful and hideous disease. His friends and even his wife finally forsook him, and the high esteem in which he had been held by everyone in the community soon turned to loathing and ostracism.

What he did not know, of course, and could not be told at the time was that God was permitting Satan to make a scientific falsification test on Job's faith in God. The old serpent, who had led to Adam's fall, had accused Job of serving God solely because of God's blessings, so God allowed him to make this test.

But Job persisted in his faith in spite of everything, and finally Satan seemed to depart for a season. Behind the scenes, however, he was continuing his attack, using one of his fallen angels (note Job 4:12–21) to deceive three old friends of Job into demeaning his character, accusing Job of such sin and hypocrisy as to incur God's wrath and judgment.

Job acknowledged more than once that he, like all men, was sinful by nature but kept insisting that he was unaware of any specific acts of sin for which he was being punished. This conflict is recorded in chapters 3 through 31 of the Book of Job. In spite of all his suffering, capped by the spiritual torment inflicted by his erstwhile friends, Job continued to have faith in God, saying: *"Though he slay me, yet will I trust in him"* (Job 13:15). He wanted to present his case to God, but could not seem to reach Him, somehow yearning for *"any daysman* [that is, 'mediator'] *betwixt us, that might lay his hand upon us both"* (Job 9:33).

Eventually the three friends gave up and quit arguing. But Satan had one more stratagem. A young religionist named Elihu had been listening to all the arguments, waiting for an opportunity to inject his own opinion into the debate. He did have considerable knowledge of spiritual matters, but was also quite arrogant and proud. He not only proceeded to claim that he was speaking as a "spirit" within him constrained him, but also that he was the very "daysman" who could be the needed mediator between Job and God. *"The spirit within me constraineth me,"* he said, and also: *"Behold, I am according to thy wish in God's stead"* (Job 32:18; 33:6).

But that "spirit" could not have been God's Spirit, for he merely led Elihu to repeat and embellish the false charges that Job's three friends had been lodging against Job, and making it even worse by claiming that he was inspired by God in doing so. The spirit in him was apparently a "lying spirit" also, like the one who had influenced Eliphaz (Job 4:12–21), for he accused Job of saying and doing several wicked things which Job had *not* said or done. (Note Job 34:7–8; 35:2–3; etc.)

Elihu's harangue continued through six chapters (32–37), and Job remained silent. He knew Elihu's charges were false, but Elihu was claiming to be speaking for God, and Job did not know how to answer.

God *did* know how to answer, however, finally breaking *His* long silence. *"Who is this that darkeneth counsel by words without knowledge?"* (Job 38:2), God said. He obviously was not addressing Job, whom He knew very well, for it was Elihu, not Job, who had been sermonizing for so long. That put-down was His only response to Elihu, but now He *"answered Job"* (Job 38:1) in a most remarkable four-chapter monologue, after which He acknowledged that all Job had said about his own freedom from sin had been *"right"* and that the charges of his friends had all been wrong (Job 42:7).

But what did He say about why Job had been suffering so severely? Almost with astonishment, we find that He said nothing at all! He did not mention either Job's suffering or suffering in general, never responding to Job's repeated questioning, nor did He deal in any way with the broad issue of why bad things happen to good people.

Instead, the entire four-chapter monologue was about the wonders and intricacies of creation — His unique special creation of all things in the beginning and His providential preservation of His creation since that time. God did this in the form of about 77 scientific questions about creation which Job (and the others) evidently should have been able to answer, but could not.

But we should realize that this exposition of the vital importance of creation *was* His answer! That is, the real solution to the problem of suffering — whether that of individuals or society in general (wars, racism, poverty, etc.) — is renewed recognition of God as Creator of the world and its inhabitants, and that He has an eternal purpose for His creation far transcending our own immediate problems. He has the right to do what He will with His own, especially since He has also become the Redeemer and Savior of all who believe Him. He has also promised that *"all things work together for good to them that love God, to them who are the called according to his purpose"* (Rom. 8:28).

Job did not have to understand, but simply to trust God, and he had continued to do that, just as God knew he would. God did rebuke Job, however, not because of any sins, but because of his lack of knowledge and concern about God's creation. God had given Adam and his descendants dominion over His creation as His stewards, but even Job (as godly as he was) had been more concerned about his own works of righteousness than about God's purposes in creation. Thus, one vital way to view our own personal problems today is to place them in the perspective of God's creative purposes for us in eternity.

As the apostle Peter said (and he also had been severely tested by Satan — note Luke 22:31–32): *"Wherefore let them that suffer according to the will of God commit the keeping of their souls to him in well doing, as unto a faithful Creator"* (1 Pet. 4:19).

We need also to keep in mind God's immediate reason for allowing Job to be so severely tested by the devil. Not only was the reality of Job's saving faith being tested, for Job's sake, but it was also being demonstrated as real and effective to Satan and to all the angelic sons of God, both those who were faithful to the Creator and those who had followed Satan in his rebellion. Some of these had even been aiding Satan in trying to seduce Job away from his faith in the goodness and justice of the Creator.

Perhaps, therefore, there are times in our lives when God also allows the devil to test the reality of our own faith, as he did that of Job and Peter. Satan is, after all, *"that old serpent . . . which deceiveth the whole world . . . the accuser of our brethren . . . which accused them before our God day and night"* (Rev. 12:9–10).

In fact, it was the apostle Paul (who had himself gone through tremendous trials all during his ministry) who said that he was seeking *"to make all men see what is the fellowship of the mystery, which from the beginning of the world hath been hid in God, who created all things by Jesus Christ: To the intent that now unto the principalities and powers in heavenly places might be known by the church the manifold wisdom of God"* (Eph. 3:9–10).

With all this in mind, when God allows us to suffer some great sorrow or hardship, and we see no immediate reason for it, let us simply continue to trust Him, as Job did, putting it into the context of His creating us for some divine creative purpose which we shall someday *"know even as also [we are] known"* (1 Cor. 13:12), and so that *"the trial of [your] faith . . . though it be tried with fire, might be found unto praise and honour and glory at the appearing of Jesus Christ"* (1 Peter 1:7).

Much of the foregoing discussion may seem to apply primarily to godly Christian believers, suggesting that *their* sufferings may be to test the reality and strength of their faith. Occasionally, no doubt, such a situation must be explained in terms of chastisement for unconfessed sin in one's life. This might even include rebuke, as in Job's case, for unconcern about God's primeval Dominion Mandate — in other words, failure to recognize the significance of his own vocation in the accomplishment of God's will and failure to try to serve *"to the glory of God"* (1 Cor. 10:31). Sufferings may also help him or her to *"grow in grace"* and to *"grow up into him in all things"* (2 Pet. 3:18; Eph. 4:15).

As far as unbelievers are concerned, such explanations may apply in part to their sufferings as well. The Lord, with His foreknowledge, may be preparing them for their future Christian service even before they have accepted Christ.

In fact, their sufferings may even lead them to accept Christ in the first place, as many have stressed in their own personal testimonies after becoming Christians. The apostle Paul is a primary biblical example. While actually engaged in persecuting the followers of Christ, Paul was suddenly struck blind, remaining that way until the Lord enabled a mature disciple named Ananias to heal his blindness. At that time, God told Ananias that Paul *"is a chosen vessel unto me . . . for I will shew him how great things he must suffer for my name's sake"* (Acts 9:15–16).

Who knows whether, as we seek to answer the questions of a potential convert about his own sufferings, God may have some special future service in mind for him? At least that is one point we can make in our own answer to him. God is indeed a God of love and purpose, and He does know the end from the beginning.

CHAPTER VII

CREATION AND THE
SCIENCE OF LIFE

The best conclusive proof that life is based on special creation and not evolution is the fact that creation is taught in the Bible, with not a hint of evolution or the long geological ages anywhere in its 66 books. These were written by 40 or more authors (all as inspired by God) over at least 2,000 years.

However, this truth may not convince a person who thinks the Bible to be entirely human in its origin, subject to all the mistakes and subjective philosophies to which human writers are prone. It may be necessary to show such a person that true science *also* supports creation and does *not* prove evolution, as evolutionists like to claim. This type of evidence, while not necessary for those who believe the Bible, will also help to strengthen their faith and witnessing confidence as well.

Accordingly, the next three chapters will focus mainly on the scientific data related to origins. I think it might be useful to begin with a summarizing critique of the most recent (probably the last) book written by the man widely acknowledged to be probably the most influential evolutionary scientist of the past century.

That would be Dr. and Professor Ernst Mayr, of Harvard.

The Dean of Evolution

With the passing in recent years of three of the most revered, modern scientific spokesmen for evolution — Isaac Asimov, Carl Sagan, and Stephen Jay Gould — Professor Ernst Mayr is left as the unquestioned dean of the modern evolutionary establishment.

Gould, Asimov, and Sagan were all three extremely prolific and brilliant writers. All three were atheistic professors at prestigious eastern universities (Gould at Harvard, Asimov at Boston University, Sagan at Cornell), and all three were effusive and vigorous anti-creationists. They were formidable opponents (but eminently quotable), and we miss them. All three died at relatively young ages.

But that leaves Ernst Mayr, long-time professor of biology at Harvard. Dr. Mayr was born in 1904 and is (at this writing) still very much alive at the century mark. Dr. Gould called him "the greatest living evolutionary biologist and a writer of extraordinary insight and clarity" (in a jacket blurb on Mayr's latest book).

Mayr's New Book

And that book is the subject of this section. Its title is intriguing — *What Evolution Is*[1] — for if anyone could speak authoritatively on such a subject, it should be Professor Mayr. In his adulatory foreword, Jared Diamond, another leading modern evolutionist, concludes: "There is no better book on evolution. There will never be another book like it."[2]

That evaluation should give any reader very high expectations. Unfortunately, however, Dr. Mayr first shows his disdain for creationism, not even considering its arguments. He simply says:

> *It is now actually misleading to refer to evolution as a theory, considering the massive evidence that has been discovered over the last 140 years documenting its existence. Evolution is no longer a theory, it is simply a fact.*[3]

He dismissed the evidence for creation as unworthy of further discussion. "The claims of the creationists," he says, "have been refuted so frequently and so thoroughly that there is no need to cover this subject once more."[4]

---

1 Ernst Mayr, *What Evolution Is* (New York: Basic Books, 2001), 318 p.

2 Ibid., p. xii.

3 Ibid., p. 275.

4 Ibid., p. 269.

IGNORING CREATION EVIDENCE

He himself, however, has apparently not bothered to read any creationist or secular anti-evolutionist scientific books or articles. Or at least that is what one would infer from the fact that none of them or their arguments and evidence are even mentioned in his book.

No mention is made by Mayr, for example, of creationist expositions of the amazing created designs in living systems, nor the effects of God's curse on the creation, or of the significance of the great Flood in understanding the geologic record. He does not even acknowledge the significance of naturalistic catastrophism or of such scientific concepts as complexity or probability. Current ideas about "intelligent design" are never mentioned. The origins of all things are due to time, chance, and natural selection, no matter how complex and interdependent they may be, according to Professor Mayr, who had been (along with Julian Huxley, George Simpson, and a few others) primarily responsible for the so-called modern evolutionary synthesis (or neo-Darwinism) back in the 1930s and 1940s.

Neither does Mayr seem aware that there are now thousands of credentialed and knowledgeable scientists (including a great many biologists) who reject evolution, giving not even a nod to the Creation Research Society, or to ICR, or any other creationist organization. He does occasionally refer to God or to Christianity, but only in passing, and always in a context that indicates that he does not believe in either one. He, like his three younger colleagues, is an atheist, and this naturally constrains him to ignore any possible theological implications of the origins issues.

THE ALLEGED EVIDENCE FOR EVOLUTION

Mayr's new book is beautifully written and does contain much good material, but it will not convert many to evolutionism, even though he does devote a chapter to what he thinks are the evidences for evolution. These evidences are essentially the same as those used almost 150 years ago by Darwin in the *Origin* (fossils, comparative morphology, embryological similarities and recapitulation, vestigial structures, and geographical distribution). Mayr adds nothing new to these arguments, ignoring the fact that creationists (and even a number of evolutionists) have long since refuted all of them. He does devote a brief section to the more recent "evidence" from molecular biology. But that also has been vigorously disputed by a number of specialists in this field, especially the supposed evolutionary relationships implied by the molecules. Even Mayr admits that "molecular clocks are not nearly as constant as often believed,"[5] but he does not mention any of the numerous contradictory relationships implied by these biochemical studies (e.g., the well-known genomic similarities of humans and bananas).

As do most evolutionists, Mayr spends much time in discussing microevolution, whereas modern creationists only reject macroevolution. He devotes five chapters to microevolution and only one to macroevolution. This particular chapter is quite long, discussing many speculative theories about how macroevolutionary changes might be produced, but there is one vital deficiency. He gives *no* example of any macroevolutionary change *known* to have happened. In other words, macroevolution seems never to have occurred within the several thousand years of recorded history. Thus, *real* evolution (as distinct from variation, recombination, hybridization, and other such "horizontal" changes) does not happen at present. Where, we would ask Professor Mayr, are there any living forms in the process of evolutionary change? He gives no examples, of course, because there are none.

As far as pre-human history is concerned, Dr. Mayr does insist that the fossil record documents past evolution. He cites the usual claims — horses, *Archaeopteryx*, mammal-like reptiles, walking whales, etc. — which are very equivocal, at best, and have all been shown by creationists to be invalid as transitional forms. Instead of a handful of highly doubtful examples, there ought to be thousands of obvious transitional forms in the fossils if evolution had really been occurring. Yet Mayr admits:

> *Wherever we look at the living biota . . . discontinuities are overwhelmingly frequent. . . . The discontinuities are even more striking in the fossil record. New species usually appear in the fossil record suddenly, not connected with their ancestors by a series of intermediates.*[6]

Professor Mayr still says the fossils are "the most convincing evidence for the occurrence of evolution."[7] Yet he also says that "the fossil record remains woefully inadequate" (p. 69). Thus, as creationists have often pointed out, there is no *real* evidence of either present or past evolution.

---

5 Ibid., p. 37.

6 Ibid., p. 189.

7 Ibid., p. 13.

We have repeatedly noted also that the scientific reason why this is so is because real evolution to any higher level of complexity is impossible by the law of entropy, which states the proven fact that every system of *any kind* "tends" to go toward lower complexity, unless constrained otherwise by some pre-designed external program and mechanism.

Yet Ernst Mayr seems either to ignore or misunderstand this key argument of the creationists. Here is what he says:

> *Actually there is no conflict, because the law of entropy is valid only for closed systems, whereas the evolution of a species of organisms takes place in an open system in which organisms can reduce entropy at the expense of the environment, and the sun supplies a continuing input of energy.*[8]

And that's all he says about one of the key arguments against evolution. This ubiquitous dodge of the evolutionists has been discredited again and again by creationists, and one would think that this "greatest living evolutionary biologist" in this "best book on evolution" would at least take notice of our arguments! At least half of America's population, according to many polls, are creationists, apparently agreeing more with us than with Mayr.

An open system and external energy are, indeed, *necessary* conditions for a system to grow in complexity, but most definitely are *not sufficient* conditions. The question is just *how* does the sun's energy produce complexity in an open system? The fact is that the application of external heat energy to an open system (such as from the sun to the earth) will *increase* the entropy (that is, decrease the organized complexity) in *any* open system, if that's all there is. This is a basic principle of thermodynamics, and neither Mayr nor any other evolutionist has answered this problem. Evolution seems to be impossible by the known laws of science.

As we look in a bit more detail at some of the most widely used arguments for evolution, consider first the supposed evidence that evolution is still going on in the modern world. The alleged evolutionary changes in England's famous peppered moth have supplied the most popular argument, but this "proof" has itself recently been severely criticized even by evolutionists.

---

8 Ibid., p. 8.

THE PROOF OF THE PEPPERED MOTH

For many years the peppered moth has adorned the pages of introductory biology textbooks as the prime example of "evolution in action." Its recent removal has also been accompanied by a sad exposure of the world of scientific academia as often a world of pettiness, inordinate rivalry, and tender egos, sometimes tempting to near-fraud in the "tweaking" of reported results.

The story has been told in a wonderfully researched book recently published by Judith Hooper entitled *Of Moths and Men.*[9] She notes in her prologue that "I am not a creationist" (p. xix). She evidently felt she had to provide this assurance because, as she said about the reaction to the developing moth scandal, "Behind the story, like a monster lurking under a five-year-old's bed, is the bogey-man of creationism."

Apparently, the creationist revival has been impacting the evolutionary establishment more than its leaders admit publicly. In fact, the major impetus behind the drive to document the evolution of the peppered moth in the first place may well have been due to the need to show that evolution by natural selection was actually happening now.

The prolific scientist writer Isaac Asimov once noted that: "One of the arguments of the creationists is that no one has ever seen the forces of evolution at work. That would seem the most nearly irrefutable of their arguments, and yet it, too, is wrong."[10]

Asimov then proceeded to recount the evidence of the peppered moth "evolving" into the *carbonaria* variety of the species *Biston betularia* by a process that had been called industrial melanism. This had indeed become the main popular "proof" of natural selection, convincing countless innocent students of the "fact" of evolution. The idea was that the "peppered" moth had evolved somehow into the "melanic moth" as a defense against bird predation during the industrial revolution in England and the resultant blackened tree trunks.

The two names most closely associated with the evolutionary myth of the peppered moth were two renowned Oxford University biologists, Dr. E.B. Ford and Dr. H.B.D. Kettlewell. Judith Hooper called Ford the "megalomaniac founder of the Oxford School of Ecological Genetics,"

---

9 Judith Hooper, *Of Moths and Men* (New York: W.W. Norton and Co., 2002), 377 p.

10 Isaac Asimov, *Asimov's New Guide to Science* (New York: Basic Books, 1984; as quoted by Hooper, see endnote 9), p. 309.

who, "by his own lights . . . had almost single-handedly rescued natural selection from oblivion in the 1920s and 1930s. . . ."[11] Bernard Kettlewell was a medical doctor and amateur entomologist who was recruited by Ford when he recognized Kettlewell's unusual abilities in the field as a student and collector of moths.

The black (melanic) moths had first turned up in England around 1858 and soon were multiplying, especially in the industrial areas. It was reasonable to attribute this rise in melanism to natural selection. But this was only speculative until it could actually be proved in the field.

Dr. Ford had become an ardent defender of natural selection in the Darwinian sense, as opposed to other evolutionary mechanisms being promoted at the time. Eventually, he became convinced that a relatively rapid natural selection had occurred in the peppered moth and could actually be demonstrated by systematic field studies.

For this fieldwork, Bernard Kettlewell was selected, and he did perform the well-known field studies which resulted in the to-be-much-publicized proof of "evolution in action." As Hooper notes: "By the close of the 1950s, the peppered moth would be *the* poster child for evolution."[12]

The noted evolutionary historian William Provine told Judith Hooper in a personal interview: "It's fun to look through all the textbooks and always this example — and I mean *always* — is hauled out."[13] Hooper says: "The peppered moth was becoming evolution's number one icon just in time for the big Darwin centennial."[14]

That event took place in Chicago in 1959, which Hooper called a "supercharged extravaganza, which encompassed five days of pageantry, televised debate, Darwin worship, and theatrical spectacle."[15] Julian Huxley, who had become an admirer of Ford and Kettlewell, was the keynote speaker, and he enthusiastically proclaimed the triumph of Darwinism and death of God. The then recent studies on the peppered moth were frequently cited by speakers there. Though Kettlewell was not present, Ford did present a paper on polymorphism.

Interestingly, Judith Hooper's comment on this great convocation is as follows: "Huxley's atheism and the general Darwinist pep rally were

---

11 Hooper, *Of Moths and Men*, p. xvi.

12 Ibid., p. 146, emphasis hers.

13 Ibid., p. 149, emphasis his.

14 Ibid., p. 165.

15 Ibid., p. 166.

noted darkly by a small group of outraged evangelicals. A stream of anti-evolution literature followed, notably John C. Whitcomb and Henry Morris's *The Genesis Flood*, the forerunner of the 'scientific creationism' movement. . . ."[16]

Furthermore, the whole neo-Darwinian paradigm was beginning to be questioned as well. Kettlewell was invited to the 1966 Wistar Institute symposium on "Mathematical Challenges to the Neo-Darwinian Interpretation of Evolution" in Philadelphia, where he heard a number of key mathematicians and biologists show that the standard theory could not possibly account for the world of living creatures in any finite time. In 1967, his friend and supporter, Julian Huxley, "was in a nursing home receiving electroshock treatments for one of his periodic depressions."[17]

After laboring on it for many years, Kettlewell finally published his magnum opus, *The Evolution of Melanism*, in 1973, but the reviews were lukewarm. Furthermore, Stephen Jay Gould, who would soon become the chief antagonist of the British neo-Darwinists of the rising generation (most notably Maynard Smith and Richard Dawkins, as well as the followers of Dr. Ford), had just published his first influential paper in 1965. His Harvard colleague, Richard Lewontin (who was, like Gould, a Marxist), published a book in 1974 which would "portray the Oxford School crowd as silly toffs with butterfly nets."[18] Even in England, younger scientists were finding they could not replicate Kettlewell's field results, and were raising questions as to why.

Kettlewell himself was having serious health problems. When he was denied election as a Fellow of the Royal Society for the third time in 1976, he became completely disheartened. He died in 1979, reputedly by suicide.

Since his death, many researchers have been raising doubts about various aspects of his research, and even those of his boss, E.B. Ford. One of the main questioners has been Ted Sargent, emeritus professor of biology at the University of Massachusetts, who insists that the famous photographs of moths on tree trunks published by Kettlewell were all fake.

Sargent's first paper expressing these doubts was published in 1976, but few seemed to notice. Eventually, however, many others also began finding flaws in Kettlewell's work. In the process, some of these critics

---

16 Ibid., p. 167.

17 Ibid., p. 186.

18 Ibid., p. 216.

have been accused of "giving aid and comfort to the enemy, the creationists."[19] We cannot discuss all these criticisms here, but the conclusion was, as Hooper says: ". . . at its core lay flawed science, dubious methodology, and wishful thinking."[20] Some went so far as to accuse Ford and Kettlewell of actual fraud, but most thought it was just poor science. Cambridge lepidopterist Michael Majerus, in his book *Melanism: Evolution in Action*, "left no doubt that the classic story was wrong in almost every detail."[21] Yet, amazingly, he still believed the basic story of the shift in coloration of the peppered moth as caused by bird predation and natural selection.

And so does Judith Hooper, for that matter. In her last chapter, she says that the fact that the peppered moth story was all wrong "does not disprove the theory of evolution. . . . It is reasonable to assume that natural selection operates in the evolution of the peppered moth."[22]

It may be surprising to her and other evolutionists that creationists have never had a problem with the traditional story, except with the claim that it was "evolution in action." It was really only "variation and conservation in action." It could hardly even be called microevolution, because the moth remained the same species throughout the process.

The words of this writer, in a book published over 30 years ago, are still relevant. "The classic example of the *peppered moth* . . . was not evolution in the true sense at all but only variation. Natural selection is a conservative force, operating to keep kinds from becoming extinct when the environment changes."[23]

Most creationists, believe it or not, have never questioned the basic story of the peppered moth. After all, a leading British zoologist, L. Harrison Matthews, in his introduction to the 1971 edition of Darwin's *Origin of Species* had already said: "The peppered moth experiments beautifully demonstrate natural selection — or survival of the fittest — in action, but they do not show evolution in progress, for . . . all the moths remain from beginning to end *Biston betularia*."

No creationist today questions the phenomena of variation and natural selection; most would not even question speciation. But, there is still

19 Ibid., p. 286.
20 Ibid., p. xx.
21 Ibid., p. 283.
22 Ibid., p. 312.
23 Henry M. Morris, *Scientific Creationism* (Green Forest, AR: Master Books: 1974), p. 51.

no evidence whatever for macroevolution or the introduction of new information into the genetic system of any basic kind of organism, including the famous moth. Evolution has always been nothing but a pagan myth.

There have been a number of such biological events in modern times that have been widely trumpeted as evidence that evolution is still going on today. Perhaps the best known and most significant is the island-to-island variation in beak size and other features of the Galapagos Islands finches. These were first noted by Charles Darwin himself and are recently being widely promoted as a prime example of modern evolution.

However, as Matthews opined about the peppered moth, the finches may show natural selection, but not evolution. Their beak sizes may "evolve" in various ways, but they remain finches "from beginning to end." The finches have changed in various ways, but never into sparrows or robins or any other "kind" of bird. Such changes might be called "microevolution," but there is no evidence whatever that these minor changes could ever develop into the changes required for macroevolution.

And the same is true for all other kinds of plants and animals. In all recorded history there is not one single example of macroevolution from one kind into a higher, more complex kind. It does not happen in moths or finches or any other creature.

In fact, this is so obvious that evolutionists have even used it as an argument against creationist explanations of how varieties proliferated after the Flood. They say that the relatively small number of species that could have been accommodated on Noah's ark could never have proliferated into the vast numbers of varieties in the present world in just the few centuries since the Flood. But this is also wrong. Microevolution (or variation) can occur rapidly, but only within the limits of the created "kind." The organic world as it is observed today is exactly the way we would expect it to be, as based on the biblical record.

HORIZONTAL EVOLUTION

Contrary to the statements of most evolutionary writers, few (if any) creationists have ever advocated the idea of absolute fixity of species. The biblical unit of biological taxonomy, of course, is the Genesis "kind" (Hebrew, *min*).

It may be worth mentioning that this fact was stressed in my first book on creationism almost 60 years ago:

> *It is well to observe at this point that the Bible does not teach the fixity of species. . . . Thus, it is probable that the original Genesis "kind" is closely akin to what the modern systematist calls a "family." And let it be stated in no uncertain terms that there is no evidence that evolution ever has occurred or ever can occur across the kinds.*[24]

As a matter of fact, no scientist has ever observed even an unequivocally new *species* evolve from another species, although thousands of species have become extinct during human history! Evolutionists have to admit that:

> *. . . it was and still is the case that, with the exception of Dobzhansky's claim about a new species of fruit fly, the formation of a new species, by any mechanism, has never been observed.*[25]

Creationists have no problem, however, with speciation, or even the "evolution" of new genera in some instances, as long as such development does not extend to the "family" (dogs, cats, horses, etc.).

According to the Bible, all present land animals are descended from the "kinds" preserved on Noah's ark during the Flood. *"Every beast, every creeping thing, and every fowl, and whatsoever creepeth upon the earth, after their kinds, went forth out of the ark"* (Gen. 8:19).

It was the "kinds" — seven of every "clean" kind and two of all other kinds — that went out to repopulate the whole earth, with all its different ecological niches. Within each kind was a created genetic system capable of considerable recombination, so different varieties could quickly develop within each kind, as the descendants migrated to different regions of the world with all their different environments. Some of these eventually became stably reproducing species or even genera — probably still capable of reuniting to produce hybrids but normally remaining distinct.

Thus, all the dogs — including domestic dogs in all their varieties, wolves, coyotes, foxes, etc. — presumably descended from the two members of the creation "dog kind." The same may well have been true of the cats and other zoological families.

This type of "horizontal" evolution (within the limits of variation created for each original kind) is often called "microevolution," as distinct

---

24 Henry M. Morris, *That You Might Believe* (Chicago, IL: Good Books, Inc., 1946), p. 48, 49.

25 Jeffrey H. Schwartz, *Sudden Origins* (New York: John Wiley, 1999), p. 300.

from "macroevolution," the total evolution of all forms of life from some imaginary primeval one-celled common ancestor.

> *Evolutionists use the term microevolution to describe the changes that take place within a persisting species and higher taxa.*[26]

Whether macroevolution is simply "microevolution writ large," as many evolutionists allege, is a matter of dispute even among evolutionists.

> *A long-standing issue in evolutionary biology is whether the processes observable in extant populations and species (microevolution) are sufficient to account for the larger scale changes evident over longer periods of life's history (macroevolution).*
>
> *Outsiders to this rich literature may be surprised that there is no consensus on this issue, and that strong viewpoints are held at both ends of the spectrum, with many undecided.*[27]

Most evolutionists still hold to the dogma that microevolution (accepted by both evolutionists and creationists) eventually becomes macroevolution if continued over millions of years. Evolutionist Paul Ehrlich is a leading advocate of this view.

> *The very same processes . . . that cause evolution within populations (microevolution) also cause populations to differentiate and form different kinds of organisms. The creation of new species is, along with evolutionary changes within species, the mechanism that generates major evolutionary patterns — such as the diversification of vertebrates into fishes, amphibian, reptiles, birds, mammals, and so on.*[28]

On the other hand, there are many evolutionists — especially among those paleontologists who are trying to understand the ubiquity of gaps between kinds in the fossil record — who realize that this assumption probably is wrong. For example, a widely used textbook on macroevolution insists that:

---

26 Elliott Sober, *Philosophy of Biology* (2nd ed, Boulder, CO: Westview Press, 2000), p. 2.

27 Sean B. Carroll, "The Big Picture," *Nature*, vol. 409 (February 8, 2001): p. 668.

28 Paul R. Ehrlich, *Human Natures* (Washington, DC: Shearwater Books, 2000), p. 46.

Macroevolution is decoupled from microevolution.[29]

The Bible does not say explicitly what the limits of variation within the created kinds (or "baramins") may be, although the repeated reference in Genesis 1 to reproducing "after their kinds" seems to suggest interfertility as a key. The term "baramin," incidentally, is a word coined from the Hebrew *bara* ("create") and *min* ("kind").

Several ICR graduate students in biology, working under Dr. Ken Cumming, have been doing laboratory research on this question for several years, and there is an active *ad hoc* "Committee on Baraminology" consisting of several leading creationist biologists at various colleges and scientific organizations who are actively doing research in this field. The ability of seemingly distinct animals within a so-called "family" (e.g., horses and donkeys, lions and tigers, dogs and wolves) to produce hybrid progeny seems to suggest this ability as at least a preliminary definition.

This type of "evolution," if one wishes to call it that, does not take a million years. Recombinations of existing genes in the created genome for the kind, under the severe environmental pressures existing in the changed world after the Flood, could accomplish it rather quickly.

On the other hand, if one must depend on mutation and natural selection to produce new species — let alone new families, orders, and phyla — as evolutionists assume, then not even billions of years would suffice!

> *Genetic variation depends on the process of mutation, and mutations are rare events. Any particular new DNA mutation will occur only once in about 100 million gametes. Moreover, when a single mutation occurs in a single newborn, even if it is a favorable mutation, there is a fair probability that it will not be represented in the next generation because its single carrier may not, by chance, pass it on to its few offspring.*[30]

Remember also that practically no mutations are ever really favorable, and that many millions of favorable mutations would be required to generate a new baramin, or even a new genus. One has to wonder if such

29 Steven M. Stanley, *Macroevolution: Pattern and Process* (San Francisco, CA: W. H. Freeman and Co., 1979), p. 187.

30 Richard Lewontin, *The Triple Helix* (Cambridge, MA: Harvard University Press, 2000), p. 91.

things ever could really happen. Evolutionism requires much faith! The creation model, on the other hand, with its global Flood and devastated post-Flood world, does seem to present a very plausible solution to these questions.

Some may think that the biblical time scale after the Flood is too short for such extensive microevolution, but this would only be the case if mutations were the required mechanism. A clue to the possible rapidity of this process under the conditions of the post-Flood world may be noted in recent studies on salmon populations.

> *Colonization of new environments should promote rapid speciation as a by-product of adaptation to divergent selective regimes. . . . Nothing is known about how quickly reproductive isolation actually evolves when new environments are first colonized. . . . We found evidence for the evolution of reproductive isolation after fewer than 13 generations.*[31]

This case might be a mini-model of the vast wave of microevolution that must have fanned out from the ark after the Flood. The continents were wide open for animal migrations and multiplication, and the created genetic variational potential in each baramin allowed rapid diversification and adaptation to appropriate habitats for all.

As far as people were concerned, it took the confusion of tongues at Babel over a century after the Flood to persuade them to move out to fill the earth as God had commanded. They also (the three sons of Noah and their wives) had the genetic potential soon to become all the diversified tribes of the world (black, brown, and white tribes just like black, brown, and white bears!). This microwave of horizontal evolution after the Flood — or wave of microevolution — constitutes the only *real* "evolution" of biological life that fits either the biblical record or the scientific data.

Since no "vertical" evolution has ever been documented in the present age, evolutionists have to resort to the fossils in the earth's crust to try to show that it has occurred during the supposed billions of years of earth history, as "documented" in the geological ages. But there are problems there as well.

---

31 Andrew P. Hendry, John F. Wenburg, Paul Bentzen, Eric C. Volk, and Thomas P. Quinn, "Rapid Evolution of Reproductive Isolation in the Wild: Evidence from Introduced Salmon" *Science,* vol. 290 (October 20, 2000): p. 516.

WHAT DO THE FOSSILS SAY?

When we take a close look at the billions of fossils now preserved in the earth's sedimentary crust, an honest answer to the question above is expressed in the title of an influential book by Dr. Duane Gish, *Evolution: the Fossils Say No!* For one thing, the animal and plant kinds of the present world are very largely represented in the fossil world. The former, in fact, are sometimes called "living fossils" — not necessarily always the same "species," but often of the same "family."

Evolutionists often consider what they call "living fossils" to be rare, the famous coelacanth fish being the best-known example. The fossils of this fish are found only in rocks older than 70 million years (assuming the standard geologic time scale to be real), but living coelacanths have been found in the Indian Ocean.

New cases of so-called living fossils do turn up fairly often. Graptolites have been considered in the past to be index fossils for the Ordovician period, 300 million years old. Yet they recently were found still living in the south Pacific.[32]

Other famous living fossils include the tuatara (supposedly extinct since the Cretaceous period until found still living in New Zealand), the Lepidocaris crustacean (only found as fossils in Devonian rocks), the Metasequoia conifer tree (thought extinct for the past 20 million years), the Neopilina mollusk (supposedly extinct for 280 million years), the lingual brachiopod ("extinct" since the Ordovician), and even the trilobite (chief index fossil of the even more ancient Cambrian period).[33]

Evolutionists tend to reserve the title of "living fossil" for those animals and plants which had been considered extinct until suddenly they turned up living today. Consequently, the vast numbers of living organisms that were already known to be in the fossil record are generally ignored as examples of living fossils. These even include those organisms supposed to be the most ancient of all. Evolution is supposed to have begun when prokaryotes evolved out of the primeval soup. It is significant, therefore, that:

---

32 Sue Rigby, "Graptolites Come to Life," *Nature,* vol. 362 (March 18, 1993): p. 209–210.

33 "Living Fossil Resembles Long-Extinct Trilobite," *Science Digest,* vol. 42 (December 1957): p. 490.

Fossils very similar to living prokaryotes are found in rocks about 3,500 million years old.[34]

Likewise, the primitive one-celled organisms called eukaryotes are supposed to have evolved from prokaryotes. But these are also still living, essentially unchanged, in the modern world.

Simple eukaryotes, resembling living unicellular algae, are first confirmed in the fossil record about 1,500 million years ago and first suspected in rocks almost 2,000 million years old.[35]

The most important modern prokaryotes are probably the bacteria and the blue-green algae, and these certainly should be considered living fossils. They have been found in abundance in 3.4-billion-year-old rocks from South America. Modern soil bacteria have been found in Precambrian rocks. One wonders why, if evolution really works, these "primitive" organisms have not changed significantly in over a billion years.

The prolific evolutionist Stephen Jay Gould has insisted that there is no evidence whatever against evolution. Yet he stresses the fact that bacteria have changed little since ancient times.

The most salient feature of life has been the stability of its bacterial mode from the beginning of the fossil record until today and, with little doubt, into all future time so long as the earth endures.[36]

The same situation applies throughout the geologic column. In the supposed "oldest" period with metazoan fossils, all the present-day animal phyla are found as fossils, largely in modern form. As Gould says:

In one of the most crucial and enigmatic episodes in the history of life . . . nearly all animal phyla made their first appearance in the fossil record at essentially the same time, an interval of some 5 million years (about 525 to 530 million years ago) called the Cambrian explosion.[37]

---

34 Colin Patterson, *Evolution,* 2nd ed. (London: Natural History Museum, 1999), p. 129.

35 Ibid., p. 131.

36 Stephen J. Gould, "The Evolution of Life," in *Evolution! Facts and Fallacies,* ed. by J. Wm. Schopf (San Diego, CA: Academic Press, 1999), p. 5.

37 Ibid., p. 38.

Speaking of the Cambrian fauna, there are many that still survive, all looking much like they did over 500 million years ago. The prominent British evolutionist Richard Dawkins has made the following comment:

> And we find many of them already in an advanced state of evolution, the very first time they appear. It is as though they were just planted there, without any evolutionary history. Needless to say, this appearance of sudden planting has delighted creationists.[38]

Indeed it has. Until recently, the phylum of vertebrates had been considered a later arrival in evolutionary history. But not now! Even the vertebrate phylum now extends into the Cambrian period, especially with the recent discovery of two fossil fish in China:

> The two new fossils . . . from Chengjiang are the most convincing Early Cambrian vertebrates ever found.[39]

The insects and other land invertebrates are also a very important group, and these practically all seem to be living fossils. With respect to the arthropod phylum (the largest in the animal kingdom), consider the millipedes, for example.

> Indeed, the oldest fossils of land-dwelling animals are millipedes, dating to more than 425 million years ago. Incredibly, the archaic forms are nearly indistinguishable from certain groups living today.[40]

The same phenomenon holds for practically all the insects.

> Compared with other life forms, insects are actually slow to evolve new families — but they are even slower to go extinct. Some 84 percent of the insect families alive today were alive 100 million years ago. . . .[41]

---

38 Richard Dawkins, *The Blind Watchmaker* (New York: W.W. Norton Co., 1987), p. 229.

39 Philippe Janvier, "Catching the First Fish," *Nature,* vol. 402 (November 4, 1999): p. 21.

40 William A. Shear, "Millipedes," *American Scientist,* vol. 87 (May/June 1999): p. 234.

41 Carl Zimmer, "Insects Ascendant," *Discover,* vol. 14 (November 1993): p. 30.

Whether bees or ants, cicadas or beetles, termites or cockroaches, the fossils of these and other insects are always practically identical with (though often larger than) their modern descendants. The same applies to the arachnids and myriapods.

We could also note that modern amphibians (e.g., frogs, toads), reptiles (crocodiles, alligators, turtles), mammals (bats, squirrels, shrews, opossums, tarsiers, etc.), and many, many others are practically identical with their fossil representatives.

Speaking of extinction, the dinosaurs come to mind. These also may have been living fossils up until modern times, except that they were called dragons. Not many people realize how closely the ancient and medieval descriptions of various types of dragons correspond with modern paleontological reconstructions of various dinosaurs. But encyclopedia articles on "dragons" have occasionally noted this characteristic. Dinosaurs were according to two of these,

> . . . *gigantic and astonishingly dragon-like extinct reptiles of past ages.*[42]

> *The dragons of legend are strangely like . . . the great reptiles which inhabited the earth long before man is supposed to have appeared on the earth.*[43]

The Bible, of course, also mentions dragons as real living animals at the time it was being written.

I shall not try here to discuss the various ages themselves, but in the young-earth model of geologic history all the alleged "ages" were actually different deposits either of the great Flood or of the residual catastrophes following it. Thus, it is not surprising that the sedimentary rocks laid down by the Flood contain fossils of most of the creatures still surviving in the present age. Still further correlation with extant plants and animals will, no doubt, be developed as more fossils are discovered.

> *The fossil record is often so sparse that . . . there are plenty of cases where groups survived for tens of millions of years without leaving a single fossil.*[44]

---

42 Article "Dragon" in *Encyclopedia Britannica*, 1949 edition.

43 Article "Dragon" in *World Book Encyclopedia*, 1965 edition.

44 Peter J. Bowler, Review of *In Search of Deep Time*, by Henry Gee (New York: Free Press, 1999). In *American Scientist*, vol. 88 (March/April 2000): p. 169.

In actuality, as documented in many books by young-earth creationists, the fossil record is not a record of long evolutionary ages, with distinctive life forms in each age, as evolutionists allege, but of just one age, that of the great Flood. No wonder, then, that practically all living organisms are represented in the rocks of the geologic column.

And in their marvelous variety and complexity they all bear witness to the wisdom and power of their Creator, while the great panorama of suffering and death (often even extinction) displayed in their fossilized preservation is a perpetual reminder, not of evolution, but of the terrible consequences of human sin on man's entire dominion.

It is well known that there are no real evolutionary transitional series found in the fossils. As noted earlier, the chief of living evolutionists, Ernst Mayr, admitted that the discontinuities were essentially ubiquitous. The fossil record consists mostly of "gaps."

A few very controversial transitional forms have been claimed — *Archaeopteryx*, the supposed part bird, part reptile, for example. Also, there are the alleged walking whale, the questionable feathered dinosaur, the various ape-like men, etc. All of these are extremely doubtful and have been repudiated by some evolutionists as well as creationists.

Furthermore, none of these are in a *series*, which illustrate the actual changes taking place, for example, all the way from a land mammal of some kind to a whale. Never can paleontologists point to even one such *series* of transitions. There ought to be many if evolution was really happening. After all, there are billions of fossils out there, including large numbers of apparently unchanging kinds.

As a result, most evolutionary paleontologists now are convinced that evolution must have taken place in rapid spurts, leaving no record in the fossiliferous rocks. In any case, there is certainly no more real observable evidence for "vertical" evolution in the fossil record of the past than in the living plants and animals of the present.

CHAPTER VIII

ORGANIZED COMPLEXITY

I t is very significant that no one has ever seen or been able to prove any example of macroevolution to ever have taken place in all recorded history. Cases of microevolution (e.g., the development of all the dogs, coyotes, wolves, etc., from one ancestral dog "kind" several thousand years ago) abound, and creationists fully accept this fact. But not one case of macroevolution to a more highly organized state of complexity is known, or even claimed, in all human history (except in magical stories, of course, like frogs suddenly evolving into princes).

And neither is there any clear case of macroevolution to be found in all the billions of fossils preserved in the rocks and sediments of the earth's crust. This indisputable fact is very hard to understand if evolution is the true explanation of all biological life forms, as evolutionists claim. Instead of *no* transitional series, there ought to be multitudes of them. In fact, it would seem natural to suppose that *every* creature of past or present represents some kind of transitional form. The ubiquitous phenomenon of "stasis," as they call it, needs explaining, if evolution is true. Why is real evolution so hard to document?

THE MYSTERY OF COMPLEXITY

The universe is full of an infinite variety of complex systems, from the almost incredible universe itself to the tiniest one-celled creature in the ocean. The most intricately involved of all is the human brain, which Isaac Asimov once called "the most complex and orderly arrangement of matter in the universe."

More incredible even than that, however, is the fact that some humans (including Asimov himself) who possess such marvelous brains, with their trillions of inter-connecting electrical circuits, still manage to imagine that the complex human brain arose by chance through mutations and natural selection!

Those of us who believe in the God of the Bible — the personal, omnipotent, omniscient God of creation and redemption — find nothing mysterious at all about the origin of the complex structure of the human brain or any of the great multitude of complex organisms and other complex systems of the world. *"Lift up your eyes on high, and behold who hath created these things"* (Isa. 40:26). *"The Lord of hosts is his name"* (Isa. 48:2). *". . . the Lord God formed every beast of the field, and every fowl of the air"* (Gen. 2:19). As to His method of creation, *"He spake, and it was done"* (Ps. 33:9). Very simple and clear — if one just believes in God!

The naturalistic creed of most evolutionists, however, requires them to account for complexity naturalistically. Somehow a scenario must be developed showing how a primeval chemical molecule could evolve into a replicating protein, then a complex protozoan, eventually a large beast, and finally a human being with an infinitely complex brain. The increase of complexity involved would seem to be incredible — but it must have happened, they insist, because otherwise God would have done it, and that would be unscientific.

The problem with trying to be scientific, however, is that science doesn't help either. Instead of a process that increases organized complexity, there is a universal scientific law that all natural processes tend to *decrease* complexity in the universe. This is the famous second law of thermodynamics, or law of increasing entropy. It is expressed in various ways, depending on type of situation — decreased energy available, increased randomness and disorganization, garbled transmission of information, etc. Entropy always increases in a closed system, and it always *tends* to increase even in an open system.

In the case of open systems, there must be an influx of energy (or ordering information) into the system from outside in order to keep it in equilibrium and for a time to offset the tendency to decay. Eventually it will decay anyway; a man, for example, may keep functioning for many years, but he will finally die. By the same principle, the earth and all its systems could survive, perhaps, for millions of years, but the sun would itself finally burn out and the earth's supply of external energy lost, so the earth and its systems also would all disintegrate and die. In fact, if present processes continue long enough, the universe itself will ultimately die.

How, then, when the whole universe is decaying and dying, struggling hard just to maintain a fragile equilibrium in which living humans and animals can be maintained for a while — how can *evolution* toward higher organized complexity ever take place at all? Well, here is their current best answer:

> *Thus, once again we conclude that an energy flow through an open system is an absolute necessity if order is to be created from disorder.*[1]

Yes, but *that* is necessary just to maintain its present order (or better, organized complexity). How can it be increased? How can a population of worms, say, be upgraded into a population of human beings?

Most evolutionists today, when pressed to answer such questions, will say that Ilya Prigogine, with his concept of "dissipative structures" in "far-from-equilibrium" thermodynamics, has provided the answer to the mystery of life's origin. That it does not really do so, however, I have tried to point out in several previous discussions, so will not repeat the discussion here.[2]

However, the author of a recent book has now taken on the ambitious project of applying the Prigogine approach, not just to the origin of life from non-life, but also to every stage of evolution, from the evolution of the cosmos to the evolution of social systems. He rather audaciously tries to make the second law of thermodynamics and the dissipation process, with its inevitable increase in entropy, the very generator of evolution and increased complexity, as well as *decrease* in entropy on the earth.

> *At all times in the Universe, and at all places, the second law of thermodynamics is the ultimate arbiter of Nature's many*

---

1 Eric J. Chaisson, *Cosmic Evolution* (Cambridge, MA: Harvard University Press, 2001), p. 47.

2 See, for example, *Science and Creation*, vol. 2 in *The Modern Creation Trilogy*, by Henry M. Morris and John D. Morris (Green Forest, AR: Master Books, 1996), p. 150–158.

varied transactions; it, and the ubiquitous process of energy flow directed by it, embody the underlying physical principle behind the development of all things.[3]

Chaisson, like Prigogine and other writers, has been able to note certain situations where a sudden increase in "order" in an energy-dissipating system has been generated in a part of that system. The special condition required seems to be "fluctuations" in the flow-through of energy under "far-from-equilibrium" conditions in that field of flow. In such unstable conditions, there also is inevitably an abnormally large amount of energy lost to the external environment — hence the name "dissipative structures."

Prigogine's classic example of such structures was the sudden development of eddies in a liquid surface caused by a flow of heat up from a source of heat at the bottom. These are "ordered" structures, but they are necessarily accompanied by increased dissipation of energy to the environment. Another oft-used example is the tornado, a highly ordered structure generated by flow of heat and/or air in the atmosphere.

Tornadoes are paragons of order through fluctuations. . . . though superbly (and locally) constructed, can be utterly (and globally) destructive. . . .[4]

How such dissipative structures, even if they are maintained indefinitely by the continuing non-equilibrium thermodynamics of the field of flow, can ever be the base on which higher and still higher degrees of complex structure can be developed is still a mystery which Chaisson does not pretend to solve in his entire book on "cosmic evolution." He, like Prigogine and other evolutionists, is adept at making broad evolutionary generalizations, but also at avoiding experimental proof.

With the whole universe running down, and with the decay process apparently even hastened by the extra energy loss required to generate increasing complexity, how can the evolutionary process possibly be sustained, all the way from particles to people?

The non-equilibrium dynamics are universally maintained, Chaisson believes — believe it or not — by the expanding of the universe!

---

3 Chaisson, *Cosmic Evolution*, p. 207–208. The author of this book is a research professor in physics, astronomy, and education at Tufts University.

4 Ibid., p. 62–63.

The very expansion of the Universe, then, provides the environmental conditions needed to drive order from chaos; the process of cosmic evolution itself generates information.[5]

But saying so doesn't make it so! We would like to see some real scientific evidence that this supposed cosmic process of universal expansion is really generating evolution. But Chaisson only provides wishful thinking.

How that order became manifest specifically in the form of galaxies, stars, planets, and life has not yet been deciphered in detail.[6]

But, even after such a profound understatement, this eminent cosmologist still claims to have developed a thought channel which evolutionists can use to guide their wishful thinking.

We thereby have a means to appreciate in the main, if perhaps not yet understand the particulars, the observed rise in complexity throughout the eons of cosmic evolution.[7]

He also says his present 274-page book is an "abridgement" of a "larger opus to come" in which all the specific evidences can be given to show just *how*, in detail, an over-all disintegration of complexity in the universe somehow really produces more complex systems all over the universe.

Right now, however, the details are all missing. Chaisson at least does acknowledge that there is much work yet to do before evolutionists will really have a rational explanation of complexity without God.

Our treatment of cosmic evolution set forth in this book is by no means complete or comprehensive, especially regarding the devilish details.[8]

I might respectfully suggest that Dr. Chaisson carefully consider whether the devil is not only in the details but in the whole concept of cosmic evolution, especially the oxymoronic idea of complexity through dissipation and evolution by entropy.

It becomes evident, therefore, that the reason why there is no observable evidence for evolution in either the fossils of the past or the living

---

5 Ibid., p. 131.
6 Ibid.
7 Ibid.
8 Ibid.

creatures of the present is because evolution, at least on the vertical or "macro" scale is impossible in terms of the universally applicable law of increasing entropy. A similar argument can be developed in terms of probability theory, since the second law of thermodynamics is actually another way of stating the laws of probability.

Evolution Mathematically Impossible

According to the most-widely accepted theory of evolution today, the sole mechanism for producing evolution is that of random mutation combined with natural selection. Mutations are *random* changes in genetic systems. Natural selection is considered by evolutionists to be a sort of sieve, which retains the "good" mutations and allows the others to pass away.

Since random changes in ordered systems almost always will decrease the amount of organization in those systems, nearly all mutations are harmful to the organisms which experience them. Nevertheless, the evolutionist insists that each complex organism in the world today has arisen by a long string of gradually accumulated good mutations preserved by natural selection. No one has ever actually *observed* a genuine mutation occurring in the natural environment which was beneficial (that is, adding useful genetic information to an existing genetic code), and therefore, retained by the selection process. For some reason, however, the idea has a certain persuasive quality about it and seems eminently reasonable to many people — until it is examined *quantitatively*, that is!

For example, consider a very simple putative organism composed of only 200 integrated and functioning parts, and the problem of deriving that organism by this type of process. The system presumably must have started with only one part and then gradually built itself up over many generations into its 200-part organization. The developing organism, at each successive stage, must itself be integrated and functioning in its environment in order to survive until the next stage. Each successive stage, of course, becomes statistically less likely than the preceding one, since it is far easier for a complex system to break down than to build itself up. A four-component integrated system can more easily "mutate" (that is, somehow suddenly change) into a three-component system (or even a four-component non-functioning system) than into a five-component integrated system. If, at any step in the chain, the system mutates "downward," then it is either destroyed altogether or else moves backward, in an evolutionary sense.

Therefore, the successful production of a 200-component functioning organism requires, *at least* 200 successive, successful such "mutations," each of which is highly unlikely. Even evolutionists recognize that true mutations are very rare, and beneficial mutations are *extremely* rare — not more than one out of a thousand mutations are beneficial, at the very most.

But let us give the evolutionist the benefit of every consideration. Assume that, at each mutational step, there is equally as much chance for it to be good as bad. Thus, the probability for the success of each mutation is assumed to be one out of two, or one-half. Elementary statistical theory shows that the probability of 200 successive mutations being successful is then $(\frac{1}{2})^{200}$, or one chance out of 10^{60}. The number 10^{60}, if written out, would be "one" followed by 60 "zeros." In other words, the chance that a 200-component organism could be formed by mutation and natural selection is less than one chance out of a trillion, trillion, trillion, trillion, trillion! Lest anyone think that a 200-part system is unreasonably complex, it should be noted that even a one-celled plant or animal may have millions of molecular "parts."

The evolutionist might react by saying that even though any one such mutation organism might not be successful, surely some around the world would be, especially in the 10 billion years (or 10^{18} seconds) of assumed earth history. Therefore, let us imagine that every one of the earth's 10^{14} square feet of surface harbors a billion (i.e., 10^9) mutating systems and that each mutation requires one-half second (actually it would take far more time than this). Each system can thus go through its 200 mutations in 100 seconds and then, if it is unsuccessful, start over for a new try. In 10^{18} seconds, there can, therefore, be $10^{18}/10^2$, or 10^{16}, trials by each mutating system. Multiplying all these numbers together, there would be a total possible number of attempts to develop a 200-component system equal to 10^{14} (10^9) (10^{16}), or 10^{39} attempts. Since the probability against the success of any one of them is 10^{60}, it is obvious that the probability that just one of these 10^{39} attempts might be successful is only one out of $10^{60}/10^{39}$, or 10^{21}.

All this means that the chance that any kind of a 200-component integrated functioning organism could be developed by mutation and natural selection just once, anywhere in the world, in all the assumed expanse of geologic time, is less than one chance out of a billion trillion. What possible conclusion, therefore, can we derive from such considerations as this except that evolution by mutation and natural selection is mathematically and logically indefensible!

DISCUSSION

There have been many other more elaborate ways in which creationist writers have used probability arguments to refute evolutionism, especially the idea of random changes preserved, if beneficial, by natural selection. James Coppedge devoted almost an entire book, *Evolution: Possible or Impossible*,[9] to this type of approach. I have also used other probability-type arguments to the same end.[10]

The first such book, so far as I know, to use mathematics and probability in refuting evolution was written by a pastor, W. A. Williams, way back in 1928. Entitled *Evolution Disproved*, it made a great impression on me when I first read it about 1943, at a time when I myself was still struggling with evolution.

In fact, evolutionists themselves have attacked traditional Darwinism on the same basis.[11] While these scientists did not reject evolution itself, they did insist that the Darwinian randomness postulate would never work.

As mentioned before, the law of increasing entropy, or the second law of thermodynamics, is essentially a statement of probabilities, and many writers have used that law itself to show that evolution on any significant scale is essentially impossible. Evolutionists have usually ignored the arguments or else used vacuous arguments against them ("Anything can happen given enough time"; "The earth is an open system, so the second law doesn't apply"; "Order can arise out of chaos through dissipative structures"; etc.).

In the real world of scientific observation, as opposed to metaphysical speculation, however, no more complex and functioning system can ever "evolve" out of a less complex system, so the probability of the naturalistic origin of even the simplest imaginary form of life is zero.

The existence of complexity of any kind is evidence of God and creation. *"Lift up your eyes on high, and behold who hath created these things, that bringeth out their host by number: he calleth them all by names by the greatness of his might, for that he is strong in power; not one faileth"* (Isa. 40:26).

---

9 James Coppedge, *Evolution: Possible or Impossible* (Grand Rapids, MI: Zondervan, 1973), 276 p.

10 See, e.g., Morris and Morris, *Science and Creation*, p. 161–201.

11 See *Mathematical Challenges to the Neo-Darwinian Interpretation of Evolution* (Wistar Institute Symposium, 1967), 140 p.

THE HUMAN BRAIN

Every part of God's marvelous universe is so complex and skillfully designed that it seems incredible that anyone could doubt God's existence. As Paul commented (Rom. 1:20), they are *"without excuse."*

Human beings are the most complex of all creatures, of course, and the human brain is the most highly organized component of men and women.

In a recent book, two eminent authors (both evolutionists) give a glowing assessment of the human mind and the brain through which it functions.

> *The human brain is the most astonishing and mysterious of all known complex systems. Inside this mass of billions of neurons, information flows in ways that we are only starting to understand. The memories of a summer day on the beach when we were kids; imagination; our dreams of impossible worlds. Consciousness. Our surprising capacity for mathematical generalization and understanding of deep, sometimes counter intuitive, questions about the universe. Our brains are capable of this and much more. How? We don't know: the mind is a daunting problem for science.*[12]

This testimony brings to mind a statement made more than 30 years ago by the atheistic biochemist Isaac Asimov, arguably the most prolific scientist writer of all time. He said that:

> ... *in man is a three-pound brain which, as far as we know, is the most complex and orderly arrangement of matter in the universe. How could the human brain develop out of the primeval slime?*[13]

Asimov's answer to this key question was that the energy from the sun somehow provided the information necessary to create life and ultimately the human brain. He had no explanation as to *how* this miracle of complexity could have been produced by the sun, and neither does

---

12 Richard Sole and Brian Godwin, *Signs of Life* (New York: Basic Books, Inc., 2000), p. 119.

13 Isaac Asimov, "In the Game of Energy and Thermodynamics You Can't Even Break Even," *Smithsonian Institute Journal* (June 1970): p. 10.

anyone else. The current authors (Sole and Godwin) are frank enough to acknowledge, simply, that "we don't know."

The mind is, indeed, "a daunting problem for science." The fact is that science can never provide the answer as long as its practitioners deny the truth of a divine creation. The Psalmist, on the other hand, gladly acknowledged God, and said in awe: *"I will praise thee; for I am fearfully and wonderfully made"* (Ps. 139:14).

He then continued with remarkable insight: *"My substance was . . . made in secret, and curiously wrought . . ."* (Ps. 139:15). The word so picturesquely translated in the King James Bible as *"curiously wrought"* is the Hebrew *raqam* meaning *"embroidered,"* or *"did needlework,"* and it is so translated in the other passages where it is used.

The idea of highly intricate needlework is most appropriate in trying to describe the amazing network of interconnected neurons in the human brain.

> *Human beings have something on the order of 100,000 genes, and human brains have more than 1 trillion nerve cells, with about 100-1,000 trillion connections (synapses) between them. That's at least 1 billion synapses per gene, even if each and every gene did nothing but control the production of synapses (and it doesn't).*[14]

But astoundingly complex as the human brain may be, it still does not explain how all this serves to produce consciousness, let alone how it can generate abstract thought and inventive ingenuity and all the myriad thoughts and reasonings of the human brain, not to mention its imaginations and even its dreams. Anthropologist Matt Cartmill acknowledges this vital gap in our knowledge.

> *The phenomenon of consciousness is the source of all value in our lives. As such, it should be at the top of the scientific agenda. Yet despite its fundamental importance, consciousness is a subject that most scientists are reluctant to deal with. We know practically nothing about its mechanisms or its evolution.*[15]

---

14 Paul R. Ehrlich, *Human Natures* (Washington, DC: Shearwater Books, 2000), p. 4, emphasis his. Dr. Ehrlich is a professor at Stanford University.

15 Matt Cartmill, "Do Horses Gallop in Their Sleep?" *Key Reporter* (Autumn 2000): p. 6.

What a marvelous paradox this is! The gift of consciousness is the basic phenomenon which permits scientists to investigate the processes of nature and develop descriptions thereof, but they have no understanding of consciousness itself.

> *The machineries of consciousness are an almost perfect mystery.*[16]

Not only does the human brain somehow generate consciousness and then complex thought processes, but also the ability to communicate those thoughts to others. The phenomenon of language (real language, not animal barks and grunts) is still another amazing phenomenon for which there is no evolutionary explanation. Languages can rather quickly "evolve" into different languages, but how did *language* evolve? And was there one original language, or have various languages evolved independently? Evolutionists do not know. If they refuse to consider God's explanation in the Bible, they will probably never know.

> *All contemporary modern humans use very complex languages. There are no "primitive" languages: the 5,000 or more spoken today are equally flexible and expressive, and their grammar and syntax are sometimes richer and more precise than that of the more widespread languages like English or Spanish, which have undergone some simplification over the centuries.*[17]

There is, therefore, no evidence whatever for any supposed evolutionary origin of human language, though each individual language can "evolve" into some different language in relatively short time (e.g., compare Chaucer's English to modern English). Yet linguists have been notably unsuccessful in trying to map out an "original" language from which the other language families have come. Neither the origin of language itself nor the origin of the major linguistic families is amenable to an evolutionary explanation. One of the world's most distinguished linguistic ethnologists admits this.

> *It is not certain that all languages have a common origin. Most linguists consider both problems insoluble.*[18]

---

16 Ibid., p. 8.

17 Luigi Lura Cavalli-Sforza, *Genes, People and Languages* (New York: North Pointe Press, 2000), p. 59.

18 Ibid., p. 142. Dr. Cavalli-Sforza is professor of genetics at Stanford.

Not really! The biblical account fits all the facts. Language is a special gift of God, imparted to the first man and woman when He created them "in His image," so that they could communicate with God and other humans. The original language families were also supernaturally imparted by God to thwart the rebellion against Him at the Tower of Babel.

Not only did God provide a means of oral communication, but also a means of communicating in writing. The first book, in fact, was apparently written by Adam himself (Gen. 5:1). After the Flood and the confusion of tongues at Babel, this ability was lost, except possibly by Noah, Shem, and any others who had not participated in the rebellion.

But the others still retained the basic mental tools to learn *how* to write, this time in their new languages. It was not long, at least in the great civilizations that developed in certain early nations, before practically everyone could read and write. Probably the earliest was in Sumeria, including Assyria and others in the Tigris-Euphrates region.

> *As many as half a million cuneiform tablets, hand size up to book-page size, are now stored in the museums of the learned, from Baghdad upriver out to Moscow and Berkeley. Surely many more are waiting to be found. These samples are of every quality: once prized accounts and receipts, schoolboys' lessons, litigation profound or droll, literary essays, erotica, mathematics — and entire ancient epics, centuries older than Father Abraham's. A mostly unread treasury, comprising the equivalent of tens of thousands of large printed volumes.*[19]

In none of these very ancient archaeological sites, whether in the Middle East, Egypt, China, or India, is there any indication of a gradual evolution of language or writing. The languages just seem to spring into existence fully developed in complex form when they first appear. So-called "primitive" languages are invariably highly complex languages, and the same is true of their written form, with the ability to read and write evidently widespread in each community.

Indeed, the human brain and human consciousness, along with the ability to express human thoughts in speaking and writing, are amazing phenomena without any adequate evolutionary explanation. The same is true of the marvelous DNA molecules in which are encoded all the

---

19 Philip Morrison and Phylis Morrison, "Information Technology, 2500 B.C." *Scientific American,* vol. 284 (January 2001): p. 109.

programmed information for the reproduction and growth of every cell of the human body.

As the Psalmist implied, our brains have indeed been very *"curiously wrought"* in our mothers' wombs (Ps. 139:15), through the intricately entwined DNA coding extending all the way back to Mother Eve and Father Adam and ultimately to the infinite mind and skillful hands of the great Designer himself.

As the patriarch Job stressed, contemplating all the wonderful works of God in creation: *"Who knoweth not in all these that the hand of the Lord hath wrought this?"* (Job 12:9).

THE ORIGIN OF HUMAN LANGUAGE AND LANGUAGES

The very idea that the phenomenon of human language and the many human languages could ever have developed by some natural evolutionary process seems so absurd to a creationist that he finds it difficult to find words in any language adequate to express the absurdity and utter impossibility of any such notion. The primeval origin of human language — the ability of men and women to communicate with one another in intelligent, symbolic, often abstract speech and writing — is a complete mystery to naturalistic scientists.

Evolutionary paleoanthropologists may claim to have certain tenuous evidences of human physical evolution in the various fragments of hominid skeletal parts that have been excavated in Africa and elsewhere. But they have no evidence whatever for the origin of language — and language is the main entity that separates man from the apes and other animals.

The authoritative *Atlas of Languages* confirms this fact and also the fact that apes can never be taught to speak.

> *Language is perhaps the most important single characteristic that distinguishes human beings from other animal species. . . . Because of the different structure of the vocal apparatus in humans and chimpanzees, it is not possible for chimpanzees to imitate the sounds of human language, so they have been taught to use gestures or tokens in place of sounds . . . but chimpanzees never attain a level of linguistic complexity beyond the approximate level of a two-year-old child.*[20]

---

20 Stephen Matthews, Bernard Comrie, and Marcia Polinsky, editors, *Atlas of Languages: The Origin and Development of Languages Throughout the World* (New York: Facts on File, Inc., 1996), p. 10.

Similarly, Lewis Thomas, the distinguished medical scientist who was the longtime director and chancellor of the Sloan Kettering Cancer Center in Manhattan has affirmed that:

> . . . *language is so incomprehensible a problem that the language we use for discussing the matter is itself becoming incomprehensible.*[21]

A man recognized universally as one of the world's greatest linguists is Dr. Noam Chomsky, professor of linguistics at the Massachusetts Institute of Technology. He himself is a thorough-going evolutionist — in fact, even an atheist and a Marxist. Yet he also recognizes the present impossibility of accounting for language by naturalistic evolution.

> *Human language appears to be a unique phenomenon, without significant analogue in the animal world. . . . There is no reason to suppose that the "gaps" are bridgeable. There is no more of a basis for assuming an evolutionary development of "higher" from "lower" stages in this case, than there is for assuming an evolutionary development from breathing to walking.*[22]

Not only is there no animal that is capable of achieving anything like human speech, but also there is, at the other end of the scale, no human tribe that does not have a true language.

> *No languageless community has ever been found.*[23]

There are no normal humans that cannot speak and no animals that ever can. This is the great unbridgeable gap between all mankind and every component of the animal kingdom.

Evolutionary scientists have made many attempts to teach chimpanzees to speak, but all to no avail.

> *But though animal trainers and investigators have tried since the seventeenth century to teach chimpanzees to talk, no chimpanzee has ever managed it. True, a chimpanzee's sound-*

21 Lewis Thomas, "On Science and Uncertainty," *Discover,* vol. 1 (October 1980): p. 59.

22 Noam Chomsky, *Language and Mind* (New York: Harcourt, Brace, Jovanovich, 1972), p. 67–68.

23 Matthews, Comrie, and Polinsky, *Atlas of Languages,* p. 7.

producing anatomy is fundamentally different from our own. But chimpanzees might still produce a muffled approximation of human speech if their brains could only plan and execute the necessary articulate maneuvers. To do this, they would have to have our brains.[24]

A recent book by an authority in this field, Terence Deacon, has the insightful title *The Symbolic Species* (published by the W.W. Norton Co.). Another authority in linguistics reviewing the book uses an even more provocative title, "Babel's Cornerstone," for his review.

> *Time after time, in sorting through the countless proposals put forward by language evolutionists, Deacon makes the right choices. Could language have come directly out of some prehuman trait? No. Does it resemble forms of animal communication? No. . . . No ape, despite intensive training, has yet acquired even the rudiments of syntax, and many language acquisitionists insist that syntax is there even at infants' one-word stage. . . . Deacon does not begin to grapple with the really difficult problems — how words emerged, how syntax emerged. But these problems lie at the heart of language evolution.*[25]

Even such a dogmatic Darwinist as Richard Dawkins, England's most influential evolutionary biologist, finds it impossible to explain the origin of human language.

> *My clear example is language. Nobody knows how it began. . . . Equally obscure is the origin of semantics; of words and their meaning.*[26]

Dawkins then comments on the high degree of complexity in each of the world's many languages, including even those of the most "primitive" tribes. He notes that:

> *. . . all the thousands of languages in the world are very complex (some say they are all exactly equally complex, but*

24 Philip Lieberman, "Peak Capacity," *The Sciences*, vol. 37 (Nov./Dec. 1997): p. 27.

25 Derek Bickerton, "Babel's Cornerstone," *New Scientist*, vol. 156 (October 4, 1997): p. 42.

26 Richard Dawkins, *Unweaving the Rainbow* (Boston, MA: Houghton-Mifflin Co., 1998), p. 294.

that sounds too ideologically perfect to be wholly plausible). I am biased towards thinking it was gradual, but it is not quite obvious that it had to be. Some people think it began suddenly, more or less invented by a single genius in a particular place at a particular time.[27]

Our distinguished British evolutionist here is coming close to a biblical perspective, though he undoubtedly would indignantly repudiate any such suggestion.

But Philip Lieberman even feels constrained to use biblical terminology as he concludes his own wistful treatment of this subject.

For with speech came a capacity for thought that had never existed before, and that has transformed the world. In the beginning was the word.[28]

Although Dr. Lieberman had no such intent when he quoted John 1:1 in this way, he actually was giving the true explanation for the origin of language. It was, indeed, by *"the Word"* that *"all things"* were created in the beginning (note John 1:3), and that would include human language. There is no better — in fact, no *other* — workable and plausible explanation.

God in Christ created Adam and Eve at *"the beginning of the creation"* (note Mark 10:6, quoting Gen. 1:27) and immediately communicated with them in language which their created brains and minds could understand (note Gen. 2:16–17, and Gen. 3:9–19). They and their descendants continued to use this created language, even speaking to God in prayer in that language (Gen. 4:26) until the great rebellion at Babel, when *"the Lord did there confound the language of all the earth: and from thence did the Lord scatter them abroad upon the face of all the earth"* (Gen. 11:9).

The people scattering from Babel probably represented about 70 basic languages, judging from the 70 ancestral tribes listed in the Table of Nations (Gen. 10). These have, in time, proliferated into many others.

In the last decade of the twentieth century, it is estimated that over 6,000 languages are spoken in the world.[29]

---

27 Ibid., p. 295.

28 Philip Lieberman, "Peak Capacity," p. 27.

29 Matthews, Comrie, and Polinsky, *Atlas of Languages*, p. 10.

Historical linguists believe all these languages have developed within about 100 language "families." As to whether these could have developed just since Babel, Dr. Les Bruce has said:

> *It is not too difficult to imagine that 70 languages have in 5,000 years diversified into 100 distinct-looking families today.*[30]

If Professor Dawkins and his fellow evolutionists really want to *know* where man's ability to speak and communicate originated, but are still unwilling to believe the clear account in Genesis, they also would do well to hear God's rebuke to Moses: *"And the Lord said unto him, Who hath made man's mouth? . . . have not I the Lord? Now therefore go, and I will be with thy mouth, and teach thee what thou shalt say"* (Exod. 4:11–12).

It was God who, as the eternal Word himself, created the marvelous gift of human language along with the mouth and tongue and all the intricately complex vocal and mental apparatus with which to use it. It is eminently reasonable to conclude that God's gift of language to man was so that He could reveal His Word and will to us and that we could then respond in faith and praise to Him.

---

30 Les Bruce, personal communication. Dr. Bruce is a research linguist with Wycliffe Bible Translators and a professor in the Graduate School of Applied Linguistics in Dallas.

CHAPTER IX

THE BIZARRE WORLD OF COSMIC EVOLUTION

When the average person talks about evolution, he is usually thinking about apes evolving into men, or at least about the origin of the various kinds of living creatures. But when naturalistic scientists think about evolution, they are including the origin of *everything* — including the earth, the stars, and the universe itself. They seem to consider themselves to be on a compelling mission to explain all things in the entire cosmos without resorting to God as the Creator of anything. But in trying to accomplish this impossible feat, they invoke some remarkable concepts.

These physicists, astronomers, and cosmologists are, no doubt, brilliant men, with doctorates from leading universities. They have facility in higher mathematics, and use it copiously in developing their evolutionary theories, so much so as to make it practically impossible for us ordinary mortals even to understand how they arrive at their cosmologies, let alone refute their conclusions.

We encounter such marvels as expanding space, quantum fluctuations of nothing into something, cosmic inflation, multi-dimensional geometry, infinitesimal strings and particles, and even multiple universes. Maybe they could be right — they are brilliant thinkers — but they offer no experimental proofs — only intricate higher mathematics. And since the ultimate purpose seems to be to dethrone God, we creationists have to be skeptical. And we are not the only ones.

Astronomy and Cosmology on Trial

A recent book has the provocative title and subtitle: *Astronomy on Trial — A Devastating and Complete Repudiation of the Big Bang Fiasco.*

The author, Dr. Roy Martin, is not a creationist, but neither is he an astronomer, so evolutionary astronomers and cosmologists ignore his criticisms. Nevertheless, his objections to the establishment's big-bang theory do echo what many people are thinking. He opens the "Prologue" to the book with the following blistering charges.

> *Astronomy, rather cosmology, is in trouble. It is, for the most part, beside itself. It has departed from the scientific method and its principles, and drifted into the bizarre; it has raised imaginative invention to an art form; and has shown a ready willingness to surrender or ignore fundamental laws, such as the second law of thermodynamics and the maximum speed of light, all for the apparent rationale of saving the status quo. Perhaps no "science" is receiving more self-criticism, chest-beating, and self-doubt; none other seems so lost and misdirected: trapped in debilitating dogma.*[1]

Martin then proceeds, page after page and chapter after chapter, to illustrate and document the absurdity of the "big-bang fiasco."

The big-bang idea is not based on observation and experimentation, as is usually true in legitimate science, but speculation and esoteric mathematics.

> *It is not a theory, and only weakly might it be referred to as an hypothesis. . . . The physical laws of conservation of matter, inertia, and others that are inviolable here on Earth, are negated in space by mathematics.*[2]

Even though Martin himself is not an astronomer, there are significant numbers of top-flight professional astronomers who also reject the big bang. Three very eminent astronomers have recently commented as follows:

---

1 Roy C. Martin Jr., *Astronomy on Trial* (Landham, MD: University Press of America, 1999), p. xv.
2 Ibid., p. 14.

> *. . . the theory departs increasingly from known physics, until ultimately the energy source of the universe is put in as an initial condition, the energy supposedly coming from somewhere else. Because that "somewhere else" can have any properties that suit the theoretician, supporters of the Big Bang cosmology gain for themselves a large bag of free parameters that can subsequently be tuned as the occasion may require.*[3]

They then draw the following reasonable conclusion.

> *We do not think science should be done that way. . . . In the currently popular form of cosmology . . . the physical laws are regarded as already known and an explanation of the later situation is sought by guessing at parameters appropriate to the initial state. We think this approach does not merit the high esteem that cosmologists commonly accord it.*[4]

These astronomers are not creationists. In fact, they believe there never was a real creation and that the universe is eternal and in a sort of "steady state." But they strongly criticize the supposed big bang.

The big bang obviously contradicts the first law of thermodynamics, with all the matter/energy of the cosmos suddenly coming into existence out of nothing — either by a "quantum fluctuation" out of the primeval void or, as some suggest, through a so-called "wormhole" from some other imaginary universe. The second law stipulates that disorder will necessarily increase in the universe, which is surely a closed system, if God is excluded, so it seems anomalous to say that the matter/energy, which spontaneously appeared in the big bang, would evolve into the highly complex universe that now exists.

The second law is also rejected by cosmologists if it interferes with their cosmological speculations. Astrophysicist Lawrence Schulman of Clarkson University and others feel that time can actually be reversed, along with the second law. Science writer Marcus Chown notes the implications.

> *The Universe may contain regions where milk would stir itself out of coffee and eggs would unbreak. . . . The idea that there may be regions where time runs backward could explain invisible dark matter.*[5]

---

3 Geoffrey Burbridge, Fred Hoyle, and Jayant V. Marlikar, "A Different Approach to Cosmology," *Physic Today,* vol. 52 (April 1999): p. 39.
4 Ibid.
5 Marcus Chown, "Unwrite This," *New Scientist,* vol. 165 (Nov. 27, 1999): p. 11.

A subsequent comment by another science writer "explains" this extraordinary concept further.

> *In his studies, Schulman assumes that the universe expands and then contracts. . . . celestial bodies with reversed time would have originated in our distant future and would already have experienced the cosmic turnaround.*[6]

Presumably, these retreating bodies in reversed time, being no longer visible, could constitute the vast amounts of "dark matter" required by big-bang cosmology.

To me, it is especially surprising that so many evangelical scientists and theologians seem quite willing to discard the statements of Scripture in order to accept the imagined "big bang" as the event of the divine creation. They are even using the "New Age" icon, the so-called anthropic principle, which presumably ties various cosmic constants in with big-bang cosmology, as evidence of this event. They should realize, however, that all this compromise not only contradicts God's Word, but also the opinions of the large majority of evolutionary cosmologists.

> *For about a decade now, an increasing number of scientists and theologians have been asserting, in popular articles and books, that they can detect a signal of cosmic purpose poking its head out of the noisy data of physics and cosmology. This claim has been widely reported in the media, perhaps misleading lay people into thinking that some kind of new scientific consensus is developing in support of supernatural beliefs. In fact, none of this purported evidence can be found in the pages of scientific journals. . . .*
>
> *Stronger versions of the anthropic principle, which assert that the universe is somehow actually required to produce intelligent "information-processing systems," are not taken seriously by most scientists or philosophers.*[7]

The author of the above evaluation is professor of physics at the University of Hawaii, obviously biased against theism, but nevertheless accurate in his appraisal of the influence of the anthropic principle.

---

6 P. Weiss, "Time's Arrow May Make U-Turns in Universe," *Science News,* vol. 157 (January 1, 2000): p. 6.

7 Victor J. Stenger, "Anthropic Design: Does the Cosmos Show Evidence of Purpose?" *Skeptical Inquirer,* vol. 23 (July/August 1999): p. 40, 42.

To come back to earth, so to speak, it is worth repeating the great truth that God's revelation of special supernatural creation of the heavens in the beginning has never been refuted by any factual discoveries of astronomy or physics or cosmology. God was there, and He knows! We do well to believe His Word.

> *By the word of the LORD were the heavens made; and all the host of them by the breath of his mouth. . . . For he spake, and it was done; he commanded, and it stood fast* (Ps. 33:6–9).

> *My right hand hath spanned the heavens: when I call unto them, they stand up together* (Isa. 48:13).

But in trying to get away from the revelation of God's special creation of the universe, astronomers do encounter many obstacles. There are many speculations, but no proofs, and no firm evidences. So why not creation?

WHAT ASTRONOMERS DON'T KNOW ABOUT THE HEAVENS

Judging from the number of published books and articles on the subject, there is a lot going on in the field of evolutionary cosmogony as astronomers and cosmological physicists are trying to learn how the universe originated and its various components evolved, including all the millions of galaxies, stars, planets, and other objects in the vast cosmos. I try to scan two dozen or more scientific journals each month, and it seems to me there is no end to the speculative writings and researches on these topics. Like *"the Lord's mercies,"* they are *"new every morning"* (Lam. 3:22–23), though hardly as beneficial. As one scientist noted rather wistfully while eulogizing science as a whole:

> *Still, even today certain major sciences offer scant prospect of practical application. Astronomy and cosmology are of little earthly use.*[8]

That's a valid point, though not completely true, of course. The visible stars have for centuries been of great use in navigation, surveying, and chronometry.

But the distant stars and galaxies, observable only through giant telescopes, have been of use only in fueling speculations about the origin and evolution of the universe. That also is the primary motivation for

---

8 Horace F. Judson, "Century of the Science," *Science 84* (November, 1984): p. 42.

the scientists of NASA and their space program, as they are trying to determine how the earth and the solar system evolved, and even how life began.

The noted columnist George Will quotes the physicist Steven Weinberg as saying:

> *Effort to understand the universe is one of the very few things that lifts human life a little above the level of farce, and gives it some of the grace of tragedy.*[9]

That is a darkly pessimistic outlook, obviously, but is the logical conclusion of any consistent evolutionary world view.

Yet with all the billions of dollars spent on such studies and all the brainpower of such large numbers of brilliant scientists devoted to it and thus sidetracked from useful research, they still don't know the answers to any of the key questions about the universe.

As far as the origin of the universe itself is concerned, the predominant belief is still the theory of the big bang. Actually, no one knows.

The big-bang concept at least postulates a beginning, but that beginning consists of an infinitesimal particle of space/time which explodes and evolves over billions of years into our present cosmos. One science writer, trying to help us understand it, says:

> *Don't imagine outer space without matter in it. Imagine no space at all and no matter at all. Good luck.*
>
> *To the average person it might seem obvious that nothing can happen in nothing. But to a quantum physicist, nothing is, in fact, something.*[10]

The author of the above article calls this notion a "grand guess." It is certainly not anything that anyone *knows!*

The so-called "grand guess" was put forth by MIT astrophysicist Alan Guth. According to this concept, the infinitesimal particle of space/time which exploded into the big bang had to first go through a period of cosmic inflation, which presumably would solve the various difficulties present in the unmodified big-bang theory. The latter is said to be a "singularity," where the equations describing the phenomena of the expansion cease to apply.

---

9 George F. Will, "Trying to Understand the Universe," syndicated column as published in the *San Diego Union-Tribune*, March 24, 2002, p. G-2.

10 Brad Lemley, "Guth's Grand Guess," *Discover*, vol. 23 (April 2002): p. 35.

> *At such places, physics dissolves into metaphysics. These*
> *mathematical points admit of no explanation; they just are.*[11]

Scientists can't explain singularities. That means they don't know how to explain the big bang, although Guth's theory is said to handle most of the difficulties, and most astronomers now accept inflation. However, that doesn't help much, so many modifications of inflation have been proposed.

> *Roughly 50 forms of inflation have been proposed, named,*
> *and studied, including double, triple, and hybrid inflation,*
> *tilted hybrid inflation, hyperextended inflation that is "warm,"*
> *"soft," "tepid," and "natural."*[12]

Even if astronomers really understood all about inflation — that, is, the extremely rapid inflation of the universe to about the size of a grape-fruit in a tiny fraction of a second prior to the explosive bang — that would not answer the question of how the universe began. That "singularity" is still there.

> *For instance, cosmic inflation . . . does not eliminate the*
> *primeval singularity but simply isolates it from today's universe.*[13]

So one thing astronomers don't know is how the universe began. They take refuge in quantum physics, saying it somehow evolved from the primeval nothingness. And, of course, they don't know that either.

> *Quantum theory also holds that a vacuum, like atoms, is*
> *subject to quantum uncertainties. This means that things can*
> *materialize out of the vacuum, although they tend to vanish*
> *back into it quickly. . . . This phenomenon has never been*
> *observed directly. . . .*[14]

In spite of not being able to observe it, Guth and others hope that it happens. Of course, they don't know. Guth believes, nevertheless, that all of this is consistent with the known laws of physics. But that raises another question.

---

11 Anonymous, "Been There, Done That," *Scientific American*, vol. 286 (March 2002): p. 25.

12 Lemley, "Guth's Grand Guess," p. 38.

13 "Been There, Done That," p. 25.

14 Lemley, "Guth's Grand Guess," p. 35.

> *"Where do the laws of physics come from?" [Guth] pauses:*
> *"We are a long way from being able to answer that one."*[15]

Yes, that would be a very big gap in scientific "knowledge"!

But maybe we should bypass the question of the origin of the universe and study more tractable problems such as the origin of stars and galaxies. These would be amenable to observation and ordinary physics, would they not?

Take galaxies, for example. The most familiar, of course, is the Milky Way, the galaxy of which our own sun is a member. It is a spiral-disk galaxy, a type very common in the cosmos. It is supposed that it began from vast quantities of gas from the big-bang explosion collapsing through gravitational attraction of the molecules in the gas.

> *Our galaxy is a highly evolved entity. . . . It is an elegant structure that shows both order and complexity. . . . The end product is especially remarkable in the light of what is believed to be the starting point: nebulous blobs of gas. How the universe made the Milky Way from such simple beginnings is not altogether clear.*[16]

It's not clear at all. They simply do not know how our galaxy began. Even less could be known about other galaxies.

What about individual stars? The standard guess is that the first stars, called Population III, were formed only of hydrogen and helium. Later stars with heavier elements were supposedly generated when these first stars collapsed, forming heavier elements in their heated interiors which then traversed space to eventually coalesce enough to form new suns. This remarkable scenario is widely believed, but did it really happen?

> *Did later stars come into being through variants on a common theme (such as the collapse of molecular clouds) or in a seething moist pit of disparate forces and mechanisms? No one knows.*[17]

---

15 Ibid., p. 38.

16 Cristina Chiappini, "The Formation and Evolution of the Milky Way," *American Scientist,* vol. 89 (Nov./Dec. 2001): p. 506.

17 Linda Rowan and Robert Coontz, "Great Balls of Fire," *Science,* vol. 295 (January 4, 2002): p. 63.

As far as those hypothetical first simple stars are concerned — those stars whose collapse eventually generated all the more complex stars — it is not even known that they ever existed.

> *Astronomers have never seen a pure Population III star, despite years of combing our Milky Way galaxy.*[18]

Our purpose here does not require discussion of the various speculations about other components of the universe (planets, satellites, asteroids, dark matter, etc.). Ignorance about these matters is also quite profound. As another prominent astronomer, Alan Sandage, once observed:

> *The study of origins is the art of drawing sufficient conclusions from insufficient evidence.*[19]

Their conclusions may vary widely from one cosmologist to another, but they all try to keep them compatible with their basic assumption of cosmic evolution over billions of years.

It is well to remember that they *do not know* how the cosmos evolved — or stars, or galaxies, or anything else. Sometimes, they even admit it. But they keep right on trying.

Some do recognize a little humor in this rather bizarre realm of cosmic evolutionary mathematical speculation.

BUBBLELAND

Astronomer Bob Berman is (so far as I know) the originator of the felicitous term "Bubbleland." This remarkable region is the domain of the imaginary worlds of the mathematical cosmologies invented by our modern astrophysicists and cosmogonists. Berman calls it the realm beyond the present reach of science.

Most of these learned scholars believe the universe began in the singularity known as the big bang, when our cosmic continuum of space, matter, and time suddenly came into existence. But where did *that* come from? According to Berman, it must have come from Bubbleland.

> *Nobody has the foggiest idea what happened the Tuesday before the Big Bang. Who can say whether there was a previous*

---

18 Robert Irion, "The Quest for Population III," *Science*, vol. 295 (January 4, 2002): p. 66.

19 Alan Sandage, as quoted by Chiappini, "The Formation and Evolution of the Milky Way," p. 515.

collapsing universe or an incipient quantum fluctuation? The whole domain is part of Bubbleland.[20]

Berman notes certain speculations about "other dimensions" and various other esoteric mathematical concepts.

In truth we have no clue. We should say we have no clue. But since there is no official category for what happens to singularities, we'll just say they enter Bubbleland and everyone will understand.[21]

Even I can understand that, but I do have considerable trouble with 11 space dimensions, quantum fluctuations of nothing into something, multiple universes, and such like.

The big bang itself somehow gets away with going against the laws of causality, probability, conservation, entropy, and even common sense. Although I had a minor in mathematics at the graduate level, I get lost in trying to follow the esoteric mathematics of relativity and quantum theory. However, there are a number of very competent scientists in these fields who *do* understand these subjects and who reject the big bang. Among those are Fred Hoyle and several others of comparable stature.

And then there is Professor Sir Fred Hoyle, Britain's greatest living astrophysicist, and the Big Bang theory's greatest adversary. . . . Together with two other respected astrophysicists, Hoyle systematically reviews the evidence for the Big Bang theory, and gives it a good kicking.[22]

The author of the above quote, Robert Matthews, is referring to the recent book by Hoyle and others, entitled *A Different Approach to Cosmology*. Summarizing their arguments for the big bang in a physics journal, these writers say, as noted previously:

We do not think science should be done that way. . . . We think this approach does not merit the high esteem that cosmologists commonly accord it.[23]

---

20 Bob Berman, "Strange Universe: Bubbleland," *Astronomy,* vol. 28 (June 2000): p. 106.

21 Ibid.

22 Robert Matthews, "Sir Fred Returns to Give Big Bang Another Kicking," *Sunday London Telegraph: Cosmology Column,* February 13, 2000.

23 Geoffrey Burbridge, Fred Hoyle, and J. V. Narlikar, "A Different Approach to Cosmology," *Physics Today,* vol. 52 (April 1999): p. 39.

Compelling as their arguments against the big bang may be, however, they will probably be ignored by most astronomers. As Matthews says:

> *I don't expect the vast majority of astronomers to pay the slightest attention to Hoyle and his colleagues: frankly, there are too many careers riding on the Big Bang being right.*[24]

Perhaps the big bang itself really resides in Bubbleland!

And what about relativistic physics in general? An astrophysicist at the University of Rochester, says:

> *General relativity consists of ten interwoven equations. Along with these ten equations come hundreds of others that must also be solved. Each of these mathematical expressions can be hideously complicated, with term after term appearing in forms that provide no simple means of solution. A single equation can fill many pages. . . . The equations of General Relativity are intractably woven together. They snake through each other in a deeply non-linear way, forming a kind of mathematical Gordian knot.*[25]

Perhaps some of the inhabitants of Bubbleland can deal with such complexity, but I simply have to wonder and doubt.

As far as quantum theory is concerned, some of its implications also seem to belong in Bubbleland. Certain observations and calculations have indicated that the expansion of the universe may actually be accelerating. One science writer calls it the "revved-up universe."

> *Many associate its energy with the sea of particles and anti-particles that, according to quantum mechanics, populates empty space. Others call it "funny energy" and propose that it relates to the quantum nature of gravity. In either case, it's exotic stuff and poorly understood.*[26]

So now we learn that Bubbleland may be a revved-up universe vibrating with funny energy and a sea of particles in empty space.

---

24 Robert Matthews, "Sir Fred Returns to Give Big Bang Another Kicking."

25 Adam Frank, "The Dynamic World of General Relativity," *Sky and Telescope*, vol. 100 (October 2000): p. 53.

26 Ron Cowen, "Revved-Up Universe," *Science News*, vol. 157 (February 12, 2000): p. 106.

Then there is the multiple-universe theory of André Lind, which imagines an unending series of stacked-up quantum waves that generate new big bangs and expanding universes cascading one after another on top of each other. This remarkable notion has become more and more popular as an answer to the anthropic principle, which has been proposed by some as evidence for divine design of the cosmos.

For example, Martin Rees, Astronomer Royal of England, has published a book entitled *Just Six Numbers*, in which he argues that there are certain key numbers associated with the physical properties of the cosmos, whose fine-tuned values just barely permit life to exist. If they were different in the slightest degree, life would not be possible. Some people think that this proves a Creator.

But then Rees also argues against any theological implications of this fact by saying that this is because there may be great numbers of universes and this just happens to be the one whose randomly developed physical constants permitted life to evolve.

Well, if anyone finds difficulty in believing (or even understanding) these various notions — and I certainly do — we could just ascribe them all to Bubbleland, and then we could understand, and step out on faith!

But there is an even more amazing hypothesis recently put forth by physicist Julian Barbour in his book *The End of Time*, based on an incredible extension or modification of the multiple-universe speculation, and also on strange mathematics that supposedly can reconcile the discrepancies between the atomic world of quantum mechanics and the cosmic world of general relativity. Describing this theory of Barbour's (who has a physics doctorate from the University of Cologne and is highly regarded by his peers), Folger says:

> We don't live in a single universe that passes through time. Instead, we — or many slightly different versions of ourselves — simultaneously inhabit a multitude of static, everlasting tableaux that include everything in the universe at any given moment. Barbour calls each of these possible still-life configurations a "Now." Every now is a complete, self-contained, timeless, unchanging universe.[27]

Thus, in Barbour's universe, time has no reality. Everything is Now.

27 Tim Folger, "From Here to Eternity," *Discover*, vol. 21 (December 2000): p. 58.

> *There is no past and no future. Indeed, time and motion are nothing more than illusions....Every moment of every individual's life — birth, death, and everything in between — exists forever.*[28]

This idea must be a resident of the deepest region of Bubbleland! How can such a brilliant physicist as Barbour believe such things?

> *Like all physicists, he strongly believes that mathematically elegant explanations tend to be true, even if they conflict with common sense.*[29]

I turn in relief to the simple, believable, understandable, *true* explanation of the wonderful universe, *"In the beginning, God created the heaven and the earth"* (Gen. 1:1). *"I am he; I am the first, I also am the last. Mine hand also hath laid the foundation of the earth, and my right hand hath spanned the heavens: when I call unto them, they stand up together"* (Isa. 48:12–13).

That clear and beautiful explanation is much too simplistic, however, for evolutionary cosmophysicists. Some of their mental inventions have become so widely noted that we do need to consider them a little further. One of the most remarkable of these has to do with creation by a quantum fluctuation in the primeval vacuum.

---

28 Ibid., p. 57.
29 Ibid., p. 60.

CHAPTER X

REALLY FAR OUT

I have already briefly mentioned this popular notion of creation by a quantum fluctuation of the original nothingness into the incipient universe. Quantum theory somehow seems to allow such a thing. This original infinitesimal cosmos then supposedly went quickly through a period of "inflation," doing the inflating at a speed greatly exceeding the speed of light, reaching about the size of a grapefruit in an infinitesimal period of time. At that point it exploded with a big bang and became the expanding universe of space-time-matter — although just how the "matter" evolved is still uncertain and is currently being speculated about by many quantum physicists and astronomers. Many non-specialists, of course, still consider the whole scenario uncertain, especially those of us who still believe in God and His written Word, the Bible.

CREATION BY FLUCTUATIONS

Our Bible-believing forefathers were very naïve. They had the simplistic notion that God was omnipotent and truthful. In their unsophisticated view of things, they believed that the Bible was God's Word and that He was able to do what He said He did, and that He said what He meant to say about what He did! They believed what He wrote when He wrote the Ten Commandments on *"two tables of stone written with the finger of God . . . according to all the words, which the Lord spake with [Moses] in the mount out of the midst of the fire"* (Deut. 9:10).

Among these words were the following: *"Six days shall thou labour, and do all thy work. . . . For in six days, the Lord made heaven and earth, the sea, and all that in them is"* (Exod. 20:9–11). *Everything* that was in the heavens was made in that primeval six-day period, or — more specifically — on the fourth day of that period when God had said that He *"made two great lights, the greater light to rule the day, and the lesser light to rule the night: he made* [note: not 'is making'] *the stars also."*

That seems easy enough to understand. God was surely able to do that, and that's what He says He did! *"By the word of the Lord were the heavens made; and all the host of them by the breath of his mouth. . . . For he spake, and it was done; he commanded, and it stood fast"* (Ps. 33:6–9). *"Thus the heavens . . . were finished, and all the host of them. And on the seventh day God ended his work which he had made"* (Gen. 2:1–2). Why are "finished" and "ended" so hard to understand?

But evolutionist astronomers say we can still see stellar evolution taking place in the heavens. We can see stars, galaxies, and planets in various stages of this cosmic evolutionary process.

No, we can't! The heavens and the earth were *"finished."* All of God's heavenly *"works were finished from the foundation of the world"* (Heb. 4:3). As long as people have been looking at the stars, they have never seen a single star evolve. We do occasionally see stars disintegrate, but that's not evolution!

Perhaps the greatest anomaly in this situation is the incredibly weak scientific case for the whole scenario of cosmic evolution. There can be no "experiments" or "observations" of stars evolving, in the very nature of the case, so it cannot be *scientific*, though it may be naturalistic — all based on mathematical manipulations, computer simulations, and atheistic or pantheistic philosophies. The British Astronomer Royal, Martin Rees, has warned about putting too much faith in these speculations.

> *In a recent lecture he warned the Association for Science Education that cosmologists are not to be taken seriously when they speculate about the universe in the first second after the Big Bang. . . . Even the existence of the Big Bang itself depends on the extrapolation of physics back to the very beginning. In other words, the shaky place given to religious concepts in many of the popular cosmologies is not based on sound science.*[1]

---

1 Fraser Watts, editor, *Science Meets Faith*, "Is Science the New Religion?" by Mary Hesse (London: SPCK Holy Trinity Church, 1998), p. 124.

The author who was quoting Dr. Rees is herself a former professor of philosophy of science at the University of Cambridge. She concludes:

> *But perhaps it is unfair to judge the significance of science in general from cosmology, which is a special case in being as far removed from and sparsely supported by the here-and-now evidence as any theories can be.*[2]

In spite of the great faith placed by certain Christian leaders in the big bang, there are many secular astronomers who reject it. Among the more obvious difficulties is its contradiction of the two universal laws of thermodynamics, but there are many others. The "inflation theory" was enthusiastically promoted for awhile in the 1980s as a means of resolving at least some of these problems. As mentioned before, this was the notion that an incredibly small mini-universe "inflated" to the size of a grapefruit in an incredibly short time before it exploded into the big bang, which then proceeded to evolve into everything else.

But inflation itself has encountered numerous problems with many modifications having to be appended to the theory.

> *Even so, there is no proof that inflation is correct; and, to add to the uncertainty, distinct versions of the theory have proliferated, as physicists grapple with the problem of finding an inflation that could have produced the universe but is also compatible with known laws of physics.*[3]

As another astronomer has recently expostulated, after trying to sort through all the problems:

> *But then nobody knows whether inflation actually happened anyway.*[4]

Since simple inflation turned out to be inadequate to generate the big bang and the cosmos, various cosmophysicists have tried to improve on inflation.

---

2 Ibid., p. 125.

3 James Ganz, "Which Way to the Big Bang?" *Science,* vol. 284 (May 28, 1999): p. 1448.

4 Peter Coles, "The End of the Old Model Universe," *Nature,* vol. 393 (June 25, 1998): p. 743.

> *The theory now comes in varieties called, old, new, chaotic, hybrid, and open inflation, with numerous subdivisions like supersymmetric, supernatural, and hyperextended inflation each a vision of just how the inflation might have touched off the birth of the universe we see today.*[5]

Then, of course, there is the problem of what started the inflation in the first place. This question led to an even more fantastic speculation. There had somehow been a "quantum fluctuation" from nothing into something, by virtue of the uncertainty principle.

> *One of the consequences of the uncertainty principle is that a region of seemingly empty space is not really empty, but is a seething froth in which every sort of fundamental particle pops out of empty space for a brief instant before annihilating with its antiparticle and disappearing — these are the so-called quantum fluctuations.*[6]

After developing these thoughts at some length, the author says:

> *If this theory is correct, then seeds of structure are nothing more than patterns of quantum fluctuations from the inflationary era. In a very real sense, quantum fluctuations would be the origins of everything we see in the universe.*[7]

Atheistic astronomers used to replace Genesis 1:1 with their version of origins as: "In the beginning, hydrogen." But that didn't really explain the hydrogen. Now, the new version has it as follows: "In the beginning, quantum fluctuations."

By no means, however, have we yet seen the end of these cosmic metaphysical speculations. As Coles says:

> *But perhaps none of the available family of models will fit all the new data. For many of us, that is the most exciting possibility of all, as we would have to move to stranger theories, perhaps not even based on General Relativity.*[8]

---

5 Ganz, "Which Way to the Big Bang?" p. 1448.

6 Rocky Kolb, "Planting Primordial Seeds" *Astronomy,* vol. 26 (February 1998): p. 42.

7 Ibid., p. 43.

8 Peter Coles, "The End of the Old Model Universe," p. 744.

Who knows? Perhaps they will someday even hit on the simplest of all — the *true* theory that, *"In the beginning God created the heaven and the earth."*

These theories of inflation and fluctuation are widely believed to have resolved some of the problems encountered with the straightforward big bang and expanding universe concept. But now we are offered still another remarkable theory called "string theory," which is hoped will someday lead to a great unified theory of everything.

The Amazing Tiny Strings

I was recently reminded of an unusual article[9] which appeared many years ago in a leading science journal. The article had the fascinating subtitle, *"Prius Dementat,"* a Latin phrase meaning "They First Make Mad." This was essentially a shortened form of an old proverb: "Whom the gods seek to destroy, they first make mad."

The content of the article was a scathing critique of the nation's many colleges of education that were then training teachers for the public schools. The author of the article had become "fed up" with the emphasis of "professional educators" on pedagogical methods rather than the substantive material which most university professors considered essential in true liberal arts education.

What reminded me of that particular article, however, was a recent paper[10] on the "string theory" of many modern physicists, written by one of the founders and leaders of that concept, Dr. Leonard Susskind, professor of physics at Stanford University. In his exposition of current developments in string theory, he made the incidental comment: "Although this phantasmagoric image seems like something out of the mind of a madman, it is hard to see how it could be wrong."[11]

Since I am definitely not an authority on string theory, it is hard for me to see how he can be so sure that it could not be wrong when he also acknowledges that: "To say all of this rigorously follows from the precise mathematics of string theory is not justified at the present time,"[12] and

---

9 Harry J. Fuller, "The Emperor's New Clothes, or Prius Dementat," *The Scientific Monthly* (January 1951): pp. 32–41. Dr. Fuller was a professor of botany at the University of Illinois.

10 Leonard Susskind, "A Universe Like No Other," *New Scientist,* vol. 180, no. 2419 (November 1, 2003): p. 34–41.

11 Ibid., p. 41.

12 Ibid.

then further admits that: "Direct observational confirmation . . . is probably not possible."[13]

Actually, in context, he was not expounding string theory in general, but drawing some remarkable conclusions therefrom. According to Susskind:

> *String theory is the most ambitious attempt of theoretical physicists to explain the laws of nature. Based on the idea that elementary particles have an extended structure that resembles tiny loops of string, it has the potential to unify all the forces in nature, including the elusive quantum theory of gravity.*[14]

No one has seen these elementary particles nor these tiny loops of string, for they are much too small. They appear only in the mathematical manipulations generated by string-theory physicists.

Probably the most significant distinctive of string theory is that it does not operate in the real universe of space-time, with three dimensions of space (length, width, depth) and one of time. Susskind explains: "Depending on one's viewpoint it either requires nine or ten dimensions of space, and one of time."[15] The fact that we cannot see these extra six or seven space dimensions is "explained" by the assumption that they are far smaller even than those elementary particles also postulated by modern physicists. Dr. Susskind says that these tiny loops of string somehow function in rolled-up, six-dimensional shapes called Calabi-Yau spaces, of which there are presumably many millions of distinct kinds from which to choose.

But then there are also many other variables involved in this process, which is called "compactification." Each such space is specified by hundreds of "moduli," as well as "branes" and "fluxes" and "vacua." "All in all," says Susskind, ". . . a generic compactification requires several hundred variables to fix it. . . . They may vary either with time or with location in ordinary space."[16]

But before we get lost in these hundreds of variables, it would be well to take an overview of the conclusion to which the author is trying to lead us in all this. He had become disturbed by what has come to be known as the "anthropic principle," and his concern that the Nobel

---

13 Ibid.
14 Ibid., p. 36.
15 Ibid., p. 39.
16 Ibid., p. 40.

prize-winning physicist Steven Weinberg, whom he calls "a tireless enemy of creationism," is in danger of accepting it. This principle is the idea that many basic constants of nature are "fine-tuned just to insure our own existence." He asserts that: "Physicists hate this idea. Especially string theorists."[17]

String theorists seem convinced that their theory, when fully developed, will be able to explain all the laws of nature and constants of nature without any need for a Creator or Intelligent Designer to establish the conditions necessary for life to be able to evolve within the 15 billion years or so since the universe itself supposedly evolved out of a quantum fluctuation of nothing into something.

But there is still this problem of the "fine-tuning" of the universe for life. Weinberg himself has expressed the hope that "string theory really will provide a basis for a final theory"[18] that would solve this problem. Weinberg does not want to believe in a divine Creator any more than do Susskind and other string-theory physicists. The problem is how to avoid postulating a Creator when there are so many evidences that our universe was indeed structured to accommodate life.

Dr. Susskind turns to two of his colleagues for a possible answer. "Suppose that, as Andrei Linde, Alexander Vilenkin, and many other cosmologists believe, the universe is vastly larger than the region that has been astronomically explored. Might it be that the cosmological constant [that is, the 'vacuum energy density' in space] is not really a constant but varies throughout the unimaginably larger space? And might it also be that the number of possible values that it takes on is so large that practically every value occurs somewhere?"[19]

That would mean that, somewhere in this vast multiverse of universes, there exists at least one universe where the laws and constants of nature do permit life to evolve. That, he thinks, would solve the problem, since that universe just happens to be the one where we live.

But can string theory really allow for such an infinite complex of universes? Yes, one of the virtues of string theory is that it can do most anything one wants it to do. "The mathematical evidence for this humongous landscape of string theory is mounting."[20]

---

17 Ibid., p. 36.

18 Ibid.

19 Ibid., p. 38.

20 Ibid., p. 41.

Linde[21] and others had already developed the idea that an infinite number of "bubbles" could form in an inflating universe. Many of these would quickly develop into "pocket universes," which would rapidly inflate and generate more bubbles, and so on. This could, indeed, seem like a "phantasmagoric image" to ordinary folk. In such a scenario, the anthropic principle, as applicable to our particular universe is just an accident. Dr. Susskind's conclusion is:

> If this view of nature is correct then there is cold comfort for those who look to the anthropic principle for a deeper meaning to their own existence. As Darwin's principle of survival of the fittest eliminated the need for the hand of God to guide evolution, so the environmental interpretation of the anthropic principle eliminates the necessity for a guardian angel to fine-tune the laws of nature.[22]

But Susskind has admitted that these inferences from string theory have not been verified by either mathematics or observation. In fact, many physicists still reject this entire theory of strange strings altogether. Eric Chaisson, for example, in his book on cosmology and thermodynamics says that, "Although the theory of superstrings is now causing great excitement in the physics community, there is to date not a shred of experimental or observational evidence to support it."[23]

Furthermore, to do away with God, this concept has to invent not only a multi-dimensional universe, but also a multi-universe polyverse! So far, at least, all these exist only in the world of mathematics and the minds of string-theory physicists.

What does the true God who created our real universe have to say about all this? We don't know directly, of course, since none of the biblical writers have even mentioned any such strange notions. As far as the implications of God's Word are concerned, our universe extends spatially without end in all three of its dimensions of space and eternally forward in time.

Four dimensions do seem to be implied in Paul's beautiful prayer for the Christian believers at Ephesus, when he prayed that they . . .

---

21 A. D. Linde, "The Self-Reproducing Inflationary Universe," *Scientific American,* vol. 271 (November 1994): p. 48–55.

22 Susskind, "A Universe Like No Other," p. 41.

23 Eric J. Chaisson, *Cosmic Evolution* (Cambridge, MA: Harvard University Press, 2001), p. 246.

> *May be able to comprehend with all saints [and that would*
> *include us as well!] what is the breadth, and length, and depth,*
> *and height; And to know the love of Christ, which passeth*
> *knowledge, that ye might be filled with all the fullness of God*
> (Eph. 3:18–19).

I don't know, but I like to think that *"height"* is included in this prayer because *"breadth, and length, and depth"* apply not only to objects on the earth, but extend forever high into the heavens, and this could suggest "time" as well. And note how Paul concludes this prayer of his for the Ephesians:

> *Unto him be glory in the church by Christ Jesus throughout*
> *all ages, world without end. Amen* (Eph. 3:21).

One of the claims has been that string theory may be able to bring harmony between certain conflicts between quantum physics and the relativistic physics of Albert Einstein. One key contention of the latter is the constancy of the speed of light (this latter has also been a problem for biblical creationism). But now even this is being re-examined by evolutionary physicists.

THE CHANGING SPEED OF LIGHT

One of the most frequent questions encountered by those of us who believe in the literal Genesis record of creation is: "How can the universe be young if the stars are old?" If a star is, say, a million light-years from earth, wouldn't it take a million years for its light to reach us?"

Creationists have tried to answer this problem in various ways. One point creationists can make is that actual geometric measurements of star distances are possible only out to about 300 light years. Greater distances are mere "guesstimates" based on a series of assumptions. However, there is no *biblical* problem with the concept of an infinite universe created by an omnipotent Creator (note such Scriptures as Isa. 55:9; Gen. 22:17; Job 22:12; etc.), so we have no basic problem with distance estimates involving millions of light years.

Others, including this writer, have stressed that God could have created the light from the stars simultaneously with the stars themselves, so that Adam could have seen the stars as soon as they were created. A major difficulty with this assumption is how to deal with post-creation stellar events such as supernovas.

An Australian scientist, Barry Setterfield, developed the idea of a decreasing velocity of light. However, most physicists reject this suggestion out of hand. A constant *"c"* is basic throughout Einsteinnian relativistic physics, which most physicists have adopted as incontrovertibly proved. There was also a question about the statistical strength of Setterfield's evidence for decreasing speed.

Based on relativity concepts, a number of physicists — most notably Dr. Russell Humphreys of ICR — have argued from Einstein's relativity theories that, at great distances, six literal days on Earth could correspond to billions of years in distant space. The problem is that one would almost have to have a Ph.D. in theoretical physics even to comprehend the physics and mathematics involved in this argument. That raises the question: Would God expect ordinary people to depend on theoretical physics to determine whether or not they could believe the Bible?

The uncertainties among cosmologists about origins has now been further pointed up by their interest in the theories of João Magueijo.[24] Magueijo is not a creationist, but is himself stressing that a changing speed of light would solve many cosmological problems, even though it would drastically modify Einstein's theories of relativity.

> *It was as if the riddles of the Big Bang universe were trying to tell us precisely that light was much faster in the early universe, and that at some very fundamental level physics had to be based on a structure richer than the theory of relativity.*[25]

The above was taken from Magueijo's new book, *Faster Than the Speed of Light*. In an earlier article he had said:

> *It now appears that the constancy of "c" is not so essential to relativity after all; the theory can be based on other postulates.*[26]

The inflationary hypothesis also has serious problems, as we have seen. Magueijo says:

> *Although cosmic inflation has acquired an aura of invincibility, alternative theories continue to attract some*

---

24 Dr. Magueijo has a Ph.D. in theoretical physics from Cambridge University and is currently a professor of theoretical physics at Imperial College in London.

25 João Magueijo, *Faster Than the Speed of Light* (Cambridge, MA: Perseus Publishing, 2003), p. 6.

26 João Magueijo, "Plan B for the Cosmos," *Scientific American,* vol. 284 (January 2001): p. 59.

*interest among cosmologists. . . . But the most promising and
provocative alternative may be the varying-speed-of-light theory
(VSL), which my colleagues and I have been developing for
several years.*[27]

Magueijo was subjected to disdain and opposition when he suggested
to his colleagues that the velocity of light might not be a constant. After
all, as he noted:

*. . . relativity's spell is so strong that the constancy of "c"
is now woven into all the mathematical tools available to the
physicist.*[28]

Nevertheless, his ideas are gradually gaining a number of important
adherents. An interviewer with *New Scientist* asked him whether the theory had yet got to the point of acceptance by his colleagues. He answered
as follows:

*It depends what you mean by accepted. I have been
commissioned by a journal to write a big review article. And
we have become respectable in the sense that there's a huge
number of people working on it now. . . . But I wouldn't say it's
mainstream yet.*[29]

Another fascinating article in the same issue of *New Scientist* deals
with the theories of an Italian scientist, Giovanni Amelino-Camelia, who
has been working on a different type of criticism and revision of Einstein's relativity, that he enthusiastically calls "Doubly Special Relativity"
(DSL).

*Einstein's special theory of relativity, which describes the
behavior of space and time and bound them together as "space-
time," has been passed down the generations as an immutable
fact. . . . But, says Amelino-Camelia, Einstein may have had
only half the story.*[30]

Magueijo has found a kindred spirit in Amelino-Camelia, combin-
ing the latter's theories with his own.

---

27 Ibid., p. 58.
28 Ibid.
29 Michael Brooks, "Hero or Heretic," *New Scientist,* vol. 177 (Feb. 8, 2003): p. 48.
30 David Harris, "After Einstein," *New Scientist,* vol. 177 (Feb. 8, 2003): p. 29.

> *João Magueijo . . . had been formulating an explanation of*
> *the evolution of the Universe. . . . But there was a heavy price*
> *to pay. . . . He was suggesting that the speed of light has been*
> *slowing ever since the big bang.*[31]

These two men and a number of other physicists have become confident that all of physics could eventually be found to fit into their revolutionary theories.

> *If these physicists are right, then Einstein's reign is coming*
> *to an end.*[32]

Now, none of this means that we now have a firm answer to the question about starlight and the age of the universe. Such an idea would be considered absurd by Magueijo. His VSL cosmology leads to various other conclusions which would be even more difficult for us to deal with (for example, it negates the first law of thermodynamics, the principle of energy conservation)!

But it does seem to reinforce our frequent observation that modern cosmology has become nothing but a morass of conflicting mathematical models, which few besides Ph.D. theoretical physicists really understand, and which they seem to replace with other models every week or so. Remember those 50 variations in the inflation model!

Another important example of cosmological uncertainty is the current notion that the stars and other measurable physical bodies comprise only 4 percent of the "matter" in space. The rest is either "dark matter" or "dark energy," neither of which has ever been observed, but which seem theoretically to be needed. But as one scientist observes referring to this unseen sea of unknown material:

> *We know little about that sea. The terms we use to describe*
> *its components, "dark matter" and "dark energy" serve mainly*
> *as expressions of our ignorance.*[33]

There are numerous other problems and controversies in cosmology. Few outside this professional clique of specialists in higher mathematics and theoretical physics really understand them. Furthermore, they often

---

31 Ibid., p. 30.

32 Ibid., p. 32.

33 David B. Cline, "The Search for Dark Matter," *Scientific American,* vol. 288 (March 2003): p. 52.

disagree with each other and repeatedly revise their theories anyway. I think we shall do well to continue to believe Genesis 1:1 quite literally.

The reference above to "dark matter" and "dark energy" will be discussed further in the next section. One wonders whether the sudden emergence of these strange topics in cosmology might unconsciously relate somehow to what the Bible calls "outer darkness."

THE OUTER DARKNESS

Astronomers have guessed that there are possibly as many as ten thousand billion trillion stars out there in the observable universe, of which perhaps five thousand can be seen without a telescope. If the universe is expanding, as many astronomers believe, there is an outer limit to this vast population of stars, as defined by the distance thus far attained by the expansion. This limit might be considered the boundary of the universe, assuming the validity of the concept of the expanding universe.

This boundary is also, practically by definition, the limit of the so-called background radiation, presumably a cosmos-filling remnant of the postulated primeval big bang which its proponents believe must have started the expansion.

> *No matter where astronomers point their telescopes, they see a distant sheet of light surrounding us. Beyond that enormous shell of radiation, astronomers can see nothing. We are caged in by this surface; the cosmic microwave background (CMB), the faint afterglow of the big bang.*[34]

Since there would be no radiation beyond this limit, there could be no stars and no light either — only outer darkness, so far as we can tell. But even *within* the known cosmos, evolutionary astronomers seem increasingly obsessed with the idea of darkness. Even with the tremendous mass of those possibly 10^{25} stars, these theorists believe that there are still vast amounts of certain mysterious kinds of matter which cannot be seen or measured. They call this *dark matter*, the gravitational influence of which they believe somehow holds galaxies and galactic clusters together.

> *For several decades, astrophysicists have postulated the existence of dark matter — objects that have mass but don't interact with light very well. . . . Scientists have calculated that*

---

34 Charles Seife, "Peering Backward to the Cosmos's Fiery Birth," *Science,* vol. 292 (June 22, 2001): p. 2236.

baryonic, ordinary matter — the stuff of stars and of people — makes up just over 4% of the energy and matter in the universe. What about the rest? Combined with observations from galaxy surveys and other sources, the CMB measurements give some rather troubling numbers. They show that about 30% of the stuff in the universe is dark matter.[35]

The unobservable matter in the universe is thus greater than all the observable matter — 7.5 times greater. Amazing!

Dark matter even comes in two flavors, hot (HDM) and cold (CDM). And all the while, astronomers and physicists have refined their dark matter theories without ever getting their hands on a single piece of it.[36]

However, that still leaves about 66 percent of the universe's "stuff" to be accounted for beyond that! In particular, there is supposedly strong evidence now that the "expansion" of the universe is accelerating near its boundaries. The gravitational influences out there seem to be driving it apart, and this would require some kind of tremendous energy whose source and character are unknown. So cosmologists just call it "dark energy"!

Astronomers have dark imaginations. They're already obsessed with another phenomenon that they call dark matter, which is entirely separate from dark energy. Dark matter is the invisible material that . . . gathers into vast clumps and exerts an ordinary gravitational tug on its surroundings. . . . The proposed dark energy, in contrast, would inhabit empty space and would be evenly distributed throughout the universe. Moreover, dark energy would exert a repulsive force — what might be called antigravity.[37]

This strange universal anti-gravity field has been given the name "quintessence" by some astronomers. No instruments have been able to measure it, or even record it, but they believe it must be there on the basis of the intensity of light from very distant supernovas, which to them suggests dark energy.

---

35 Ibid., p. 2237.

36 Steve Nadis, "Out of Sight, Out of MOND," *Astronomy,* vol. 29 (August 2001): p. 28.

37 Ron Cowen, "A Dark Force in the Universe," *Science News,* vol. 159 (April 7, 2001): p. 218.

Where would such a strange field come from? . . . An exotic
possibility is that quintessence springs from the physics of extra
dimensions.[38]

Some six or seven extra dimensions (in addition to length, width, depth, and time) have been mathematically predicted in string theory, but this also is quite an illusory concept to many, as we have noted.

In any case, the picture now occupying the minds of many evolutionary cosmologists is that of an immense universe with multitudes of stars and other objects in great variety, but which actually comprise only a minute part of the matter and energy of a very "dark" universe.

Dark energy would complete a picture of the cosmos in
which more than 98% of the matter and energy is of some
exotic, unseen form.[39]

And, since the law of entropy apparently is of universal extent, even the visible stars will eventually disintegrate into darkness, or worse.

To be sure, approaching gravitational equilibrium (in
addition to thermal and chemical uniformity) would mean a
Universe full of black holes.[40]

Dark matter, dark energy, and ultimate black holes everywhere certainly sound foreboding — if true. And that's just the known universe! What about the darkness outside of that?

It is well to remember that a great deal of modern cosmology, especially when its practitioners are trying to predict its destiny and retrodict its origin, is sheer mathematical manipulation and evolutionary philosophical imagination. "It ain't necessarily so!"

But it *is* significant that these speculations lead so often to words like "darkness" and "blackness." These are biblical terms, too.

Speaking of those teachers and leaders who would promote anti-biblical doctrines of God and His great salvation through the Lord Jesus Christ, the apostle Peter warned that *"these . . . speak evil of the things that*

---

38 Jeremiah P. Ostriker, and Paul J. Steinhart, "The Quintessential Universe," *Scientific American,* vol. 284 (January 2001): p. 50.

39 Ron Cowen, "Starry Data Support Revved-up Cosmos," *Science News,* vol. 159 (April 7, 2001): p. 212.

40 Eric J. Chaisson, *Cosmic Evolution* (Cambridge, MA: Harvard University Press, 2001), p. 166.

they understand not . . . to whom the mist of darkness is reserved for ever" (2 Pet. 2:12–17).

Similarly, Jude compares them to *"wandering stars, to whom is reserved the blackness of darkness for ever"* (Jude 13).

The Lord Jesus himself referred to *"outer darkness"* as the ultimate home of the lost. In His familiar parable of the talents, the judgment on the servant whose unfruitfulness had proved he was not a true servant was to *"cast ye the unprofitable servant into outer darkness: there shall be weeping and gnashing of teeth"* (Matt. 25:30; see also Matt. 8:12; 22:13).

The outer darkness will also be *"a world of iniquity . . . set on fire of hell"* (James 3:6), where all vestiges of goodness and love and light are gone forever. No wonder Jesus urged men to *"Fear him which . . . hath power to cast into hell"* (Luke 12:5). He also spoke of this as a place of *"everlasting punishment"* (Matt. 25:46). See chapter XII for further discussion of this unpleasant, but vital, topic.

God's created universe is also eternal with all its multitude of stars, and the lake of fire will occupy only a small, probably remote, region in comparison.

> *Praise ye him, sun and moon: praise him, all ye stars of light. . . . He hath also stablished them for ever and ever: he hath made a decree which shall not pass* (Ps. 148:3–6).

And all who are saved — those who believe His word and have received His great salvation through faith in Christ — shall live and praise Him for ever.

> *And they that be wise shall shine as the brightness of the firmament; and they that turn many to righteousness as the stars for ever and ever* (Dan. 12:3).

Although many have chosen the way that leads to outer darkness, there will also be many living forever in the Holy City on the new earth. *"And there shall be no night there . . . for the Lord God giveth them light"* (Rev. 22:5).

CHAPTER XI

THE DARKNESS OF EVOLUTIONISM

In addition to the darkness of outer space and the prospect of eternal darkness as the home of the lost, it does seem to us who believe in Christ and the Bible that those who don't are already in a state of scientific, social, and moral darkness. *"God is light and in him is no darkness at all"* (1 John 1:5), so how could it be otherwise for those who deny or ignore God as Creator in their scientific studies and moral decisions? They all fight vigorously against creationists and even among themselves, for example. Yet they can be incredibly arrogant in their repeated insistence that evolution is true science and creation merely a religious crutch for the naïve who cannot really understand the subtleties of evolutionism.

THE DIVIDED HOUSE

A fascinating book[1] was published in England in 1999 with the intriguing title *The Darwin Wars*. The author, Andrew Brown, though himself an atheistic evolutionist, in 1995 won the Templeton Prize as the best religious affairs correspondent in Europe.

The title of his book does not refer to the long warfare between evolutionists and creationists, as one might first suppose, but rather to the

---

1 Andrew Brown, *The Darwin Wars: How Stupid Genes Became Selfish Gods* (London: Simon and Schuster, 1999), 241 p.

internecine battles between various groups of evolutionists against each other. Although they close ranks when doing battle with creationists, they wrangle bitterly among themselves.

The most publicized recent battle was between the neo-Darwinians and the punctuationists. Richard Dawkins (of Cambridge University in England) was the best-known protagonist for the New-Darwinists and the late Stephen Jay Gould of Harvard University for the punctuationists.

> *These two parties need names, and I propose to call them Gouldians and Dawkinsians.*[2]

Like the gingham dog and the calico cat, these two groups seemed bent on eating each other up. The Gouldians argued vigorously that the fossil record proves that evolution did not occur slowly and gradually and progressively, as neo-Darwinianism requires. The Dawkinsians, on the other hand, insisted vehemently that there is no possibility genetically that sudden evolution after long periods of "stasis" (i.e., no change) could ever happen at all, as the punctuationists allege. Both are right!

One prominent Gouldian makes the following flat assertion that paleontology proves stasis, followed by wide extinction events, followed by rapid evolution of new kinds.

> *I make the very strong claim that nothing much happens in biological evolutionary history until extinction claims what has come before.*[3]

This scenario then postulates that rapid evolution suddenly generates a new complex of flora and fauna to fill the vacant ecological niches.

But there is no biological mechanism that can do such marvelous things. Dawkins had correctly pointed out the following fact:

> *Complexity cannot spring up in a single stroke of chance. . . . Gradualness is of the essence. . . . If you throw out gradualness, you throw out the very thing that makes evolution more plausible than creation.*[4]

---

2 Ibid., p. 56.

3 Niles Eldredge, *The Patterns of Evolution* (New York: W.H. Freeman and Co., 1998), p. 4.

4 Richard Dawkins, "What Was All the Fuss About?" *Nature*, vol. 316 (August 22, 1985): p. 683.

And so Gouldians and Dawkinsians are actually (although unintentionally) helping to prove creationism, one disproving gradualism, the other disproving punctuationism. The house of evolution is badly, and eventually fatally, divided.

Niles Eldredge, the partner of Gould in their notion of stasis and punctuated equilibrium, has acknowledged this internal warfare.

> *Geneticists and paleontologists are still very much at each other's throats.*[5]

Since evolution and creation are really world views, these battles among biologists also involve sociological and psychological controversies. Modern sociobiology, for example, tends to correlate with neo-Darwinism and social Darwinism, while Marxist movements with their penchant for revolution tend to favor punctuationism. Edward O. Wilson, a colleague of Gould's at Harvard, is considered the world leader in sociobiology (the application of animal behaviors to human societies). His followers and those of Gould have been involved in serious clashes.

One of these took place in the hallowed halls of Harvard University itself, involving a group of Gouldians in a Marxist club euphemistically named "Science for the People."

> *The supporters of Science for the People were quite happy to intimidate their opponents. In the worst incident, a group of black student protestors mounted the platform at a scientific meeting where Gould and Wilson were debating and drenched Wilson (who had a broken leg at the time) with water. . . . They then chanted, "Wilson, you're wet!" for a while.*[6]

Remember that both Edward Wilson (along with most of his sociobiologist disciples) and Stephen Gould (with most other advocates of punctuated equilibrium) were doctrinaire atheists and anti-creationists. Although they could be bitter antagonists within evolutionism, they were and are of one mind in opposition to God and creation.

A notorious comment by John Maynard Smith pointed this fact out beautifully. Smith is an eminent British neo-Darwinist, who was a mentor of Richard Dawkins. With respect to Gould, he had the following to say:

---

5 Eldredge, *The Patterns of Evolution*, p. 10.
6 Brown, *The Darwin Wars*, p. 71.

Because of the excellence of his essays, he has come to be seen by non-geologists as the preeminent evolutionary theorist. In contrast, the evolutionary biologists with whom I have discussed his work tend to see him as a man whose ideas are so confused as to be hardly worth bothering with, but as one who should not be publicly criticized because he is at least on our side against the creationists.[7]

Another notorious debate involving Gould was with Steven Pinker, an evolutionary linguist and sociobiologist at MIT. Science writer Martin Brookes gives us the background.

The dispute over evolutionary psychology is just the latest incarnation of the nature/nurture debate. . . . Pinker has joined the high-profile team of Dawkins and Daniel Dennett. . . . Gould stands on the opposite side of the ideological fence. . . .[8]

The comments of Brookes about the debate itself are fascinating.

For an argument about science, you would be hard pressed to find an exchange of views so full of hollow rhetoric, pompous quotations, and insults. . . . The spat between Pinker and Gould . . . has no apparent function other than intellectual one-upmanship. It is precisely because there is so little evidence for either of their views that they can get away with so much speculation and disagreement.[9]

Brookes seems to agree with us creationists (though he would probably be appalled at such a suggestion!) that there is "so little evidence" for either neo-Darwinism or punctuationism, that both have to rely on "hollow rhetoric, pompous quotations and insults" to defend their beliefs.

Another combatant in the internal wars among evolutionary biologists is the growing body of evolutionary pantheists, who admit there is much evidence of intelligent design in living things, but then maintain that this is the result of Gaia, or cosmic consciousness, or Mother

---

7 John Maynard Smith, in a review of *Darwin's Dangerous Idea*, by Daniel Dennett, published in *New York Times Review of Books*, as cited by Andrew Brown, *The Darwin Wars*, p. 60.

8 Martin Brookes, "May the Best Man Win," *New Scientist*, vol. 158 (April 11, 1998): p. 51.

9 Ibid.

Nature, or anything other than a personal Creator. One of the most articulate leaders of this group is Lynn Margulis, who is especially critical of such neo-Darwinists as Richard Dawkins, John Maynard-Smith, and others of like faith.

> *Neo-Darwinian language and conceptual structure itself ensures scientific failure. Major questions posed by zoologists cannot be answered from within the new-Darwinist straitjacket.*[10]

Then quoting Gabriel Dover, she agrees that:

> *The study of evolution should be removed from teleological computer simulations, thought experiments and wrong-headed juggling of probabilities . . . the new-Darwinist synthesis should not be defended to death by blind watchmakers.*[11]

The last phrase is a reference to Richard Dawkins famous book, *The Blind Watchmaker.*

If their importance justified it, these internal squabbles among biologists could be elaborated at great length. Similar bitter in-house arguments are common among evolutionary geologists and evolutionary astronomers. But they all stand united against creationism! Otherwise, they would have to believe in God and a future judgment, and this they are all unwilling to face.

We who *do* believe in God, creation, judgment, and redemption by Christ can at least remind them of the words of our Lord Jesus Christ: *"If a kingdom be divided against itself, that kingdom cannot stand. And if a house be divided against itself, that house cannot stand"* (Mark 3:24–25). Some day, the House of Evolution will fall, *"and great* [shall be] *the fall of it"* (Matt. 7:27).

EVOLUTIONARY ARROGANCE

There seems to be something about evolutionism that generates arrogance in many of its spokesmen. The concept is so wide-ranging that it purportedly can explain everything scientifically, from the origin of the cosmos to the origin of religion. Perhaps because it seems to eliminate the need for God, science itself becomes "god," and some evolutionists

---

10 Lynn Margulis and Dorion Sagan, *Slanted Truths: Essays on Gaia: Symbiosis and Evolution* (New York: Springer, Verlag, 1997), p. 100.

11 Ibid., p. 271.

think they have become its official prophets and priests. One of the communicants, in fact, calls them its "shamans." He says,

> We show deference to our leaders, pay respect to our elders and follow the dictates of our shamans; this being the Age of Science, it is scientism's shamans who command our veneration. . . . Scientists [are] the premier mythmakers of our time.[12]

One of these great shamans, arguably the premier living evolutionist, is Professor Ernst Mayr of Harvard. He tells us that evolution can even answer the great "Why?" questions of life. Many people of normal intelligence, including most scientists, have acknowledged that science can deal with questions beginning with "What?" and "Where?" and "How?" but not "Why?" The latter requires a theological answer, or at least philosophical. But not Shaman Mayr. He says:

> There is not a single Why? question in biology that can be answered adequately without a consideration of evolution.[13]

After all, says Shermer, "cosmology and evolutionary theory ask the ultimate origin questions that have traditionally been the province of religion and theology" and evolutionism is "courageously proffering naturalistic answers that supplant supernaturalistic ones and . . . is providing spiritual sustenance. . . ."[14]

The investment of these leaders of the evolutionary faith with such pontifical authority, however, tends to generate in them an attitude of profound impatience with such heresies as creationism. Instead of opposing the creationists with scientific proofs of macroevolution, they resort to name-calling and ridicule. A professor at a Missouri university fulminated at the "lunatic literalism of the creationists,"[15] especially "the weirdness produced by leaders such as Henry M. Morris."[16]

And even such an articulate and highly revered evolutionist as the late Stephen Jay Gould, in a voluminous book of 1,433 pages published

---

12 Michael Shermer, "The Shaman of Scientism," *Scientific American* (June 2002): p. 35.

13 Ernst Mayr, *What Evolution Is* (New York: Basic Books, 2001), p. xiii.

14 Shermer, "The Shaman of Scientism," p. 35.

15 Taner Edis, "Darwin in Mind," *Skeptical Inquirer,* vol. 25, no. 2 (March/April 2001): p. 36.

16 Ibid., p. 35.

just before his death, referred angrily to "the scourge of creationism."[17] He had refused many invitations to debate a qualified creationist scientist with the self-serving and misleading explanation that it would be a mistake to dignify creationism and its scientists in this way.

Dr. Massimo Pigliucci, who has lost a number of debates with Dr. Gish and other creationists, laments the fact that "many Americans are still enchanted with dinosaurs such as John Morris and Duane Gish of the oxymoronically named Institute for Creation Research."[18]

Although Dr. Gould would never debate a creationist scientist, despite the inducement of large financial incentives to do so, he was quick to criticize them in print, calling them "fundamentalists who call themselves 'creation scientists,' with their usual mixture of cynicism and ignorance."[19] Gould often resorted, in fact, to the standard debate technique of name-calling and *ad hominem* arguments commonly used when one has no factual evidence to support his position.

In his gigantic magnum opus, Dr. Gould provides a valuable historical review of the development of evolutionary theory, including the many conflicts among the evolutionists themselves, but in his 1,433 pages neglected to provide a single *proof* of macroevolution. The same was true of the esteemed Ernst Mayr, who, in his own recent textbook,[20] could cite no such proof. Yet he had the gall to make the pronouncement that "every knowing person agrees that man is descended from the apes."[21]

We ignorant creationists, since we theoretically know nothing about the subject, thus, according to Gould, have "always relied, as a primary strategy, upon the misquotation of scientific sources."[22] We not only are ignorant, but also by him are assumed to be liars. Strange that, in his 1,433 pages, not to mention his copious other writings, Dr. Gould failed to cite a single example of such misquotations.

Creationists are fallible human beings, of course, and it is possible that a few mistakes could be discovered among the thousands of quotes we have used from the evolutionists, but they would certainly be rare

17 Stephen Jay Gould, *The Structure of Evolutionary Theory* (Cambridge, MA: Harvard University Press, 2002), p. 984.

18 Massimo Pigliucci, "Defending Evolution, as Strange as It May Seem," *Evolution*, vol. 56, no. 1 (2002): p. 206.

19 Gould, *The Structure of Evolutionary Theory*, p. 101, footnote.

20 Mayr, *What Evolution Is*.

21 Ernst Mayr, "Interview," *Omni* (March/April 1988): p. 46, emphasis supplied.

22 Gould, *The Structure of Evolutionary Theory*, p. 986.

exceptions, as well as unintentional. They certainly could not obviate the tremendous case that has been built up against evolution just from admissions of evolutionists.

It would be easy if space permitted to multiply examples of the evolutionists' use of ridicule and insulting names in lieu of scientific evidence. But another type of evolutionary arrogance consists of their repeatedly professed amazement that anyone of intelligence could ever disagree with them.

One writer laments that even after the pope reaffirmed the commitment of the Catholic Church to evolution in 1996,

> Forty percent of American Catholics in a 2001 Gallup poll said they believed that God created human life in the past 10,000 years. Indeed, fully 45 percent of all Americans subscribe to this creationist view.[23]

Two eminent authors of an important article in the journal, *Evolution*, assume that this simply indicates "a lack of . . . understanding of evolution by the general public" and then suggests that the cause of this ignorance may be "the way the media communicates evolution and anti-evolution."[24]

Perhaps these authors were writing this with tongue-in-cheek! It would seem they must know that practically all the media strongly promote evolution and that the "general public" has been taught only evolution in public schools and secular colleges all their lives. Evidently all this brainwashing somehow has failed.

But why would the public favor creation? Only a statistical minority of the "general public" attends church and Sunday school. Could it possibly be that evolution is so contrary to evidence and common sense that people intuitively know that evolution is wrong? And could it be that many of these have studied the evidences for themselves and thereby found that evolution is not really scientific after all?

---

23 Roger Doyle, "Down with Evolution," *Scientific American,* vol. 286 (March 2002): p. 30.

24 Brian J. Alters and Craig E. Nelson, "Perspective: Teaching Evolution in Higher Education," *Evolution,* vol. 56 (October 2002): p. 1892. Dr. Alters was the lead author of *Defending Evolution* (Boston, MA: Jones & Bartlett, 2001), 261 p., an anti-creationist book which was reviewed in the September 2001 issue of ICR's *Acts & Facts.* Dr. Nelson is a professor at the University of Indiana who has unsuccessfully debated for evolution several times.

Higher education doesn't seem to help much. Alters and Nelson have made a fairly extensive survey of this kind of study.

> *Research results show that there may be surprisingly little difference in performance between majors and non-major introductory biology students. For example, in an ecology and evolutionary biology pretest of 1,200 students, biology majors scored only 6% higher than non-majors. When the same students were posttested on the first day of the following semester, the researchers concluded "that majors, who received a much more rigorous treatment of the material, came through the semester with the same degree of understanding as the non-majors".*[25]

This strange intransigence on the part of science students when subjected to evolutionary teachings, they think, must be caused by religion!

> *The more deeply ingrained the religious teachings, the more the evidence was viewed through lenses different from those of students without contradictory religious beliefs.*[26]

Well, that does make sense. If evolutionists can just persuade students to be atheists, it should be easier to make them become evolutionists!

There will always be a problem, however, in convincing students who believe that scientific generalizations should at least be based on scientific facts.

Even more difficult will it always be to convince students who believe that the biblical account of creation is the true account as revealed by the Creator himself.

In the absence of either a divine "evolution revelation" or real scientific *proof* of macroevolution, it is hard to understand this pervasive attitude of intellectual superiority (even over thousands of fully credentialed creationist scientists) as anything but evolutionary arrogance.

BEHIND THE DARK CURTAIN

One might think that, if evolution were really true, belief in evolution would contribute to mental peace and stability. On the contrary, however, commitment to evolutionism seems actually to generate serious mental and even physiological problems in an abnormally significant number of its leaders.

---

25 Ibid.
26 Ibid, p. 1898.

The most influential founders and proponents of modern evolutionism were not always objective and unemotional scientists. Most of their modern followers would like for us to think of them as interested only in discovering and teaching truth. Instead, they often seem to have been driven by very unscientific feelings and motivations. This observation does not apply to all evolutionists, of course, but such nonscientific purposes seem too common to be merely coincidental. It almost seems that some unseen powers were pulling strings behind the curtain.

For example, Thomas Huxley (without whose strong public advocacy Darwinism may well have died unnoticed) was not the cool scientist most writers have assumed. Adrian Desmond has written a biography of Huxley with the intriguing title of *Huxley: The Devil's Disciple*, and a reviewer makes the following cogent observations.

> *We hear much of Huxley's rage and ferocity: Desmond makes it easy to picture the manic power and intensity of his moods. . . . In portraying Huxley's mental life as frequently bordering on madness, Desmond leaves us no doubt that dark passion fed his ambition. . . . Beatrice Webb, Fabian author and Huxley's close friend, described him as "supremely sad" and as someone whose work amounted to "philosophic clashes between disabling fits."* [27]

Consider also Julian Huxley, the grandson of Thomas Huxley. Sir Julian was probably the leading evolutionist of the 20th century. He was made the first director-general of UNESCO and later was selected as the keynote speaker at the famous Darwin Centennial Celebration at the University of Chicago in 1959. He had also been the first head of the biology department at Rice University where I received my undergraduate education and later served on its faculty. Huxley was gone by the time I got there, so I never met him, but his influence on the university had been profound.

He also had significant mental problems. A reviewer of a recent book about Huxley based on the proceedings of a conference held at Rice wrote:

> *Kenneth Waters sets out a clear chronology of Huxley's life from his birth . . . to an abortive engagement that landed him*

---

27 Jane Camerini, "The Power of Biography," *Isis*, vol. 88 (June 1997): p. 308.

in a sanatorium. . . . Huxley . . . had two sons and a second
nervous breakdown, this one caused apparently by his feelings
of inadequacy as a teacher. . . . A third nervous breakdown
did not keep him from becoming the first director general of
[UNESCO]. . . . He also had three more nervous breakdowns.
. . . [28]

Huxley was an outspoken atheist and humanist, as well as a strong political leftist.

Alfred Russel Wallace, the "co-discoverer" with Charles Darwin of the theory of evolution by natural selection, was a confirmed spiritist — in fact, Wallace was one of the leaders of the revival of "spiritualism" in England that was taking place at the time. He wrote articles and books defending the ancient pagan belief that people could actually communicate with spirit beings (the Bible calls them demons).

In fact, he "discovered" natural selection in a very strange way. Wallace related this experience as follows:

> *The whole method of species modification became clear to*
> *me, and in the two hours of my fit I had thought out the main*
> *points of the theory.* [29]

That is, Wallace, with no scientific education and little contact with scientists at all, invented in two hours the whole evolutionary scenario that Charles Darwin, in the midst of England's most distinguished scientific community, had been working on for 20 years. The noted science historian Loren Eisely said concerning this experience:

> *A man pursuing birds of paradise in a remote jungle did not*
> *yet know that he had forced the world's most reluctant author*
> *[that is, Darwin] to disgorge his hoarded volume, or that the*
> *whole of western thought was about to be swung into a new*
> *channel because a man in a fever had felt a moment of strange*
> *radiance.* [30]

---

28 David L. Hull, "A Recent Huxley," *Science,* vol. 262 (November 12, 1993): p. 1079.

29 Alfred Russel Wallace, *The Wonderful Century: Its Successes and Failures* (New York: 1898), p. 140.

30 Loren C. Eiseley, "Alfred Russel Wallace," *Scientific American,* vol. 200 (February 1959): p. 81.

These dark influences also were present in the careers of the two most influential pioneers of evolutionary psychology, Carl Jung and Sigmund Freud.

> . . . Jung was an arrogant, belligerent, and intensely selfish man who destroyed several people's lives in pursuing his selfish ambitions. . . . Jung's ideas were heavily influenced by the popular German volkisch cults.[31]

Another reviewer of a recent book on Jung writes:

> It is from his discussions with Philemon [Jung's spirit guide] . . . that Jung received his most profound insights about the nature of the human psyche.[32]

Jung was thus inspired by his "spirit guide" — which most certainly was *not* God's Holy Spirit!

Similar influences were deeply involved in Freud's life, also. Paul Vitz, of New York University, has written an insightful biography of Freud. One reviewer notes the following:

> . . . threats of Freud's unconscious hostility toward the faith, which, as Vitz details, was a consequence of a curious preoccupation with the Devil, Damnation and the Anti-Christ. . . . Vitz even questions if Freud made a Faustian pact with the devil.[33]

Then there was Karl Marx, the spiritual father of the evil system called communism, which has slain and enslaved millions in Russia, China, and many other countries. Marx was a doctrinaire evolutionist and follower of Darwin, who permeated economics and the social sciences with evolutionary principles. Richard Würmbrand, a pastor formerly imprisoned under Communist persecution in Siberia, convincingly documented the fact that Marx was not merely an evolutionary atheist, but more likely

---

31 Linda Gamlin, "Mastery over Mind," *New Scientist,* vol. 159 (July 18, 1998): p. 46.

32 William Grigg, "Apostle of Perversion," *The New American,* vol. 14 (April 27, 1998): p. 37–38, citing *The Aryan Christ: The Secret Life of Carl Jung,* by Richard Noll (New York: Macmillan).

33 G.A. Cevasco, "Freud Versus God," reviewing *Sigmund Freud's Christian Unconscious* (New York: Guilford Press, 1988) in *Intercollegiate Press,* vol. 24 (Fall 1988): p. 39.

an evolutionary Satanist, who may also well have made some kind of Faustian pact with Satan.[34]

Charles Darwin himself was never involved in spiritualism or occultism of any kind, so far as we know. Yet, through most of his life, he was plagued with a mysterious illness, especially after he gave up his nominal belief in Christianity and began consciously searching for a naturalistic explanation of the apparent design in nature.

> *Throughout his life, Darwin was plagued by, in his own words, "vomiting . . . shivering, dying sensations, ringing in ears," as well as heart palpitations, blurred vision, and hysterical crying fits.*[35]

There have been many different hypotheses published as to the basic cause of this long illness. The most thorough study was made in a book-length analysis by Colp.[36] After reviewing all the different possibilities, Colp concluded that Darwin's complex of illnesses was emotionally induced, caused by his persistent advocacy of evolution, knowing the harm it would inflict on human relationships.

Space does not allow discussion of the madness of the ardent evolutionary philosopher Friedrich Nietzshce, with his "God is dead" propaganda, or the dedicated Darwinist Adolph Hitler, and his obsession with astrology and occultism, or others whose influential achievements on the worldly plane have been accompanied by traumatic physical problems and questions in relation to the moral and spiritual plane.

It may be difficult to define precise cause-and-effect relations in these phenomena, but we need at least to remember that *"God is not mocked: for whatsoever a man soweth, that shall he also reap"* (Gal. 6:7). All the men mentioned above are now dead and facing divine judgment, for *"it is appointed unto man once to die, but after this the judgment"* (Heb. 9:27). In the meantime, we who profess Christ as our Creator, Savior, and Lord can rejoice that *"God hath not given us the spirit of fear; but of power, and of love, and of a sound mind"* (2 Tim. 1:7).

---

34 Richard Wurmbrand, *Marx and Satan* (Westchester, IL: Crossway Books, 1990), 143 p.

35 John Bowlby, *Charles Darwin: A New Life* (London: W.W. Norton, 1990), copy on book jacket.

36 Ralph Colp Jr., *To Be an Invalid: The Illness of Charles Darwin* (Chicago, IL: University of Chicago Press, 1977).

EVIL-UTION

There is yet another aspect of the darkness of evolutionism. Christians have often felt that, if a person believes he or she is simply an evolved animal, that person will often tend to act like an animal and philosophize on such a presupposition.

Christians who have lived through eight decades or more (as of this writing, I am over 85) have seen society's standards of morality deteriorate in ways that would have seemed incredible, say, 50 years ago. As evolutionism has become the dominant teaching in our schools and colleges, those evil doctrines and practices whose rationale is based on evolution have inevitably followed. In terms of its impact on society — especially a society once founded on principles of biblical morality as ours was — evolutionism has indeed evolved into evil-utionism (as the British pronounce it!).

Even when immorality becomes scandalously common among our public leaders, many evolutionary authorities still assure us that this is normal evolutionary behavior.

> *Biologists suggest President Clinton has followed the genetic program handed down by human evolution: have as much sex with as many females as possible in the Darwinian quest for hereditary survival.*[37]

But are those biologists who offer such explanations merely certain obscure biologists, who have some personal agenda to promote?

Not at all. The same article that makes this observation quotes Michael Ruse (probably Canada's leading Darwinian philosopher) and Richard Dawkins (certainly England's most articulate evolutionist) as promoting this concept.

> *"What Darwin says is that the most dominant male gets the first crack at the women," said Michael Ruse. . . . Darwinism has argued that survival is the main goal of organisms, and part of that quest is to produce as many offspring as possible.*[38]

This evolution-driven impulse is working against the current concern of liberalism about the supposed population explosion and also over the AIDS epidemic generated by such sexual promiscuity.

---

37 *Washington Times,* March 1999, p. 5.
38 Ibid.

Nevertheless, these evolution-based lusts are quite natural, they say. The *Times* article then quotes from an article by Richard Dawkins in the *London Observer*, as follows:

> *We lust because our ancestors' lust just helped pass their lustful genes on to us — What else does a man become a great chieftain for?*[39]

Since such behavior is part of our evolutionary genetics, they argue that we must not legislate against it, even though it is producing too much population. The remedy, they say, is not to return to biblical morality, but to promote "safe sex" and abortion (perhaps also infanticide and euthanasia), and even homosexuality. These practices are said to be common in the animal world, so are part of acceptable evolutionary philosophy.

The practice of homosexuality (formerly considered a crime, and firmly condemned in the Bible) is now considered not only acceptable but even desirable by most evolutionists. A recent large volume[40] goes to great lengths to show how normal it is in an evolutionary context. A recent review of this book in the prestigious journal *Nature* says,

> *The species-by-species accounts of adult mammals and birds of the same sex courting and mounting each other, living in pairs, defending joint territories and raising young together are fully documented and referenced. . . .*[41]

Similarly, a review in *New Scientist* commends the extensive research of the author.

> *And not just primates, according to a compendium of animal homosexuality, just published in Britain by Bruce Bagemihl, an independent scholar and author based in Seattle. . . . The result is a species-by-species profile of more than 470 species. . . . "Nearly every type of same-sex activity found among humans has its counterpart in the animal kingdom," he concludes. His take-home message is simple: Homosexual behavior is as "natural" as heterosexual behavior.*[42]

---

39 Ibid.

40 Bruce Bagemihl, *Biological Exuberance: Animal Homosexuality and Natural Diversity* (New York: St. Martin's Press, 1998), 735 p.

41 Paul H. Harvey, "A Bestiary of Chaos and Biodiversity," *Nature,* vol. 397 (February 4, 1999): p. 402.

42 Gail Vines, "Queer Creatures," *New Scientist,* vol. 163 (August 7, 1999): p. 33–34.

Now, even if all this turns out to be true among animals, there is still no proof whatever that man has evolved from such animals, and thus no proof that our "behavior" is a product of evolution. According to the Genesis record of creation, men and women were created to *"have dominion"* over the animal world (Gen. 1:26, 28), not to copy its behavior. In fact, the Word of God calls homosexual behavior an *"abomination"* (Lev. 18:22) and those who practice it *"dogs"* (Deut. 23:17–18), evidently because of the similarity of such behavior to that of these animals. If, indeed, they are now trying to make it seem "natural," as a product of evolution, then here is another reason to call this philosophy *"evil*-ution."

An even more egregious application of what the authors call "evolutionary psychology" has recently been vigorously promoted in a controversial book called *A Natural History of Rape*.[43] According to this view, the growing incidence of rape (both female and male) in our society — like all other sinful sexual practices (sinful, that is, in the biblical sense) — is understandable in terms of the widespread acceptance of evolutionism. After all, if, as noted above, it is a natural evolutionary drive for males to "produce as many offspring as possible" with "as many females as possible," then when this instinct is thwarted by a reluctant female, or a disapproving society, men must resort to rape. Even homosexual rape is supposed to have an evolutionary rationale in terms of struggle and dominance.

From a Christian point of view, or even from any moral perspective whatever, such reasoning seems atrocious. But the authors (and many defenders of the book) advance it in all seriousness, as the only logical conclusion from the "fact" of evolution.

The practices of sexual promiscuity, homosexuality, and abortion are already widely promoted and accepted as "normal" and even "good" in our culture, in the name of evolutionism. Infanticide, and euthanasia are being increasingly advocated, on the same basis. And now even rape?

Of even greater concern is that so many churches, colleges, and seminaries of the mainline denominations have accommodated their teachings

---

43 Randy Thornhill and Craig Palmer, *A Natural History of Rape* (Cambridge, MA: MIT Press, 1999). Thornhill and Palmer are professors at the University of New Mexico and the University of Colorado, respectively. See also an interview with Thornhill by David Concar in *New Scientist*, vol. 164 (February 19, 2000): p. 45–46.

to sexual "freedom," abortionism, and even homosexuality (thankfully, not yet to rape!). These evils are even infiltrating a number of evangelical institutions.

The prophet Isaiah warned against this trend toward pagan compromise among his own Israelite people long ago. *"Woe unto them that call evil good, and good evil; that put darkness for light, and light for darkness; that put bitter for sweet, and sweet for bitter!"* (Isa. 5:20).

Well, as the Bible warns: *"In the last days perilous times shall come. . . . Yea, and all that will live godly in Christ Jesus shall suffer persecution. But evil men and seducers shall wax worse and worse, deceiving, and being deceived"* (2 Tim. 3:1–13).

Undoubtedly, many of those who practice such things do so because they have been "deceived" into thinking they are natural and normal. The nature inherited from Adam naturally tends toward the folly of sin and unbelief. So, as the Scripture goes on to say, *"They shall turn away their ears from the truth, and shall be turned unto fables"* (2 Tim. 4:4). And there is no more fabulous fable than evolution! With its alleged escape from God and His constraining will, there comes great temptation to accept evolution — and the shadow, "evil-utionism" that follows it.

Not only in the area of morals, but also in the wide-ranging philosophies of Communism, Nazism, racism, imperialism, and human greed in general (all of which have their pseudo-scientific rationales in evolution[44]) has the evolutionary fable deceived men into the ultimate sin of rejecting God as Creator and the Lord Jesus Christ as Savior and coming King.

As long as life lasts, of course, every sinful belief and practice of any man or woman can be forgiven and transformed into true saving faith and Christian character. The sole condition is *"repentance toward God and faith toward our Lord Jesus Christ"* (Acts 20:21). *"God commendeth his love toward us, in that, while we were yet sinners, Christ died for us"* (Rom. 5:8). *"Therefore if any man be in Christ, he is a new creature: old things are passed away; behold, all things are become new"* (2 Cor. 5:17).

---

44 See my book, *The Long War Against God* (Green Forest, AR: Master Books, 2000), 344 p., for firm documentation of this fact.

CHAPTER XII

GOD'S PLAN AND ETERNITY

G od is surely a God of love and grace and mercy. As Peter wrote: *"The Lord . . . is longsuffering to us-ward, not willing that any should perish, but that all should come to repentance"* (2 Pet. 3:9). Furthermore, Christ has paid the penalty for all sinners of all times, so that anyone who wants to be forgiven and saved can indeed *"come to repentance."* It is an eternal and immutable fact that *"He is the propitiation for our sins: and not for ours only, but also for the sins of the whole world"* (1 John 2:2). And He has promised that *"him that cometh to me I will in no wise cast out"* (John 6:37).

Nevertheless, although salvation is the free gift of God's grace, a gift must be accepted before it becomes a possession. The unspeakably sad and astounding truth is that *most* people either neglect or even refuse ever to accept that gift. *"My Spirit shall not always strive with man,"* God has said (Gen. 6:3), so most people are still unsaved sinners when they die, and therefore will enter eternity separated forever from God. *"For if ye believe not that I am he, ye shall die in your sins"* (John 8:24).

THE LAKE OF FIRE

The subject of hell is seldom taught or preached these days, even in fundamentalist churches. Most people believe that hell (if there is such a place) is for monsters of wickedness such as Adolph Hitler, but not for themselves. Many don't believe in hell at all, and resent any preacher (or writer!) who teaches that hell is real and will be well populated. A recent authoritative poll found that:

> *Majorities of about two-thirds of all adults believe in hell and the devil, but hardly anybody expects that they will go to hell themselves.*[1]

But they are wrong! Most people *will* go to hell. Jesus Christ said so!

I don't like to say such a thing, and would not dare to do so, except for the fact that Jesus Chrsit said it, and people desperately need to know how *not* to go to hell. After all, the Lord Jesus Christ was the Creator of all things (Col. 1:16; John 1:3; etc.), and it was He who said that a place of *"everlasting fire, prepared for the devil and his angels"* would also be the place of the *"everlasting punishment"* of multitudes of people (Matt. 25:41, 46) in an age to come.

This place of everlasting fire is also called *"the lake of fire,"* and is evidently synonymous with hell's final location. Wherever and whatever it is, hell will not be located on (or in) the earth. This present earth is to be destroyed by fire (2 Pet. 3:10) and to have *"fled away"* (Rev. 20:11) before God created the new heavens and the new earth. Since the *"beast"* and the *"false prophet"* are said to be cast into the lake of fire *before* this earth's destruction, whereas Satan is said to be thrown into it *after* that destruction (Rev. 19:20; 20:10), the fiery lake must be located away from the earth. One suggestion is that it could be somewhere on a star (after all, stars are actually vast lakes of fire) far, far away from earth, out in *"the blackness of darkness"* of the infinite cosmos (Jude 13).

More important than its location will be its occupants. The *"devil and his angels"* will be there, Jesus said, but also all those men and women whose names are *"not found written in the book of life"* (Rev. 20:15).

And who are these? *"But the fearful, and unbelieving, and the abominable, and murderers, and whoremongers, and sorcerers, and idolaters, and all liars, shall have their part in the lake which burneth with fire and brimstone: which is the second death"* (Rev. 21:8).

---

1 "Harris Poll: The Religious and Other Beliefs of Americans, 2003," *Skeptical Inquirer,* vol. 27 (July/August 2003): p. 5. This poll is claimed to be highly reliable, having used the same methods employed by the Harris organization when it forecast the results of the year 2000 elections with great accuracy. It was conducted in January 2003, surveying over 2,200 Americans online.

Probably most "good people" would agree that *"murderers and whoremongers"* deserve hell — but *"the fearful, and unbelieving . . . and all liars"*? Would that not include just about everyone? And who are those "good" people — those who presume to judge who deserves to go to hell — anyway?

In the antediluvian world, we are told that *"all flesh had corrupted his way upon the earth"* (Gen. 6:12). During the period of God's greatest blessings in Israel, the wisest of men, Solomon, had to acknowledge that *"there is not a just man upon earth that doeth good, and sinneth not"* (Eccles. 7:20). The apostle Paul agreed that *"there is none that doeth good, no, not one"* (Rom. 3:12). And even Christ himself said that *"there is none good but one, that is God"* (Mark 10:18). *"For whosoever shall keep the whole law, and yet offend in one point, he is guilty of all"* (James 2:10). God is *"of purer eyes than to behold evil"* (Hab. 1:13), and so cannot allow even one unforgiven sin into heaven. It begins to look as if the lake of fire will have many, many occupants after all!

There is a way to escape hell, of course, even though literally everyone really *deserves* to go there. But not many people are willing to escape hell *that* way. None other than the Lord Jesus Christ himself said that *"narrow is the way, which leadeth unto life, and few there be that find it"* (Matt. 7:14). At the same time, He said also that *"broad is the way, that leadeth to destruction, and many there be which go in thereat"* (Matt. 7:13).

Please note that the man who said these things was not only the God who created all of us, but also the one who has provided the way of escape from hell, and who will be our final judge — and *He* has said that most people will stay on the broad road leading to the lake of fire! Most of these undoubtedly will be men and women who assume they are "good" (at least most of the time!) and are not expecting to go to hell when they die (how many funeral services can we remember when the preacher ever said *that* was where the deceased would go?).

But consider several specific categories of people who are in such danger.

(1) What about all those who don't believe in hell, or any religion at all? "According to recent surveys, 39 percent of Americans — 111 million of us — belong to no church, synagogue, mosque, or other religious institution. . . . an unprecedented 14 percent of Americans tell pollsters that they are atheists, agnostics, secular

humanists, or simply disinterested in religion. That's about 40 million Americans. . . ."[2]

That's in America! In Europe, the percentages would be greater. These people are all headed for hell, because Jesus said: *"If ye believe not that I am he* [that is, God], *ye shall die in your sins"* (John 8:24). *"The fool hath said in his heart, There is no God"* (Ps. 14:1; 53:1; also note Rom. 1:22).

(2) Then, there are the billions of people who believe in false religions. What about them? Many are "good" people. Nevertheless, they are all lost and bound for hell. They all reject Christ, and *"there is none other name under heaven given among men, whereby we must be saved"* (Acts 4:12). Remember that Jesus himself said: *"I am the way . . . no man cometh unto the Father, but by me"* (John 14:6). It is not that they are all ignorant about Jesus. Most of them know His claims and have either rejected or ignored them. Those who follow the Koran, for example, know that, even though Mohammed acknowledged Christ as a prophet, he denied repeatedly that He was the unique Son of God, that He died for our sins, and that He rose from the dead. Jesus said: *". . . he that believeth not is condemned already, because he hath not believed in the name of the only begotten Son of God"* (John 3:18). Mohammed, therefore, is a lost sinner, and so are all those who believe him rather than God in Christ.

(3) There are also many who profess to be Christians but will eventually be sent to the lake of fire. *"And if any man shall take away from the words of the book of this prophecy* [that is, not only from the final book of the Bible, but in context, the words of Scripture as a whole], *God shall take away his part out of the book of life"* (Rev. 22:19). In addition to these sober words of warning to those who would tamper with the inspired words of the Bible, it was also Jesus who said, *"Many will say to me in that day, Lord, Lord, have we not prophesied in thy name? . . . and in thy name done many wonderful works? And then will I profess unto them,*

---

2 Promotional brochure for the Council for Secular Humanism. The Harris Poll, cited above, has even found that, among professing Christians, 1 percent do not believe in God, 5 percent do not believe in heaven, and 18 percent do not believe in hell.

I never knew you: depart from me, ye that work iniquity" (Matt. 7:22–23).

We might well ask (as did the disciples when Jesus said that it was *"easier for a camel to go through the eye of a needle, than for a rich man to enter into the kingdom of God. . . . Who then can be saved?"* (Matt. 19:24–25). The fact is, however, as Jesus said: *"With God all things are possible"* (Matt. 19:26).

God has made our salvation possible and easily available through the incarnation, substitutionary sacrifice for our sins, and glorious victory over death in the bodily resurrection of His only begotten Son, Jesus Christ. What we could never earn by good works, He has provided as a free gift! *"For all have sinned, and come short of the glory of God; Being justified freely by his grace through the redemption that is in Christ Jesus"* (Rom. 3:23–24).

"Believe on the Lord Jesus Christ, and thou shalt be saved" (Acts 16:31). Paul calls this magnificent offer *"the glorious gospel of the blessed God"* (1 Tim. 1:11), so how could anyone refuse such a gift of divine love?

But aren't there other ways to be saved? What about Buddhism and Islam and other philosophical systems that seem to make good sense? No: *"There is a way which seemeth right unto a man, but the end thereof are the ways of death"* (Prov. 14:12).

As Paul pointed out long ago to the intellectuals at Athens, all such questions should have been settled by the bodily resurrection of Christ. *"God . . . now commandeth all men every where to repent. Because he hath appointed a day, in the which he will judge the world in righteousness by that man whom he hath ordained; whereof he hath given assurance to all men, in that he hath raised him from the dead"* (Acts 17:30–31).

Only Jesus Christ, of all men who ever lived, has shown that He has the power to defeat our greatest enemy, death (the evidence of His resurrection is compelling, for all who care to look). Therefore, He is God, and we will do well to believe both His warnings and His promises. Would anyone dare call Him a liar by insisting on some other way? There could be no greater sin, and those who commit this sin will undoubtedly remember it forever there in their fiery prison.

But what about those who have never heard about the Savior and His great gift of love? The fact is that *everyone* knows enough to be saved, if he will act on the light he has. Jesus Christ, the Creator is *"the true Light, which lighteth every man that cometh into the world"* (John 1:9). For those who will act on whatever light they have — whether in the evidence of creation or the witness of conscience or whatever remnants of truth may have been preserved in their particular religion — then God will presumably send whatever additional light is needed to enable belief unto salvation. The Scriptures provide the experience of Cornelius as a case in point (Acts 10). Most men, however, fail to act on whatever light they may have, and God says they are *without excuse*" (Rom. 1:20).

No doubt, some receive more light than others (in fact, no two individuals, even in "Christian" nations, have been given identical amounts and types of light), and therefore the Bible teaches there will be degrees of reward in heaven and degrees of punishment in hell (note, for example, Luke 12:42–48), but the one great divide between heaven and hell is one's response to Christ's great sacrifice and proffered gift of love. *"He that believeth on the Son hath everlasting life: and he that believeth not the Son shall not see life; but the wrath of God abideth on him"* (John 3:36).

The City with Foundations

In sharp contrast to the lake of fire, which the Bible says is the future home of the wicked (that is, those whose sins have never been forgiven because of their wicked refusal to accept their Creator as their personal Savior), the Bible also promises a wonderful city as the future home of the righteous (that is, those to whom has been imputed the perfect righteousness of the Lord Jesus Christ, who had created them and then suffered and died in their place to redeem them forever).

That future city is called *"the holy city, new Jerusalem."* The apostle John, supernaturally translated in his spirit into the future by the Holy Spirit, was permitted to see that city *"coming down from God out of heaven"* (Rev. 21:2) to the new earth: *"for the first heaven and the first earth were passed away"* (Rev. 21:1). He then proceeded, in the last two chapters of the Bible, to describe the wonders of that great city where we shall dwell someday.

The city is not "heaven," as some have thought, for John saw it coming down *out of heaven*. It is evidently in heaven today where probably our Creator and Savior is preparing and making it ready. When Christ was here on this present earth, He promised His followers that He would *"go and prepare a place for you . . . that where I am, there ye may be also"* (John 14:3). Perhaps it is almost ready, for many signs indicate His coming is near.

And indeed, when He comes back as He said He would, *"so shall we ever be with the Lord."* That will be the most blessed aspect of our future home. But we shall also see again all those who have preceded us to their present heavenly home, for when He comes, we *"shall be caught up together with them…to meet the Lord in the air"* (1 Thess. 4:17).

At my highly advanced age (85 as of this writing), most of my friends are already there, as are my parents, my two brothers, and even my son Andy, so I'm happily looking forward to being there, too, whether at the Lord's personal return or through physical death before His coming. And that beautiful city and home are also awaiting me there!

Long before the Lord Jesus was here on Earth, His ancient followers, such as Abraham, also, *"looked for a city which hath foundations, whose builder and maker is God"* (Heb. 11:10). Therefore, God was *"not ashamed to be called their God: for he hath prepared for them a city"* (Heb. 11:16).

And what foundations it has! *"The wall of the city"* had *"twelve foundations"* supporting *"a wall great and high,"* and those *"foundations of the wall of the city were garnished with all manner of precious stones"* (Rev. 21:12, 14, 19).

Some expositors think that all this is symbolic of something or other, but I am one who has been called a "naïve literalist," so I have to believe it will be exactly as John saw it. It does have certain spiritual remembrances built into it as well, for the 12 gates in the great wall are inscribed with *"the names of the twelve tribes of the children of Israel,"* and the foundations themselves are inscribed with *"the names of the twelve apostles of the Lamb"* (Rev. 21:12, 14).

As far as personal homes are concerned, Jesus called them *"mansions"* (John 14:2), but they may not be what we usually mean by that word. The Greek word is *mone*, normally used as a prefix meaning "sole" or "alone." We use its English derivative "mono" the same way. It stresses uniqueness or individuality of the object connected with it. It is used only one other time in the New Testament, in John 14:23. There, Jesus also promised that, even in this present life: *"If a man love me, he will keep my words: and my Father will love him, and we will come unto him, and make our abode with him."* We can probably infer from this that, whatever our unique "abode" in heaven may be, it will be like a "mansion" to us, because God's "presence" will also abide there. That can seem true even now if we truly love Him and keep His words, because the indwelling Spirit of God is here within each believer now.

The city as a whole will be marvelous in size and beauty. It is also called *"Paradise."* The paradise of Eden will be restored and made even better than at first (note Luke 23:43; 2 Cor. 12:4; Rev. 2:7)! The *"tree of life"* will be there — not a single tree as in Eden, but many such trees, lining the banks of a great river emerging from the throne of the Lamb (Rev. 22:1–2).

In size, the city will be a tremendous cube, 12,000 furlongs on each side. The word "furlong" is from the Greek *stadios;* this works out to mean that the city is about 1,380 miles long, wide, and high (see Rev. 21:16). The *"streets"* of the city, like the city itself, are of pure transparent gold, like pure glass (Rev. 21:18, 21). These must be both horizontal and vertical streets, the latter presumably somewhat like elevator shafts. There will be no need for "lifts," of course, nor even for automobiles or carriages of any kind. Our new bodies will enable us to travel very swiftly throughout all levels of the city and even throughout the universe. Christ will have transformed *"our vile body, that it may be fashioned like unto his glorious body"* (Phil. 3:21), so we will probably be able to go easily and quickly wherever He can go.

Now all this is admittedly hard to visualize or even imagine. It would be very hard to believe at all, if it were not for the fact that our Lord Jesus Christ (who created the universe itself) is building the city. Our mighty cosmos, with its incredible size and infinite complexity, also would be impossible to imagine had He himself not created it and then given us the Mandate to study at least the terrestrial part of that cosmos, describe it, use it, and have dominion over it.

Speaking of this universe, the Bible makes it clear that the stars and other components of the cosmos will never pass away (e.g., Ps. 148:1–6). God is not capricious, so must have a purpose for everything He has created. Since we know from astronomy as well as the Bible that *"one star differeth from another star in glory"* (1 Cor. 15:41), the purpose for each star must be unique to itself, and, therefore, so must also its structure and functions be different from all others.

Now, although the Bible does not say it specifically, it seems reasonable that we shall be able to learn much more about the universe in the ages to come than we can ever do in this life. Surely the Lord does not intend for us to sit around just singing and playing harps through all eternity. He gave the first man work to do in his immediate home at the beginning in Eden, even before there was any sin. The Bible does say that in the new earth *"his servants shall serve him"* (Rev. 22:3). That's us, not just the angels!

In fact, I like to believe that God's primeval Mandate to have dominion over the earth may be enlarged eventually to cover the whole creation. Would it not be a wonderful future to be able to travel to distant stars and plants, explore them, and then write about their nature and uniqueness in God's plan for a book in God's library? Others could read our reports, and we could read theirs, and all would still further increase our awe at God's great creation and our love and devotion to Him.

The universe and its intricate complexities are infinite, and the time to study them will be endless. *"O the depth of the riches both of the wisdom and knowledge of God! How unsearchable are his judgments, and his ways past finding out!"* (Rom. 11:33). We shall never lack for challenging, enjoyable, and useful work to do in these ages to come.

This is not to suggest that everyone will always be out exploring the cosmos. God will no doubt assign many different forms of service to His redeemed and glorified servants — depending probably on their God-given talents and also on their faithfulness in this present life. There will have been differing rewards presented at the judgment seat of Christ, and He has promised that His rewards will be given to every man *"according as his work shall be"* (Rev. 22:12). Our future work probably will be somewhat in relation to our former work. The Lord's several parables dealing with faithfulness and diligence in service in this life stress that these characteristics will be proportionately rewarded in the future life after His coming. *"For whosoever hath, to him shall be given, and he shall have more abundance"* (Matt. 13:12). *"Blessed is that servant, whom his lord when he cometh shall find so doing"* (Luke 12:43). *"For the Son of man shall come in the glory of his Father with his angels; and then he shall reward every man according to his works"* (Matt. 16:27).

One of the most wonderful aspects of these ages to come in God's holy city is that *"there shall in no wise enter into it any thing that defileth"* (Rev. 21:27). Unutterably sad, however, is the contrasting state of those whose eternal residence will be in that far off *"world of iniquity"* (James 3:6), called the lake of fire. For there, near the very end of the Bible, the Lord Jesus had said concerning those sent to that grievous place: *"He that is unjust, let him be unjust still: and he which is filthy, let him be filthy still"* (Rev. 22:11). In addition to the vast numbers of lost souls of unsaved men and women, Satan and all his demonic hordes will be there.

Modern sinners and unbelieving intellectuals should remember that John the Baptist long ago was warning people to *"flee from the wrath to come"* (Matt. 3:7; Luke 3:7), and that warning is more urgent today than ever. The coming of the Lord almost certainly *"is near, even at the doors"* (Matt. 24:33).

For a time, no doubt, even in the holy city we shall have tears to shed, especially for unsaved friends and loved ones who have been imprisoned forever in that awful lake, but then *"God shall wipe away all tears"* (Rev. 21:4), and the glories of life in the new Jerusalem and the new earth will be so magnificent that *"the former shall not be remembered, nor come into mind"* (Isa. 65:17).

I am personally looking forward not only to learning more about God's creation but also just resting for a while! And not only to seeing loved ones and old friends again and sharing with them all our (and their) experiences, but also getting to meet and talk with Noah, and Elijah, and John the Baptist, and Timothy, and all our other heroes of the faith, and then eventually to meet and know all the saints of all the ages. What wonderful times of fellowship, as well as service, await us in that beautiful city soon coming down.

It is also fascinating to note that the Bible apparently predicts more than just one future age. The apostle Paul refers at least twice to *ages* yet to come. I love especially the promise of Ephesians 2:7 — *"That in the ages to come he might shew the exceeding riches of his grace in his kindness toward us through Christ Jesus."* Then there is the great doxology of Ephesians 3:21 — *"Unto him be glory in the church by Christ Jesus throughout all ages, world without end. Amen."*

Unless one of these ages yet to come is the millennial age, with possibly another being the prophesied period of great tribulation on earth, the Bible is silent about the nature of these future ages. Christians are, in fact, divided about whether or not even those two ages should really be considered as part of this present age instead. Probably most, however, including myself, do think that the millennial age, at least, is still in the future and will take place on this present earth after Christ's return.

In Revelation 20:2–7, a thousand years (that is, a millennium) is specifically mentioned six times, during which time Satan will be bound in the bottomless pit, and the Beast and False Prophet will have been cast into the lake of fire. It is hard to see how this could refer to the present age, since the devil still *"walketh about, seeking whom he may devour"* (1 Pet. 5:8) at this present time.

Furthermore, a number of Old Testament passages speak of a future age here on this earth, in which many attributes of the earliest ages will be restored (longevity, peace between animals and men, worldwide belief in the Lord as King, etc. — see Isa. 65:25; Hab. 2:14; Zech. 14:9; etc.). Although there will still be sin and death in the world (Isa. 65:20), it is difficult to apply these characteristics to this current age. Accordingly, this *may* be one of the future ages.

But the implication seems to be that there may be many ages to come, so some are tempted to speculate as to what they may be. One speculation is that, in some future age, God may allow other populations to come into being on other planets, with these to be guided by the pilot experiment, so to speak, here on earth, with the immortalized "graduates" of earth's learning process as their kings and priests, thereby preventing the introduction of sin in such future societies.

Another speculation is that, after one or more ages of suffering in that world of iniquity, the human inhabitants of hell would finally come to repentance and accept Jesus Christ as *their* Savior and Lord, being finally brought back to earth to renew fellowship with their friends and family members who had been saved back in the gospel age. Those who have suggested this have argued that the Hebrew and Greek words translated "eternal," "everlasting," and the like don't necessarily always mean "never-ending."

There could be other speculations. But the most we can say about any of them is that they are speculations with no real evidence except wishful thinking. When the biblical authors wrote of *"everlasting punishment"* and *"eternal fire,"* etc., they used the same word as when they wrote about *"everlasting life"* and *"the eternal God."* It does seem safer to assume that, if God is *eternal,* then so will be His *"vengeance of eternal fire"* (Jude 7).

We can safely leave all these undefined "ages to come" to God who, for His own good reasons, has not chosen to tell us about them yet. We do have, however, enough information about that soon coming age in the holy city in the new earth, with its solid and sure foundations, to look forward to it with great anticipation and eternal joy.

Don't miss it! *"For here have we no continuing city, but we seek one to come"* (Heb. 13:14).

OCCUPYING UNTIL HE COMES

As discussed in the previous two chapters, each man and every woman is destined to spend the coming future age either in the lake of fire or else headquartered in the new Jerusalem, the promised city with sure foundations — hell or heaven. The decision as to which it will be is to be made personally by each individual, by either rejecting (or neglecting) Christ's wonderful gift of forgiveness and salvation or else by volitionally coming to Him in true repentance and faith.

That decision must be made while in this life, of course, and no one knows how long that opportunity will last. Sooner or later, either Christ will come or death will come — and that will be that! The Lord Jesus has promised to return someday to bring this age to a glorious and triumphant climax, and then to bring in that wonderful future age, with its new earth and its fantastic capital city, the new Jerusalem.

Obviously, no one knows when He will be coming back to do this, although He had indeed suggested many signs that might indicate His coming is near. In fact, He has specifically said: *"When ye shall see all these things, know that it is near, even at the doors"* (Matt. 24:33). On the other hand, there is nothing to prevent His coming even before such signs appear. He had repeatedly warned His followers, even in that very first Christian generation, always to watch for His coming. *"Watch therefore, for ye know neither the day nor the hour wherein the Son of man cometh"* (Matt. 25:13). John, the beloved disciple, near the very end of the apostolic age, wrote these words: *"And now, little children, abide in him; that, when he shall appear, we may have confidence, and not be ashamed before him at his coming"* (1 John 2:28).

And just how do we *abide* in Him (that is, "continue" in Him)? John undoubtedly was thinking here of Christ's unforgettable farewell message to His disciples in the upper room just before His arrest and crucifixion — the message on the true vine and its branches, in which the word "abide" (also the same word translated as "remain" or "continue") was used at least 12 times.

But he may also have been thinking of that key parable recorded in Luke 19:11–27, the so-called "parable of the pounds." That parable, spoken as He was about to enter Jerusalem for the final week before his death, used the figure of a nobleman leaving for *"a far country"* to receive *"a kingdom, and to return."* Perhaps his listeners were remembering how King Herod had received his "kingdom" from the emperor in Rome. In any case, the nobleman in the parable was said to have left his possessions in the care of his ten servants, instructing them to *"occupy till I come"* (Luke 19:13), meaning in effect to carry on his business affairs, so that they would continue to be profitable while he was away.

The word *"occupy"* is significant. It translates a Greek word (used only this one time in the New Testament) from which is derived our

English word "pragmatic." The instruction to his servants thus plainly shows the nobleman's intent that his servants were expected to carry out the daily "practical" affairs of the business diligently and faithfully while he was gone, no doubt following his instructions as to how they were to do it.

But this is a parable, so the nobleman and his servants clearly depict some greater truth, as designed by Christ to correct the notion held by the disciples *that the kingdom of God should immediately appear*" (Luke 19:11).

The symbology clearly suggests Christ's imminent departure back to heaven, whence He will return eventually to establish the promised kingdom. He had to go to a *"far country."* The parallel parable of the talents (Matt. 25:14–30), included in His discourse on the Mount of Olives, related to His second coming and delivered after He was already in Jerusalem for that final week, not only implied that He would be going to *"a far country,"* but also might be gone for *"a long time"* (Matt. 25:14, 19). The servants in this parable also were expected to "trade" with the talents entrusted to them, so that their master's business would be profitable while he was away.

Clearly, if the Lord Jesus is represented in these two parables by a man going away to a far country, then those servants left to carry on his business affairs while he is gone must mean those of us who are now His servants here on earth. And these are *pragmatic* affairs, the business of running the office or the farm or the classroom or the household — whatever it is He has given us to do to carry on His work. They are not necessarily *spiritual* affairs — praying, singing, witnessing, etc. — although these are important, too.

And this brings us around again to His very first commandment — the Dominion Mandate. We are to "occupy" until He comes. That is, we are to do the best we can, in His name, in the particular job He has given us to do. If He has told you to be a pastor or a missionary — that is fine. Do it *"heartily, as unto the Lord"* (Col. 3:23). Likewise, if He has made you a teacher, or a research scientist, or a business man, or a homemaking wife and mother — or whatever — do *that* job *"heartily, as unto the Lord."* Every honorable occupation, carried out in the name of our great God of creation and redemption, is included under His primeval Dominion Mandate. It can even be viewed as also fulfilling His Missionary Mandate as well, as we pray and witness, too, in that particular calling and responsibility. This motivation honors Him and becomes a component part of His purpose in creating the earth and making us His stewards thereof.

But that is not all. Both these parables (that of the talents in Matt. 25:14–30 and that of the pounds in Luke 19:11–27) promise rewards for pragmatic faithfulness and diligence in carrying out Christ's work here on earth while He is away in heaven. These rewards have their fulfillment in *"the kingdom of heaven"* (Matt. 25:14) or *"the kingdom of God"* (Luke 19:11), both terms being probably essentially synonymous, and both surely having to do with the age to come, although the specific job assignments are being fulfilled in this present age.

Then note that the rewards for faithfulness are threefold. First (and this to me would be the most gratifying) will be the joy of hearing the Lord say: *"Well done, thou good and faithful servant"* (Matt. 25:21, 23). Second, there will be an assignment in the future age somehow related specifically to our service in this age. *"Thou hast been faithful over a few things, I will make thee ruler over many things"* (Matt. 25:21, 23). In the parallel parable of the pounds, the *"many things"* are specifically called *"cities"* over which the recipient is to *"have authority"* (Luke 19:17). Finally, the faithful servants will be told: *"Enter thou into the joy of thy Lord"* (Matt. 25:21, 23).

These rewards clearly apply to the future age and to our future service for our Creator and Savior in that age. Remember also that the last chapter of the Bible says that in that age: *"And there shall be no more curse . . . and his servants shall serve him: And they shall see his face; and his name shall be in their foreheads"* (Rev. 22:3–4).

The particular service will no doubt be assigned to each individual by the Lord himself (as in the parable). Obviously, not all His servants can be assigned to rule over a number of cities, but the principle of relatedness will apply — that is, our future service will somehow relate to our former service here on this present earth. Furthermore, the rewards are not to be based on *quantity* of results in our work here, but *quality*. *"Every man's work shall be made manifest: for the day shall declare it, because it shall be revealed by fire; and the fire shall try every man's work of what sort it is"* (1 Cor. 3:13).

What sort it is, not *how much* it is! For example, a woman who has been a faithful wife and mother, a *"virtuous woman"* such as described in Proverbs 31:10–31, consistent also in daily life and witness to the saving gospel of Christ, might well be given a future assignment commensurate (in prestige and honor, at least, if not in prominence) to that of a great scientist or a great evangelist. A dedicated Christian teacher could well be honored as much as a famous pastor, and a sacrificial witnessing shopkeeper as much as a faithful missionary. The Lord no doubt, as the *"Judge of all the earth"* will be careful to *"do right"* (Gen. 18:25) with His rewards.

In that future age, of course, many new types of activities perhaps will be developed as the whole cosmos becomes available for exploration and use. On the other hand, many present vocations will no longer be needed, with all the ramifications of sin gone forever. There will be no crime or war, so no police or soldiers will be needed. The same will apply to lawyers and probably also to medical doctors (since sickness and death will have been expunged completely). On the other hand, engineers and scientists will be widely used in many fields. Teachers will be used in many fields, as will architects and agriculturalists and people in all the building and communications trades.

The world will certainly be different in a multitude of ways, yet there will be a definite continuity of sorts. The earth and the heavens will be essentially unchanged, except that all the effects of sin and the Curse will be gone, and righteousness and divine love will be manifest everywhere.

But all of that is still mostly hidden in the inner counsels of the godhead. *"The secret things belong unto the Lord our God: but those things which are revealed belong unto us and to our children for ever, that we may do all the words of this law"* (Deut. 29:29). We don't need to know any of the details at this point in time. It is enough to know that He has promised to *"shew the exceeding riches of his grace"* through Christ Jesus to us *"in the ages to come"* (Eph. 2:7).

Right now, it is simply our responsibility to *"occupy"* until He comes. Each of us as a Christian believer has been given specific work to do under both the Dominion Mandate and the Missionary Mandate, so we need to be doing it, and doing it *"with [our] might"* (Eccles. 9:10) as *"to the Lord"* (Col. 3:23). *"Whether therefore ye eat or drink, or whatsoever ye do, do all to the glory of God"* (1 Cor. 10:31).

In Paul's day, some believers were actually called to be bondservants, or slaves. Even that occupation, if faithfully performed, could honor the Lord and thereby contribute to His Dominion Mandate. Joseph's willing service in his slave position was later used by God to make him a ruler over Egypt. Furthermore, he could also obey the Missionary Mandate, witnessing to his fellow servants and perhaps even to his master.

Whatever God's calling may have been for each of us, we can and should use it as our personal contribution to the implementation of the

Dominion Mandate and also such opportunities as are available to witness for Christ, as He commissioned in His Missionary Mandate. As Christians, we have a direct commitment to both, under Christ our Creator and Savior.

This double responsibility implies a lifelong commitment to study — both of God's Word and also of His world — or at least that part of it which relates directly to our particular calling. Scientists, technologists, and educators would certainly seem to have very great responsibility under the Dominion Mandate — perhaps even more than those in most other fields. To *"have dominion"* over God's creation requires knowledge about it, first of all, and this implies the work of research scientists. Then to use that knowledge in actually exercising that dominion requires the development of structures, machines, and other systems by engineers and other technologists. Then teachers, of course, must transmit the knowledge gained by the scientists and developed by the technologists from generation to generation.

Science, technology, and education thus play key roles in carrying out God's Dominion Mandate. This has been discussed to some degree in this book's early chapters, but I must hasten to repeat again the truth that every honorable vocation can and must contribute to the Dominion Mandate.

But then we are also each to obey the Missionary Mandate as well. If Christians are indeed to *"preach the gospel to every creature"* (Mark 16:15), then it is crystal clear that every Christian must be doing it. One can *"preach the gospel"* to one person or to a congregation of thousands, but it must be the true gospel being preached! Therefore, every Christian needs to know the gospel thoroughly, with answers to the various questions and objections that people tend to raise. This also requires life-long study, not just by professional theologians but by every serious Christian believer. Certainly he must be thoroughly acquainted with the truths about Jesus Christ — especially His finished work on the cross and then the impregnable evidence for His resurrection. More study!

He must also know the arguments of the great adversary, and how to deal with him. These cluster around the philosophy of evolution, which is Satan's attempt to explain the world without God and even ultimately to take the place of God as supreme ruler of the universe. But evolutionism is not only utterly contrary to God's Word, but also vacuous scientifically and deadly spiritually. It is utterly contrary to all the solid data of biology, geology, astronomy, psychology, and every other natural or social science. It is Satan's grandest deception, and must be rejected and exposed as the deadly delusion it is, by Christians everywhere.

This age-long war between God and Satan will all end when Christ comes again and the future ages begin. Soon will come the great separation, with multitudes dispatched to a fearsome home completely separated from the light and love and grace of God, the place called in the Bible the *"lake of fire."*

But there will also be *"a great multitude, which no man could number, of all nations, and kindreds, and people, and tongues,"* who will stand before Christ in that day (Rev. 7:9) and who will be led by Him *"unto living fountains of waters,"* where God himself *"shall wipe away all tears from their eyes"* (Rev. 7:17).

I have touched on many subjects in this book, and there is much, much more that *could* be written about each of them. But I hope that each reader will at least be a little better able to comprehend in some measure and appreciate in greater measure this wonderful plan of God in creation. We do need to think way beyond our own little situation and our own personal salvation to see something of God's great plan for all of us in the ages to come. We need somehow to learn to view things from *His* magnificent perspective, not just from our own very localized and limited point of view. His wonderful plan ranges all through time and all the endless ages to come. And — wonder of all wonders — we shall be there, too!

INDEX OF SUBJECTS

INDEX OF NAMES

INDEX OF SCRIPTURES